Successful Parishes

How They Meet the Challenge of Change

Thomas Sweetser

WINSTON PRESS

Cover design: Dean Vietor

ISBN: 0-86683-694-2

Library of Congress Catalog Card Number: 82-51165

Printed in the United States of America

5 4 3 2 1

Winston Press, Inc.
430 Oak Grove
Minneapolis, Minnesota 55403

Successful Parishes is dedicated to the creative, caring, and conscientious pastoral minister, whether priest, deacon, religious or lay person, married or single. I mean it as an affirmation of your work and your dedication to the Church and parish and as a way of letting you know in your moments of discouragement and loneliness that your work *does* make a difference.

Contents

Foreword

Recently a pastor asked me what single issue I would identify as most critical in today's parish ministry. With little hesitation, I said "relationships." The development of relationships is indeed at the heart of the Christian life and, therefore, of the life of a parish. This includes relationships with God, family, friends, fellow workers and fellow citizens, between men and women, generations, and races. Nevertheless, relationships within the Church are, like other relationships, undergoing serious change.

Sometimes we talk about this problem of relationships as one of roles, for roles are sets of relationships and the mutual expectations arising from them. Yet these roles and expectations are hard to define. Parents wonder what to expect from each other and from their children, and the same is true of men and women, citizens, fellow workers, and friends. The difficulty is even greater in the Church, where we struggle to define the respective roles of laity, bishops, priests, sisters, and others, as well as the relationships among pastors, parishioners, principals of schools, parish councils, and parish staffs.

Obviously, such shifts in relationships are not unprecedented in the Church. They are implicit in every ecclesiological and cultural shift and inevitable in our time of rapid and widespread change. Historical precedent can be more illustrative than consoling, for we do not work out our relationships in theory, or in general, but very much "in particular." When significant shifts occur, we are required to become deliberate about our relationships, clearly spelling out what each person or group expects from the other. To do this, we need to talk and listen to each other carefully. And we need to know that no change in relationships can ever be uni-directional. Even if the initiative for change comes from one partner, the partner's response changes him or her and calls for a new response by the initiating partner.

All of this is going on in parishes. Father Sweetser's book may be viewed as an exploration of changing relationships in parishes. It is particular and thematic. The particulars he uses to illustrate the seven fictional parishes may differ from those with which the reader is familiar. Nonetheless, the particulars help to identify the constellations of needs, gifts, and behavior that bear examination. When he becomes general or thematic in the second part of each chapter, he contributes perspectives and suggestions that could be helpful to all who are trying to work out the new relationships. And work is what it takes.

One pastor involved in a large and active parish team told me that the group must take the time at the beginning of every year to clarify and develop the relationships among themselves. If they do not, those relationships are sure to go amok before the pastoral year is concluded. The asceticism of working out carefully and faithfully the relationships involved is a key part of ministerial spirituality these days. Without such discipline, all the talk about new ministries, lay ministry, collegiality, and the rest is just talk. The challenge of parish relationships is a demanding one.

Father Sweetser addresses most of the key aspects or expressions of this challenge: staff or team relationships, small groups in parishes, planning, relationships between staffs and councils, the voluntary character of parish participation, new ways in which adults relate to faith and church, and the broadened understanding and sharing of ministerial responsibility in parishes. This book will be useful for those in parish leadership who use it, not as a substitute for their own experience and insight, but as an occasion for reflecting on their own experience and for sharpening their own understanding.

—Philip J. Murnion

Preface

The Lord has directed me in strange ways. Fifteen years ago I had no intention of working with parishes. My background was in physics as a high school teacher. My doctoral studies were in sociology and theology in preparation for work in urban planning or perhaps campus ministry.

Then my adviser asked if I would like to be part of a research project he was planning. It was to be a study involving a number of parishes and religious groups—Catholic, Protestant, Jewish—and the focus was on the interaction between cultural and religious values in local faith communities. At first I wasn't interested, but the more I thought about it, the more intrigued I became. Consenting to be part of the project changed the direction of my life and ministry.

I was responsible for the Catholic parishes in the study, and I began to learn why some parishes succeed and others don't. At the conclusion of the project I began thinking that my experience might be helpful to other Catholic parishes since I now had a method for getting in touch with the needs and desires of the parishioners. So I approached the National Federation of Priests' Councils to see whether they would sponsor this project of parish research and planning. I also asked my Jesuit provincial if he could free me from other commitments long enough to try out the project. I received support and encouragement from both quarters, and the Parish Evaluation Project was born.

That was in 1973. Since then I have learned much more about parishes, and the more I worked with parishes the more I wanted to write a book about my observations and reflections.

I spent a day in the Parish Project offices in New York talking with Father Phil Murnion and Ms. Suzanne Elsesser about my ideas and insights into parish life. When I told them I wanted to write a book on the subject, their reaction was enthusiastic. That was the push I needed.

Now the book is finished. Many people have helped me along the way. My family—especially my mother and my sister Marion Garvey—has provided not only support but constructive criticism as well. I am also indebted to my companions in the Parish Evaluation Project Office, Ms. Meredyth Wessman and Ms. Carol Wisniewski, for bearing with my ups and downs and in typing and retyping the manuscript. My friends have also been pillars of strength through it all, especially Sister Ruth Kleitsch and John and Ellen Scorzoni. Suzanne Elsesser deserves special thanks for the many hours she spent in editing the final text. I am also indebted to the people at Winston Press, especially Wayne Paulson and Pat Lassonde for carrying this project through to completion.

To all of you I say, "Thank you. Without you there would be no book *Successful Parishes*."

CHAPTER ONE

Current Trends

I have been working with Catholic parishes during the last fifteen years both as evaluator and as resource consultant. I have been both encouraged and discouraged by what I have found.

I have been encouraged because of the way in which both staff and parishioners have responded to the Spirit in their midst as they struggle to renew the parish and to draw that community closer to an embodiment of Christ's Church on the local level. But I have been discouraged by the lack of vision and creativity among parish leaders—priests, religious, and lay—as they struggle to keep the parish afloat amid rising costs and continual demands on their time and talents.

This book is meant to help parish leaders and workers by offering them ideas, insights, and alternatives that will bring them hope and show them how to focus their energies more effectively. To that extent, the book is a "how-to" resource for parish workers. I will build each of the next seven chapters around a story, each about a different type of parish. Woven into these stories are real situations I have experienced in my work with parishes. No one story is entirely true; each is partly the creation of my imagination. Nevertheless, the substance of each is very real.

All the stories have happy endings as the parishes face crises and resolve them. In the real world, however, a parish community is *always* going through ups and downs, and this may be happening in many areas of the parish at once, with few solutions bringing happy endings. The youth program may be at an all-time high while the adult education program or congregational music may be in the depths. Such is the human situation. The parish is at once a complex collection of interacting groups and individuals and a faith community that is striving to respond to the invitation of the Lord in its midst. I hope that this book will help parishes to remain alive and continue to grow into communities of believing and caring Christ-followers.

Before I begin the stories, I will outline the seven trends I have noted in Catholic parishes today, for these trends inspired and underlie the stories. Let me explain what I mean by each of these trends and where I find evidence of its appearance on the American Catholic scene.

1. *Facilitating Leadership:* An important aspect of parish that has changed in recent years, and will continue to change, is the concept of leadership. We are seeing a shift from an authoritarian approach to a facilitating one. The parish leaders provide the occasion for people to come together to share their faith vision, experience the work of the Spirit in their midst, praise God together, and gain strength to continue their work of service to others. It is difficult to be a praying, caring, serving person all by oneself.

Just a few years ago the parish seemed the best way to work out people's faith commitment. Today people are not so sure of that; they need to regain trust in the parish as a truly workable religious organization. And exercising "facilitating" leadership looks like the best way to renew that trust. Parishioners are not seeking the answers from parish leaders so much as a framework within which to experience God and make a faith commitment. Facilitating leadership provides the place, the occasion, and the motivation for authentic Christian worship and service.

In a growing number of parishes, the focus is on the pastoral team, which includes priests and professional religious and lay leaders. This is known as team ministry. Still other parishes are investigating alternatives to the hierarchical experience of leadership as they attempt to move toward a more communal, horizontal form that shares the leadership with lay volunteers. Most American Catholic parishes continue to operate on the hierarchical model, in which leadership rests on the shoulders of the pastor. I have experienced parishes which were led by strong, charismatic figures—benevolent, though creative, dictators. Great things happened in the parish as long as the dynamic leader remained. But once the person left, the parish fell apart, unable to function on its own.

I have also come across situations in which the structure was so loose that there was no direction or planning at all. But many examples of successful facilitating styles of leadership do exist. I have encountered a number of successful models of team ministry in which the staff members share equally in the ministering of the parish. Each person on the team has an area of responsibility and competence. For the larger questions concerning priorities and future directions of the parish, the team—ordained, religious, and lay alike—shares in the decisions. In observing one such team in operation, I was most impressed by its emphasis on prayer. Each meeting began with extended prayer, and after the meeting the team went to the church to pray together and to share the afternoon liturgy with the parishioners. Then the team had supper together. Prayer days were built into the calendar, and the team members encouraged one another to have an active prayer life of their own.

A number of parishes now have lay administrators who free the pastor and staff to spend more time in liturgical, sacramental, and spiritual ministry. In parishes that do not have a resident priest, others—permanent deacons, religious, and lay people—are running the parish and holding prayer services when a priest is not available to preside at Mass. Parish Councils are assuming a greater share in planning future directions for the parish. Parishioners are contributing their talents to run meetings, facilitate groups, and provide professional services such as health care, legal aid, budgeting, and teaching. As more and more lay people take part in the decision-making of the parish, the pastor and professional staff must learn to exercise a form of leadership that will facilitate this lay involvement and provide a framework for it to continue. Therefore strong parish leadership is as essential today as ever, but the definition of leadership has changed from an authoritarian to a facilitating form of behavior.

2. *Basic Communities:* Another trend in parishes is the emergence of small groups called "Basic Christian

Communities." People find it difficult to be part of a parish community where they feel alone among five thousand, or even one among five hundred. As a result there has been a tendency toward smaller, more familiar worshiping and sharing groups. This has varied according to the location and makeup of the parish, but the desire for face-to-face groups, where people know each other by name, is still strong.

In small town communities and inner-city parishes, where the number of parishioners is small, it is of course not so difficult to form personalized parish groups. In suburban parishes, though, the effort to form parish "basic communities" has not been easy since there is so much else vying for people's attention. Parish groups are low on the priority lists of most of the parishioners.

Nevertheless, the desire for parish subcommunities will not go away. People experience many large, impersonal, highly-structured organizations in their daily lives and do not want the parish to be like that. People need the support and friendship of others they know personally if they are going to remain active members of the parish. The ethnic parishes of the American Catholic past survived because they touched this need for belonging and for personal involvement. This sense of belonging must be recaptured and nurtured in the parishes of the 1980s.

In the past, Catholic parishes were created in such ethnic communities. There was a built-in community of language, customs, fear of the new world, and the desire to "make it" in a new and strange society. Ethnic parishes are still developing among the most recent immigrant groups, the Hispanics, and it is in Hispanic parishes that the formation of Basic Communities has been most successful.

But for most Catholic parishes, the surrounding culture has broken down the ties that formerly bound the parishioners together. Parish leaders are now trying to find ways of reuniting the people. They are looking for new kinds of bonds to tie people together; but today those bonds will be common interests and shared values more than language, culture, or security needs. Persons with a common interest like to spend time sharing with others of the same mind or experience. It is not enough to divide a parish into geographical subsections. Without a common interest or shared concern, people will not come together in small groups.

The most successful examples of small parish groups have been those that touched a common interest or significant concern among the people. That is why parish subgroups have sprung up around marriage encounter groups, divorced-separated persons, single parents, parents of school children, even Bible study or prayer groups.

Many informal small groups composed of persons who spend time together and share common concerns already exist in a typical parish. These center around sports events, card parties, volunteers who help out at parish socials, or parents who are waiting to pick up their children. The parish that is able to capitalize on these natural groupings will have the most success in fostering parish subcommunities.

For example, most parishes have unique groups that come to different Masses, and there is a chance to follow up on that clustering. One parish capitalized on its Sunday family Mass by inviting families to help plan the liturgy and in this way provided a feeling of belonging and closeness. Family groups came together two weeks in advance to pray over the readings and plan the liturgy. The groups then contacted other families to help with the Mass by constructing a banner based on the theme, by doing the readings as a family, by bringing up the gifts, or by choosing the songs. Groups of families experienced a sense of solidarity as they worked together to plan the Mass and join in the celebration.

Parish leaders should not feel it is their job to sustain or prop up the parish subcommunities. Rather it is their job to provide the framework, the invitation, the conducive environment, and the right occasion for small groups to form. The people themselves will make the decision whether it is worth their while for the group to continue to meet. The groups may not turn out just as the leaders had hoped. They may end up less organized, less focused, less defined than the leadership had wished. But this may also be a sign of success, since communities that come closer together and form deep and lasting ties are like families. Organization is not always the hallmark of a loving and caring family.

One parish decided to foster the formation of small groups through a three-stage process. The first stage was *social*. People were encouraged to invite their friends for a social event in their homes, whether potluck supper, lawn party, or cards. This happened at least four times during the fall. Some of the groups were from a certain area within the parish, while others drew from all parts of the parish and beyond parish boundaries. If the socializing groups stayed in existence for the four meetings, the next stage was *spiritual*. During the winter months, the groups were expected to have four meetings, each centered on a biblical theme such as prayer, vocation, discipleship, or kingdom. The parish staff provided the materials for the meetings, but it was up to the group to determine the best time to meet and best way to use the themes for discussion. If the groups continued meeting through the scriptural phase, then they entered the final stage, that of *service*. The people were encouraged to identify one area that would be of service to the parish or the larger community. In this way the small communities were given a purpose outside of themselves. This area of service was an outgrowth of their reflection on the Scriptures and on the fun they had in their socializing. The groups were expected to spend the spring months working on these service projects and to reflect on the experience together for at least four meetings. After the experience was over, two members from each of the groups, no matter how far they had progressed in the process, met with the parish staff to talk over the experience and make plans for the coming year.

3. *Linking Groups:* There is a growing trend in parishes to build bridges between different interest groups so as to discourage the formation of cliques. There is a delicate balance between fostering small, personalized groups and keeping these groups open to new people and new directions. For example, a parish that contains a number of cultural subgroups, such as Mexican, Puerto Rican, Polish, Italian, or Haitian groups, might try to encourage each subgroup to come together and gain support and identity from others who speak the same language and have similar interests. But at the same time the parish leaders must look for occasions that would draw people

of different cultures and backgrounds together.

Some parishes sponsor cultural fairs or ethnic dinners that feature different cultural dishes, or they sponsor joint school and religious education projects, or talks attended by many parish subgroups on topics such as parenting, teenage drug addiction, or neighborhood security. Even parishes that are homogeneous in educational and cultural backgrounds are seeking ways to bring parish subgroups together. Many religious education programs, for instance, are stressing the family as a whole, rather than dealing with each age group separately. Family programs are seeking ways of including single and widowed people in their activities so that different age and interest groups can benefit from one another. Sacramental programs that include parents in the Baptism, First Communion and Confirmation preparations are being used in many parishes. This linking of groups flows beyond the parish boundaries as parishes share programs and resources with other churches. This is an effort to break down provincial and in-group attitudes. Catholic parishes benefit from the experience and ideas of Protestant churches and synagogues and neighborhood groups. Some parishes are sponsoring joint activities and programs with other churches and organizations in an attempt to work more closely with religious and cultural groups.

I have worked in a small-town Catholic parish that arranged such a program. It did not have the resources to offer both a family-centered religious education program and a religious education program for each age level, so it linked up with the neighboring town's Catholic parish. One parish offered a family education program while the other offered education classes for each age group. The experiment met with limited success because many people had difficulty crossing parish boundaries and attending activities in another parish. But it was a beginning.

Another parish in a suburban area discovered that its teenagers were spending more time in the Protestant church than in their own Catholic parish. That was because the youth program in the Protestant church had an imaginative youth director who created an environment that attracted large numbers to the activities and programs. The staff at the Catholic parish approached the youth director and asked if a joint project could be planned that would include both parishes. This led to a revitalization of the youth program in the Catholic parish as well as improvement in the relationship between the Catholic and Protestant parishes in other activities.

With the rising cost of personnel and materials and the declining number of priests and religious available for parish ministry, sharing of programs and resources will become more prevalent in the years ahead. It also signifies a unity of faith and purpose that Christ prayed for in the last discourse of John's Gospel, "That they may all be one."

4. *Parish Planning:* Another trend in parishes is the effort to do effective long-range planning. Most of the parish planning of the 1950s and 1960s concerned such questions as whether to build an addition onto the parish school, how large the new church building should be, or how to provide more living space for the sisters teaching in the school. Planning meant blueprints. As it became clear in the late sixties and early seventies that expansion was no longer possible, parish planning became crisis-prevention, that is, how to cope with the changes taking place in the liturgy, school enrollment, the drop in vocations, or the divergent expectations of the parishioners. As each crisis descended upon the parish, the troops were rallied to deal with it, and once that one had passed they gathered their strength for the next onslaught. This type of coping could not be endured for long, so it gave way to attempts to look at the parish from a larger perspective. It led to forming parish visions and goals and planning ways to realize them.

Parishes of the 1980s are seeking new ways to serve their people. Since the parish community is composed of people with diverse needs and expectations, any effort to meet these needs and expectations must be done carefully, with well-thought-out models of parish planning. The models being used are as diverse as the parish situations in which they are being put to use. But successful models have certain ingredients in common.

Desirable Ingredients

One such ingredient is that successful parishes listen to their people, both the old and the young, the active and the inactive, the traditional and the progressive. This listening process is done through surveys, parish forums, phone interviews, or neighborhood meetings. Whatever the method, no plans or changes are made without letting the people in on them from the beginning and encouraging the people to "own" the planning process.

Such listening leads to a second common ingredient of effective parish planning: the formation of short-range, achieveable goals. The goals come in response to the listening phase. The parish leaders listen to the needs of the people and then try to respond to a common desire or expectation. This gives the parishioners a feeling that they do matter and their ideas are being acted upon. Such simple actions as toning down the organ, changing a phone-answering service, picking up debris on the grounds, or improving the public address system in the church can make a difference. The energy expended is small compared to the positive response such actions receive from the people. This listening and responding to desires stimulates a parish community and provides everyone with a sense of hope.

These short-range goals, however, must fit into a larger context. Parish staffs and councils are learning how to dream— a third ingredient necessary for effective planning. What will the parish look like by the end of the 1980s or 1990s? What would we want it to look like if we had all the necessary money and personnel? How much control do we have over the future of the parish? Will it be twice as large or half the size it is now? What will be the vehicle or vehicles for religious education in the parish? Will it be the school, the family, special groups? How will the parish reach out to others and include them in its life? These questions help focus present efforts. If a parish knows where it is heading and why, it is much easier to settle questions of budget, spending priorities, staff positions, and parish emphases.

The fourth ingredient necessary in parish planning models is leaving room for the Spirit. The parish is more than a well-managed business; it is a faith community. Parish planning must be attuned to the Spirit from beginning to end. The Spirit, however, has a way of disrupting our best-laid plans and pointing out new directions. Parishioners must be ready for this and must respond generously and with open hearts to the invitations of the Spirit. This may mean taking risks and trying out new territory. Vatican Council II was one such experience. The explosion of lay ministry in recent years is another. Such urgings of the Spirit can turn a parish toward new avenues of operation. Effective parish planning must make room for these changes of direction.

The fifth ingredient—acting as a model community—rests on the premise that who we *are* is far more important than what we *do*. Parish planning works because people trust their leaders. Parishioners have an intuitive sense about their priests, religious and lay leaders. If the people sense a deeply caring, sensitive leadership, one that is aware of parish needs and is in prayerful contact with the Lord, then they are more likely to accept and respond to whatever plans are made. This kind of mutual caring between people and leaders is the immeasurable ingredient in successful planning whose presence will spell success for a program in one parish and whose absence will spell failure in another, although the programs may be identical.

Finally, effective planning means providing the right atmosphere or environment in the parish. If the liturgies, activities, and programs are conducted in such a way as to give the people a sense of hope, of future, and of vitality, all else will follow suit. Chairs arranged in a circle or in rows facing a desk in preparation for a meeting say far more about how the parish is being run than any amount of words or ideas exchanged during the meeting.

To sum up, good parish planning, whatever model or method is used, has more chance for success if the planning includes: listening to the people; responding immediately to at least a few of the more pressing needs; dreaming about what could happen in the future and working toward accomplishing some part of that dream; giving the Spirit room to work in the parish; looking more to who the leaders *are* than what they *do*; and working at creating the best environment for growth and interchange.

5. *Adult Spirituality:* Another notable trend in parishes is the emphasis on adult spiritual development. Many parishioners hunger for a deeper relationship with their Lord, and they want to know how to include the Lord in their relationships with their spouses, children, and friends. They want more than a child's understanding and experience of their faith, one that relates a growing knowledge of the Lord found in prayer to a growing sense of concern and care for the needs of other people.

Not so long ago, in the era of large Catholic families and flourishing Catholic schools, the focus of religious education and parish spirituality was the children. The "sisters" took care of religious formation, and once a person graduated from Catholic high school, the person was set for life. That has changed. Both in and outside of the Church there is an emphasis on adult education. As families shrink to one or two children and as more people decide not to have children or not to get married, the focus is shifting from children to adults. They are looking for a religious experience that speaks to the needs, crises, and desires of their adult life. What they often find is a staff and lay leadership unable to satisfy their needs or longings. Here are some examples.

A parish council president, mother of six children, decided she didn't know enough about the Church or new trends in theology. No one on the parish staff was able to give her much help. So after completing her term of office she gave up her active involvement in the parish and enrolled in a local Catholic seminary class in theology. She expected to stay only a semester or two. She ended up studying for three years and receiving a Master of Divinity degree. She now spends much of her time counseling seminarians and helping them understand their future role as parish priests.

A couple with a large family have been looking for ideas on how to pray. They did not find what they were looking for in the three parishes they had joined in recent years. They assumed responsibility themselves for the religious education of their children and established family religious rituals in their home in connection with special feasts and birthdays. They had made a few retreats in the past, but the retreats didn't seem to speak to their situation. Then they decided to make an individually directed retreat together, in which each saw the same director individually during a four-day weekend and also spent time in private prayer. For a couple of hours each day they prayed together and talked over their future. The individual and joint prayer led to an experience of discernment about what the Lord was asking of them. It became clear to both of them that the Lord was calling the wife to some type of ministry, and that both the husband and wife were to prepare themselves for this new work when it came into view. What is unique about this experience is that this individually directed retreat and the resulting process of discernment are being experienced by married couples and single people, and not just by priests or religious.

Such examples of lay people discovering new levels of religious experience and adult spirituality can be repeated in impressive variety. Proof of this thirst for spiritual growth among parishioners lies in the popularity of programs devoted to adult spirituality such as Genesis II, Romans 8, Marriage Encounter, the Charismatic Renewal, and the Cursillo Movement. Proof also can be found in the enthusiastic response to parish renewal programs such as *Christ Renews His Parish* or *Renew*. Priests and religious are themselves experiencing a new conversion and revitalization as they try to keep up with the growth in holiness among the people.

6. *Shared Ministry:* By this is meant people other than priests and religious sharing in the spiritual, educational, liturgical, and leadership ministry of the parish. Laypersons are becoming accepted as co-ministers with priests as they share the responsibility of conducting worship services, caring for the needs of the parishioners, and providing direction for the parish. This has changed the complexion and scope of the American parish considerably.

An example of this shift is Communion in the hand. It is a simple gesture that is now commonplace but one that is amazingly rich in its symbolism. It is no longer the sole privilege of the priest to touch the sacred species. Ordinary, nonordained people, even children, can now take the body and blood of Christ themselves, and can have contact with and control over them. This contact with the Eucharist indicates a new status for lay people. They are once again recognized as worthy to touch the bread and the cup and even worthy to bring the Eucharist to others.

The "worthiness" of non-priests to be ministers reaches into every aspect of parish life. Family men are ordained deacons, women are assisting the priest at the altar, lay people are hired as parish administrators, parishioners are being trained as ministers to the sick and dying. The parish itself may be staffed by a team in which religious sisters, brothers, deacons, and lay persons are on an equal level with the priests as co-pastors. Parish ministry, in other words, is no longer "owned" by the priests, nor is it the priests' sole responsibility. Ministering *belongs* to all who are willing and able to share this role of service. This is an astonishing shift in a short time.

Three aspects of shared ministry call for special attention. One is the permanent diaconate. It is still struggling to learn its place in the American Catholic Church. On paper it looks like a partial answer to the shortage of priests and seems to provide at the same time the link between the clergy and the laity. For the deacon possesses the legitimacy of ordination as well as the credibility of a parishioner. Translating this theory into practice, however, has not been easy. The deacon is often confused and frustrated about his role and position of leadership in the parish. In some parishes he has become "a little cleric" who does the same jobs as the priests, except for presiding at the Eucharist and granting absolution. He has also been accused of taking away the ministries that lay people could be doing. People hold back from volunteering because they believe that the permanent deacon is now ordained to take Communion to the sick, lead prayer meetings, and direct parish programs.

As with any new position or ministry, there will be confusion about the deacon's role in the parish until we experience more of his unique contribution and until there is more acceptance of the diaconate in the Church as a whole. The training the deacons are receiving before and after ordination is opening up new areas of ministry, both within and outside the parish.

A second emerging area of shared ministry is the role of women in positions of leadership in the parish. On parish staffs their positions range from those of being religious education coordinators and directors of music or youth programs to co-pastors sharing many pastoral responsibilities with the priests as equal members of parish teams.

Of all the roles women play in the parish, their role at the altar for the weekend liturgies has the greatest impact on parishioners because the largest percentage of them see it. Some parishes vest women and men lectors and ministers of communion in albs to symbolize their joint role with the priests in the Mass. As people become used to seeing women assuming these liturgical roles, they become more accepting of women's joint position with priests as liturgical ministers.

Pastoral care is another area in which women minister along with priests. Many parishes have a program of lay ministers to hospitals and homes, in which the parish visitors console the sick, bring them the Eucharist, and report to the priests if anyone wants absolution or anointing. The majority of these visitors to the sick and shut-ins are women.

Women are also active in forming parish social action committees or human development groups to care for the poor and needy in the area, to sponsor families immigrating from other countries, and to raise the consciousness of the parish community in regard to peace and justice issues.

In most of the parishes I have worked with during the last ten years, the majority of the people involved in shared ministry have been women. As women become more involved in parish ministry, they themselves begin asking questions about their leadership role in the parish and the Church. This leads to the issue of the ordination of women to the diaconate and the priesthood, a question that has only recently surfaced on the parish level.

When I began surveying Catholic parishes in the early 1970s, the question of the ordination of women was not included because no one thought of it. Since then it has come up so often that a question about attitudes toward the ordination of women had to be included in a 1978 revision of my questionnaire. I suspect that one issue for the '80s may no longer be the place of women in parish ministry, but how to include more men in the running and decision-making of the parish.

A third area of shared ministry in which people other than priests do the ministering is "peer ministry." In this approach, people of the same age or subgroup take responsibility for ministering to one another. This is especially valuable for teenagers or young adults—groups that are often difficult for adult staff members to reach. Instead of the staff running the youth program, for instance, a small core group of young people assumes the responsibility of becoming ministers to others of their own age and interests. Since this core group is in touch with what people of their own age like and what problems they face, they plan activities that will relate better to those likes and needs.

This same concept of peer ministry, which has been used in Alcoholics Anonymous for years, can apply to senior citizens, divorced-separated, or handicapped parishioners. The right environment, the right occasion, and the right place for the peer groups to get started are necessary. The parish staff provides the support and occasional direction, but peer group members plan and conduct programs on their own.

The rise of shared ministry provides new hope and promise for Catholic parishes, but there are inherent difficulties. People can become so interested and involved in parish ministry that they do not leave enough time for their own refreshment or for other commitments associated with their jobs and families. To solve this problem, one of the important ministries performed by staff and lay leaders is the continual recruiting of new people to fill vacancies in the parish ministries. These new volunteers will allow the overworked ministers time to rest and take care of their individual and family commitments.

7. *Alternative Directions:* Twenty years ago it was important for American Catholics to know the geographical boundary lines of their parish and to attend that parish. This was especially important when it came to having a new baby baptized, arranging a wedding or funeral, or enrolling a child in the Catholic school. Although parishes did differ one from another, especially if they served ethnic groups, there was still

the common Latin language for the Mass and sacraments, common rubrics, common belief, and of course the Baltimore Catechism.

That has changed now. People feel freer to choose the type of Mass and the kind of religious education or even the parish they will attend. This new independence in choosing one's style of worship and parish involvement is the result of many religious and cultural changes. The trend in the Catholic Church in recent years, which was supported by the bishops at Vatican II, has been to put more stress on the communal aspect of the Catholic religion and less stress on the central authority of the Church. There is no longer such great emphasis on conformity or on the need for every Mass to be done in exactly the same way.

On the cultural side, the American Catholic Church is no longer a separate subculture in American society. As a result, Catholics are assuming many of the same religious character-istics as their Protestant and Jewish neighbors. Even Hispanic groups, the most recent ethnic minority to gain prominence in the American Catholic Church, are becoming assimilated into the larger society as more Hispanic immigrants learn En-glish and take positions of leadership and authority in their work and in the professions.

One reason why American Catholics are becoming more identified with the general American culture is that they feel free to choose their own mode of religious worship and the way they will practice their religion. This trend toward greater freedom of choice has many expressions in a Catholic parish. For instance, people want smaller groupings so that they can feel they belong to a community. The decision-making and administration of the parish are more democratic in structure, and therefore laypersons have more of a say in what is hap-pening in the parish. Correspondingly, there is the growing need to find people to lead and minister to groups such as the youth, singles, divorced-separated, elderly-retired, to name but a few of the many groups now served in a typical parish.

This new freedom is manifest in the parishioners who are making more choices about their own beliefs, styles of worship, and forms of parish involvement. In short, the emphasis on free choice influences the structure and operation of the modern Catholic parish as it tries to respond to a variety of needs and desires among its people.

These, then, are the seven trends I have noticed in American Catholic parishes: facilitating leadership, basic communities, linking groups, parish planning, adult spirituality, shared ministry, and alternative directions. The fictitious, composite parish stories that follow are related to each one of these trends and provide concrete examples of how a parish can put each into operation. The stories take place in unique types of parish communities, such as predominantly Black or Hispanic congregations or parishes located in urban, suburban, or rural areas.

CHAPTER TWO

Part 1: The Black Experience

St. Joseph's is a small parish with a huge church. It began over a hundred years ago. At that time the parish was thriving in the midst of a new and growing city. Now the church, the school, and the rectory stand in a decaying section of the central city. The original parishioners, all of whom were white, have moved away from the area. They have been replaced by a predominantly Black population.

A few years ago it looked as if the parish would close. The church building was leaking and was impossible to heat in the winter. The school was still in operation, but the families of the Black students, most of whom were not Catholic, could not afford to continue it. The number of priests went from four down to one as the pool of available diocesan priests shrank. Only the pastor remained.

About 150 people came to the one Sunday Mass, and though the parishioners were determined to keep the parish open, the pastor was getting tired. He felt he could no longer cope with the rising costs and the deterioration of the parish. With much regret and some feeling of guilt, he asked for a new assignment, knowing that this would probably mean the end of St. Joseph's parish.

The diocesan personnel board did not know what to do. Should the parish be put on the assignment list for a new pastor? Would anyone want to accept such a difficult position? The board decided to go ahead and list the parish, expecting no one to consider it. To their surprise, however, not one but *two* priests asked to be reassigned to this center-city parish, but with the stipulation that they could go into the parish as a pastoral team. The two priests also made it clear that if they were given the parish their team would include others besides themselves. Their intention was that all team members would be on an equal footing, sharing the operation and decision-making of the parish and, in so doing, provide new hope and new directions for St. Joseph's.

After some discussion the personnel board gave the priests permission to try it out for two years. The bishop gave the experiment his blessing. It would be a part-time assignment for each of the priests, so that the equivalent of one full-time priest would serve the parish. The bishop asked that the other half of their time be devoted to parish development and renewal in the diocese as a whole. The two priests were grateful for the chance to work together in the parish, but they decided not to accept the assignment until they had had a chance to ask the people of St. Joseph if they wanted a pastoral team approach instead of a single pastor.

At the next Sunday Mass the priests introduced themselves and explained to the people what they had in mind. They made it clear that this was an experiment and that it all depended on whether the parishioners wanted to be part of this adventure. At the end of their presentation the congregation broke into applause, and the Mass was delayed half an hour because of the spontaneous outburst of joy from the people. The small congregation filled the church with singing, clapping, and spontaneous prayers. They prayed that this would not only assure the continuity of the parish but that it would also bring it new life. The parish sisters and lay teachers who had attended the Mass invited the whole congregation to the school hall after Mass as a way of keeping the celebration alive and to give the priests an opportunity to meet the people. The priests were amazed at the positive reaction; any fears they had about not being accepted by the parishioners vanished.

The priests went back to the personnel board and told them they were willing to accept the new assignment. They asked the diocese to continue to subsidize the parish and in this way show the parishioners that the Church is still interested in people who are without money, prestige, or privileged position.

The priests moved into the rectory on May 1, the feast of St. Joseph the Worker, and started to search for others who might want to join them as members of the pastoral team.

After talking to the teachers of the school, the priests discovered two women who seemed interested. One was a sister who lived in a small community of sisters in the neighboring parish. She had worked in the neighborhood for a number of years. The other woman, who was Black, had taught in the parish school for the last five years. The two priests invited the women to be part of the pastoral team, and after much discussion the four decided to give it a try. The diocese agreed to pay the salaries of the two women as a sign of its support of the pastoral team approach. The team had hopes of finding a fifth member, perhaps a parishioner who would be willing to become a permanent deacon in the parish, but at the moment no such person could be found.

The four team members did not know one another well, nor did the priests know the parishioners. The team decided to tackle the problem of getting to know one another first. They spent two days away from the parish sorting out their own expectations for the parish and for one another. It was hard for the laywoman, a mother of four, to spend a night away from her family, but she realized how important this time was for the growth of the new team.

At the meeting the priests said they were not only looking for a chance to share the ministry and decision-making of the parish with others, but they were also anxious to share a lifestyle that would provide for personal growth, something neither of the priests had experienced in his previous assignment. In their previous parishes they had got along well with the pastor, but it was a lonely existence. Each priest had been on his own with little chance for personal interchange or growth. The priests wanted a style of team ministry that included shared meals, prayer, and recreation, as well as a sense of responsibility and accountability to one another.

The two women, on the other hand, made it clear that each of them had a good living situation of her own so they were not looking for a type of team ministry that would require extended personal interaction and commitment. The team members spent two days discussing their different expectations and finally agreed on the amount of time each of them would spend working in the parish and the time that would be spent together as a team.

The two priests were forced to alter their expectations. They decided to work at forming a closer community between themselves, which would include time for prayer, recreation, and mutual support. The team of four agreed to meet each week for support and interaction. These meetings, however, would be limited in order to leave time for the primary reason for the pastoral team's existence—ministering to the people in the parish.

Once the team had dealt with its own expectations, it was time to start on the second issue: getting to know the parishioners. The team started thinking of what could be done to revive the parish and give it hope for a more promising future. Getting to know the people was not difficult if this meant only those parishioners who came to the Sunday Mass. That was only 150 people. But the team wanted to get to know all the people in the neighborhood as well. The four team members concentrated on the Mass-goers first. Everyone who came to the Sunday Mass was asked to put on a name tag. The priest who presided at the Mass allowed extra time for the greeting of peace so everyone could walk around the church and greet the other parishioners. The team provided coffee and donuts in the rectory after Mass so that people could get to know them and give them ideas about the parish.

The coffee-and-donuts discussions revealed untapped talent among the parishioners. One person volunteered to start a gospel choir, and she had a friend who could play the organ. A group of people agreed to be the new greeters at Mass. They would welcome people and make sure everyone had a name tag. They would also take care of setting up for Mass and taking up the collection. Others agreed to organize people to do the Scripture readings and to practice with the readers before Mass.

Once the team and the Mass-goers got to know one another and the parishioners began to take charge of some aspects of the Mass, the next step was to reach out to the neighborhood. The two women on the team already knew many people in the area, but they felt that a systematic canvass of the neighborhood would be helpful. Through her years of teaching in the parish school, the married person on the team had come in contact with many families who were not parishioners. These families had learned much about the Catholic faith through their children. The team guessed this might be the time to contact these families and tell them about the new emphases and direction in the parish.

At the Fourth of July Mass and barbeque the team announced its plan to visit every home within the boundaries of the parish and asked for volunteers to help in this effort. The door-to-door canvass would take place in September. Twenty-five people agreed to help.

On the four weekends of September, each member of the team paired up with a parish volunteer and went door-to-door to every house and apartment in the neighborhood. The team member and parish volunteer explained to each householder the new activities and direction at St. Joe's. They encouraged everyone, Catholic, Protestant, and uncommitted, to come to any or all of the functions in the parish. If the pair encountered people who said they were Catholics but were not attending Mass, or people who said they were interested in learning more about the Catholic faith, they encouraged them to join a new program for parents of the school children. That program not only explained the teachings and customs of the Catholic faith but provided time for sharing prayer, Scripture readings, common concerns, hopes, and fears.

The home-visitors asked the people what they thought were the more pressing problems of the neighborhood and what could be done to solve them. The parishioners who accompanied the team members helped the latter understand the significance of what the people had told them. The parishioners themselves gained much in the process, especially a sense of importance as co-workers or co-ministers with the team members. Of the twenty-five who volunteered, sixteen eventually became key figures in revitalizing the parish. As the team members looked back on this exhausting month of visiting, they agreed that it was one of the most difficult but also one of the most rewarding experiences of their ministry in the parish.

The visiting gave direction to the parish in many ways. It gave new hope to the neighborhood. The diocese had always said it was interested in the people of the area, but the visiting proved that the concern was not an empty claim. The Church was *listening* to the people. Many of those who were visited already knew about the Catholic faith from attending Catholic school. Some had been baptized but had long ago given up attending Mass because it had not met their needs. The visiting reawakened their interest and desire to attend church. The team members also had a chance to meet other religious leaders in the area, most of whom ran storefront churches or held services in their homes. Since that time many of these preachers and ministers have provided valuable information to the team about the needs of the area and have made suggestions on how to minister to a predominantly Black community. The sixteen laypersons who helped with the parish visiting became aware that they were important to the life of the parish: They had the ability to become leaders in the community. Besides discovering this wealth of talent, the team uncovered new areas of need that are still providing direction to the team and parish lay leaders. These visits also gave them ideas about how to deal with some of the problems: poor quality and high-priced foods in the area's stores, lack of heat in apartments, drug traffic, over-crowding, burning of vacant property, and gang warfare.

After meeting the people in the neighborhood, the team began to deal with the immediate needs of the parish. Four parish groups were formed, each including a member of the pastoral team and from five to twelve parishioners. One group of ten people dealt with changing the image of the parish and with reaching out to the neighborhood. Its task was to let people know that St. Joseph's was there for the people. The first order of business was to put up a large sign on the corner of the church property telling everyone who went by that St. Joe's was alive and growing. The sign made the parishioners feel proud to belong to St. Joe's. As the sign's message changed each month, it soon became a topic of conversation.

This group's next task was to follow up on the home visits by inviting those interested in learning more about the Catholic faith to be part of the new information program. It was to be run jointly by the parish team, the school teachers, and some of the home visitors. Its aim was not only to explain the teachings of the Church but also to encourage people to join the parish. The second phase of this follow-up was to focus on one need in the neighborhood and to organize people to deal with it. Housing occupied the committee's attention for the first year. The group members encouraged people to keep their homes looking nice. They pressured the city to tear down or rehabilitate abandoned buildings. They called upon landlords, especially those who lived outside the neighborhood, to take care of neglected property by making badly-needed repairs. Eventually, the people in the neighborhood got the message that St. Joe's was concerned about human needs and not just about getting more people to join the Catholic Church.

The second group had the responsibility of planning liturgies and parish activities. Most of the parish functions and organizations had fallen apart during the gradual decline of the parish. This group was to rekindle interest in parish activities. Bingo had endured and had kept the parish school afloat in recent years, but little else was going on to draw people together. The group split into two subcommittees, one to plan the Masses and the other to plan parish get-togethers.

The group planning the Mass discovered that many of the parishioners had been Baptists at one time and that their Baptist background influenced their religious practice. For instance, they were familiar with and frequently used the Bible for prayer and reflective reading. They did not mind spending more than an hour at Mass each Sunday. Using this knowledge, the liturgy planners tried to put more emphasis on the Scripture readings at Mass and to spend more time explaining the meaning of the Sunday readings. This group also started a Bible study and prayer group that met once a week. The parishioners were encouraged to participate in the Mass, not only by singing and reading at Mass, but also by making petitions at the prayer of the faithful, by contributing to the prayer of thanksgiving after Communion, and occasionally by "giving witness" to the meaning of the Scripture from their own experience. The people especially liked using both species of bread and wine for the Communion rite. The Mass planners trained volunteers to take Communion to the sick and shut-ins following the

Sunday Mass. The new spirit of participation and involvement by the people at the Sunday Mass began to catch on. Even the skeptics who had felt the situation at St. Joe's was hopeless were beginning to change their minds.

The other subgroup of the liturgy and activities committee had its hands full planning get-togethers for the parish. This subcommittee contributed to the rebirth of St. Joe's parish perhaps more than any other of the four groups. For one thing, the subcommittee discovered something that should have been obvious but had been missed. The people's involvement in the parish did not coincide with the school year—that is, active in the fall, winter, and spring and inactive during the summer months. The people of St. Joe's were anxious to have parish functions during the summer but not in the winter months of December to March, when it was too cold to attend. Come spring, and especially summer, the people were eager to participate in parish picnics, bazaars, barbeques, carnivals, and fund-raisers. All the subcommittee had to do was give the people the occasions to come together from April to October and enjoy one another; all they needed was a place and an excuse to meet. People spent all day preparing barbequed ribs over a charcoal fire or putting together special hot dishes for a potluck supper. That tradition started the first summer the committee began its operation and has continued to this day.

The third parish group set out to uncover potential leaders. There had never been a parish council, nor is there one now. Parishioners are still not certain whether this is what is needed. The team knew from the beginning, however, that they themselves could not hope to take care of all that had to be done. Nor did they wan. to. They saw their ministry as providing the stimulus and the environment for people to assume the responsibilities of leading the parish groups and activities.

The lay leaders, however, did not feel they were able to run meetings and lead groups by themselves. The group was able to find many natural leaders in the parish. But when approached, these people said they did not feel qualified to be leaders. They needed training to increase their confidence and allow their talents to be put to use. To this end the four team members held leadership training sessions. The sessions gave the new leaders skills in running good meetings, constructing agenda, solving problems, fostering group decision-making, and dealing with group conflicts. They began by practicing these skills on one another. Slowly they began to assume responsibility for running parish meetings and planning activities. Many of the new leaders had become aware of their leadership abilities in the original parish visiting program with the pastoral team. Their confidence grew as they acquired more skill and experience leading groups. During this time it was difficult for the team to be patient and not to take over the running of meetings for the sake of greater efficiency. Nor was it easy for the lay leaders to overcome their own feelings of inadequacy. But each time a project or meeting that was planned and run by the lay leaders succeeded, they gained confidence to take up the next activity.

The fourth group's responsibility was the upkeep of parish buildings. The diocese had promised to subsidize the parish, especially for the first two years of experimentation with the pastoral team. In addition, two suburban parishes had pledged financial support. The work of this committee was to determine the most creative way to use those monies.

The first order of business was the church building. It needed new plumbing, plaster, and paint. Moreover, the building was too big for the congregation. Should it be torn down? The committee finally decided to use the building by making it water and wind tight, and then put a smaller "church" inside. First, all the pews and furnishings were removed. The roof was repaired, the windows sealed, and the pipes replaced. Next an inexpensive geodesic dome was constructed in the center of the church. This inner church will seat 300 people. A plain wooden altar will be in the center. The triangular panels of the dome, the movable chairs and the decorations will all be in bright colors. Only this inner "church" will be heated and air-conditioned. This inner structure will be for liturgical celebrations and religious functions. The larger, outer church will be used for socials in the warmer months. Initial costs for this adventure are high, but the money saved on heat and utilities will make it worthwhile in the long run.

Renovating the church has been an exciting project and the committee members have learned about architecture, heating, lighting, and building codes in the process. The work is now in progress. The parishioners are doing much of it themselves and have invited the two suburban parishes to join them in the project.

The school building was and still is an unsolved problem. It is expensive to maintain, but it provides an important service to the neighborhood, because the parish school offers quality education unmatched by the public school. The diocese has pledged to keep the parish school open, at least for the next few years, as proof of its commitment to the people of the central city.

The next order of business for this group is the rectory. The priests find it too large for the two of them, so they have asked the maintenance committee to think up alternative uses for it. The priests are thinking about moving into an apartment down the street from the church. This would give them a chance to separate their work from their living and would also keep them in close contact with the people, especially if they go through with their plan of doing their own cooking and shopping.

The sister on the team already lives in an apartment along with other members of her religious community. She finds this a help in acquiring enough distance from the parish to keep a sense of perspective. The homemaker on the team helped the priests write a proposal and a budget for their plan to move into an apartment. They appreciated her insights and, most of all, a copy of her "quick and easy" recipe book. They sent the proposal to the chancery and received permission to move into the apartment for a one-year trial period. The bishop made it clear that the rectory could not be sold and that whatever use was made of it the priests would have the option to move back into it at the end of the year, if they so wished. The priests were delighted and invited all the parishioners to help them move out of the rectory. So many helpful people came that it turned into one of the greatest celebrations in the history of the parish.

The maintenance committee has received many suggestions for use of the rectory, ranging from a home for the elderly to a day-care center for children of working mothers.

The work of the pastoral team and of the four committees—outreach, liturgy-activities, leadership, and maintenance—has given the parish a future. The two-year period of experimentation is coming to an end. The diocese has allowed the team to extend its involvement in the parish for another two years. An evaluation group that included both diocesan personnel and parishioners has just sent a report to the bishop about the work of the team and the hopes for the future of the parish. The following statements were among the comments that the bishop made in response to the report.

The team approach has not only turned the parish around but has provided the parishioners with a living example of what it means to be a parish community. The presence of both women and men on the pastoral team, working together for the good of the parish, is an important aspect of the example of community the team gave to the parishioners.

The attempts by the team to instill a feeling of worth, responsibility, and leadership into the parishioners was an important step toward the assurance that the present direction of the parish would continue, even when one or more of the team members leaves the parish.

The outreach project that sought out people interested in the Church and tried to respond to their needs not only was a help to the parish but turned out to be one of the best examples of evangelization in the diocese.

The diocese will continue to support the attempts of St. Joseph's parish and the pastoral team to minister to the people of the central city. The diocese feels it is receiving much in return for its financial support in learning how to give new life to a parish and hope to its people.

Part 2: Facilitating Leadership

As I mentioned earlier, an example of the general trend of facilitating leadership is the *team ministry* approach chosen by the leaders of St. Joseph's parish. The term has different meanings. What I mean by team ministry is that all members of parish staff, including the priests, share equally the leadership role of the parish. Each person on the staff has an area of competence and responsibility, but no one person is considered the head of the parish staff. All have equal voice in the important decisions of the team and of the parish. One person may be considered the administrator and is the spokesperson for the parish and team to the diocese. Another person may be responsible for the liturgies and prayer life of the community; another may be in charge of education; another the pastoral care and outreach ministry. But no one person has greater authority than another. They share the pastoral ministry as peers.

People choose to be part of team ministry for a variety of reasons. Their reasons lie on a continuum between wanting to be an example of Christian community to the parish and wanting to pool staff energies and talents in performing parish ministry. Those who choose team ministry because they want to be an example of community stress the internal aspects of team interaction. They want to ensure that enough time and attention is devoted to getting to know one another, to mutual support, prayer and shared activities, and to making decisions as a group. By the care and support they show one another, the team members become an example of Christian community to the parish as a whole. This example challenges other groups and organizations to become Christian communities themselves.

As I have suggested, people also choose team ministry because they want to share with others, on an equal basis, the joys, responsibilities, and burdens of parish ministry. Rather than work alone in an area of parish ministry, team members work together on projects. They make decisions as a group about what needs to be done in the parish, and they share the responsibility of getting the work done. This emphasis on sharing stresses the outer life of the team—that is, the way the team relates to the parish. People who choose team ministry from this perspective want to be sure that enough time and energy are devoted to work among the parishioners. They feel that time spent in team prayer and discussion should not get in the way of the reason for the team's existence: ministering to the needs of the people.

Team members may be at different places on the continuum I mentioned, and because of this, their expectations of one another will vary. Those who are on the "forming Christian community" end will expect an emphasis on group sharing and interchange. Those who are on the "parish ministering" end will expect an emphasis on working together on parish projects. Members can also change position on the continuum depending on their needs and expectations at a given time.

In our story of team ministry at St. Joe's, the priests were looking for a life-style that would provide human interaction and emotional support, things they had lacked and missed in their previous assignments. The two women, on the other hand, were anxious to get on with the work that had to be done in the parish. Because the women had family and community experiences of their own, their personal involvement with the team, while important, was limited to the times the team had agreed to meet for shared prayer and planning.

It can happen that after a pastoral team is in operation for awhile, the expectations of the members change. Suppose that at a meeting of the team at St. Joe's one of the priests wants to plan the next leadership training session, while the sister on the team is looking for support from other members of the team because she is having difficulty dealing with the pressures of her work. The priest is on the task-oriented end of the continuum, and the sister is on the community-building end. Each person is looking to the team for help but with a different set of needs and expectations.

It is this dual aspect of parish team ministry, which includes both group interaction (forming Christian community) and task-oriented duties (ministering to the people), that makes team ministry a more demanding form of parish staffing than the traditional pastor-supporting staff form. Despite this, people continue to seek out the team approach, because they feel team ministry comes closer to their understanding of Church and of Christian community.

Since the team concept of ministry is new to the Church, we are still learning how to cope with its demands and difficulties. As more people experience team ministry and become members of different parish teams, their struggles and problems will become easier to manage. They will be better aware of what to expect and what not to expect from team ministry. Until people have more experience with pastoral teams, a few guidelines might help make the transition to team ministry easier.

The first guideline is to allow time to deal with important issues. These should be addressed even before the team begins its ministry in the parish.

Dealing with Preliminary Issues

One job for a new team to face is to get to know the parish. What kind of people are in the parish or the neighborhood? What is the history of the parish: its ups and downs, its triumphs and failures, its previous pastors and styles of leadership? This knowledge will influence the way the team performs its ministry to the parish, as well as the way the team members will interact with one another. The same four persons who made up the pastoral team at St. Joseph's would relate to the parish and to one another differently if they had chosen a suburban parish or an Hispanic parish rather than a parish with a predominantly Black congregation. The approach of "have team, will travel" is not enough, no matter how well members of the team relate to one another. The parishioners and the neighborhood shape a team; after all, they are the reason for the team's existence. If the team is not aware of the hurts, joys, traditions, and past crises of the parishioners, it will miss many opportunities for ministering to the needs of the people. Most important is the situation of the parish just prior to the team's arrival. What was the staff like? How did the people relate to the pastor, if there was one? Are they now grieving his departure? Are there customs and commitments that the parishioners are used to or will demand of the team? Were there any recent crises or blowups that have shaped people's opinions or caused divisions in the parish? One of the first tasks of the St. Joe's team was to learn about the people and the neighborhood *before* making any plans or starting new programs.

Another important issue or task, besides getting to know the parish, is for each team minister to form a clear idea of what his or her own dreams and expectations are for the team and for the parish. And then persons must be able and willing to describe these dreams to the team in an understandable way. This is important because team ministry includes both the inner-directed or community-building aspect and the outer-directed or ministering aspect. These expectations will change once the team starts to develop a history together, but spelling out these expectations at the beginning will save the team time and energy later when it is in the midst of parish business. So many parish concerns take up the team's time that little is left over for dealing with interpersonal matters between team members.

It also helps if team members discuss the issue of their understanding of Church. Avery Dulles' *Models of the Church* (Doubleday, 1974) can help clarify various approaches to ministry and definitions of Church. Each team member may place a different emphasis on community-building, liturgy, pastoral care, or social awareness, and this will influence both the interactions among team members and the corporate image of the team in the parish.

Team members need not all agree about everything. This is a beauty and an advantage of a team: that the members manifest in their own emphases and priorities for the parish the rich diversity of the Church and its mission. But it is important that team members have a chance to talk about their agreements and disagreements *early* in their experience so that each person's reaction to a suggested parish emphasis or program can be understood and accepted by other team members.

Another important issue for a new (or changing) team to deal with is role definitions and time commitments of each member. A team is not a family and cannot survive with a loose structure as can a family. It must have well-defined areas of responsibilities, job descriptions, and time commitments. But neither is team ministry a business. There must be a balance between establishing areas of responsibility and commitment, and allowing room for flexibility and change. At St. Joe's, the women on the team could devote less time to team interaction than could the priests. Because the women had other commitments to a family and to a religious community, they could not promise unlimited time to the team and parish. The priests also had other commitments connected with the diocese that kept them from devoting all their time to St. Joe's. The team members had to sit down and clarify what was expected from each person, what aspect of the ministry was the primary responsibility of each team member, and how much time each person was expected to spend on team interaction and on parish tasks. This is especially true if the team includes persons who are part-time and have commitments that lie beyond team ministry.

Because of the demands that team ministry places on them, team members should be given regular and frequent periods away from the team and the parish in order to maintain their own dedication, commitment, and personal well-being. The amount of time that each person may need away from work will vary, but it should be spelled out both at the beginning of the team's formation and whenever a new member joins the team. Two full days per week free from parish and team commitments would be an appropriate norm to establish at the beginning; it could be adjusted as individuals gain more experience in team ministry and interaction. As you will recall, it was because of this need for time away that the two priests decided to move out of the rectory and into an apartment.

Finally, a pastoral team should be aware at the beginning of its ministry that an inner-outer (team and parish) tension will inevitably arise. People have only a limited amount of energy available for any task. If a person is part of a team, then some of this energy will be expended trying to support, confront, and relate to other members of the team. Some of this energy will also go into planning, organizing, and conducting parish programs. Unless the team members have spent time deciding how their energies will be expended, they will feel pulled in two directions at once. Either they will be so exhausted from carrying out their ministry in the parish that they won't have the psychic energy left over for team discussions and interaction, or they will use up so much energy dealing with the interpersonal conflicts and growth of the team itself that they will become worn out and unable to perform their work in the parish. These two aspects of team ministry—group interaction and parish ministry—should be a help to each other rather than an obstacle.

One way to reduce the tension between the needs of the team and of the parish is to look at the schedule of parish commitments at the end of the summer. In many parishes most of the commitments are crowded into the period between the middle of September and the middle of November. From Thanksgiving to the middle of January some of the pressure on the team from parish programs subsides. This may be a good time for the team to spend in group interaction. Usually the parish tempo picks up again during February and March, but after Easter the pace may slow down somewhat and the team can spend more time together. In some parishes the summer is a good time for long-range planning, personal interchange, and incorporating new members. Summers are important periods for teams to deal with deeper issues that could not be handled during the busy months of September through May.

These, then, are six issues that should be faced when a team begins its ministry: learning the parish and its history; knowing one's own dreams and desires; spending time discussing each person's expectations for the team and the parish; learning one another's understanding of Church, including the areas of agreement and disagreement; establishing clear role definitions and time commitments; and preparing for the inner-outer tension between the demands of team interaction and those of ministering to the parish.

These same issues must be addressed any time a new member joins the team. This is necessary because any new member creates a new team. I am not sure who first said it, but it still rings true: "Apathy is someone working on someone else's goals." If a team does not refine its goals each time a new person is included, then that person is not a member of the team.

Once the team has faced the preliminary issues, other guidelines will help assure its success. It is helpful, for instance, *to have an outside observer sit in on at least some of the team meetings.* If communication among members becomes strained or if vested interests become so strong that team members can no longer relate to one another or perform their ministries in the parish, then a facilitator can help the team over these hurdles. Even when the team members are working well together, it helps to have an objective observer provide feedback. This person need not be a professional group facilitator. A staff member from a neighboring parish or a friend of someone on the team could provide this service. The team observer should be someone that all members trust, however, and one who listens well and can give honest and helpful opinions. Having an outside observer present for at least some of the team meetings helps keep team and parish problems in perspective. Team members can become so involved in the parish and in their own interaction that they can miss the obvious. It is easier for someone who does not have a personal investment to point out a problem, offer a tentative solution, or find humor in what the team considers serious.

Another help to team ministry is to *establish criteria for parish and team success or failure.* Teams start out with dreams for their own interaction and for team ministry in the parish. Dreams are important. But it is also necessary to establish realizable goals. Meeting these goals is one way of knowing that the team is coming closer to its dream.

A team goal might be to grow closer together into a Christian community. To tell whether the team is doing that, ask: Does the team continue to meet regularly, and do the meetings go deeper than giving reports on what each person is doing in the parish? How well do the members support the projects and ministries of one another? If a crisis arises or an important decision is to be made, how well does the team pull together? On the other hand, does the team dissolve into a collection of individuals, each person working alone? If so, the dream of community has not been realized.

What are some criteria for judging the effectiveness of the team's ministry in the parish? Do more people show up for meetings, liturgies, adult education than before the team began functioning? Do they contribute more money to the parish than previously? Do more people volunteer for service projects in the parish and neighborhood? Does the council work together better?

Whatever criteria of success are used, the team needs ways of knowing that it is accomplishing what it has set out to do. Otherwise the members can become discouraged and give up. Team ministry is not easy: It is demanding and takes much energy. But it can be a satisfying and enriching way to minister in a parish. Setting realistic goals and knowing whether those goals have been achieved (by applying established criteria) can give a team a sense of accomplishment and a feeling that whatever the energy expended, it is worth the effort. The pastoral team at St. Joe's did set goals for itself and did see improvement, both in the parish and in its own growth. The four team members felt a sense of pride and accomplishment as they saw new leaders emerge in the parish community and saw the parishioners gain hope in the parish.

A team should not be self-sufficient. It should *be accountable to others outside itself.* These "others" could be the parish council, or a diocesan evaluation committee or personnel board. If the team does not have to answer to any body outside itself, then one of two things can happen: Either the team can become so discouraged with its own interaction and attempts at shared ministry that it gives up the effort altogether, or the team can become so powerful that it is impossible to change its own way of acting.

If the team becomes discouraged, then an evaluating group outside the team can offer support in its low moments. It can help pick up the pieces when the team falls apart and help it get started again. If the team becomes too powerful, then an outside group can "blow the whistle" and keep it accountable to the parish. Not that any team would want to become that powerful or self-sufficient. But a team can become so close-knit and efficient that the parishioners feel overpowered. The team can then control the parish. The ministry performed by such a team might be well done, but its self-sufficient image will be counterproductive. When this happens, a diocesan, regional, or parish group must be engaged that can call the team to accountability for the benefit of the team itself as well as for the parish as a whole.

It is possible, however, for the evaluating group to get in the way of a team's ministry. For example, some dioceses have a policy that if one member of a parish team leaves, then the whole team must disband. This is a waste of experience and talent. It puts an unnecessary burden on team members to stay together, regardless of the desire of individuals to seek another position. Parish teams must be given freedom to change their composition according to their own rhythm and needs. The team ministry continues in the parish although the makeup of the team changes. The periods of transition when persons leave or join the team can be growth-filled moments. It would be unfortunate to deny a team the experiences of new growth by disbanding it when a change occurs.

The team should *arrange for each member to spend an extended period away from the team*, with pay. This leave is granted to each member on a rotating basis. The one who is on this sabbatical is still considered a member of the team and is expected to return with new skills and insights, with renewed commitment and strength. This keeps the team alive and open to new developments from beyond the parish. If the team is small and resources are limited, it might be possible to link two teams together. In this way, a neighboring parish could "cover" for the missing member or a parish program could be held in common with another parish for the duration of the person's absence. It is so important that people have time away from the pressures of the work that some creative alternatives for accomplishing this should be considered. This is also true for regular and frequent team days away from the parish so that personal interchange and parish planning can take place without interruption.

Team members should *consider putting a time limit on* their *commitment to the team.* Because of the demands of this form of parish staffing, people cannot be expected to do a good job indefinitely. A successful team can allow people to leave and can make room for new members without disrupting the operation of the group. Because strong interpersonal bonds are created among team members, members often find it difficult to leave the team or to allow others to join. An openness and flexibility among team members, however, can be an example to the parish community: The team acquires the reputation of being a welcoming group, one that is willing to change and to be responsive to the Spirit's challenge and call.

The team members might make a commitment of three years to the parish and to one another. After that time each person's involvement could be evaluated and renewed for another three years. Renewal after six years, however, would be subject to more serious discussion that would weigh the advantages and drawbacks of continuing on the team.

Another advantage of viewing team ministry as a limited commitment is that it opens the way for others to assume positions on the team. This was the direction that the St. Joe's team was heading as it sought out one of the parish men to become a deacon and to become a part-time member of the pastoral team.

To sum up, suggestions that I think should be considered while the team is in operation are: Allow time to deal with important preliminary issues; include an outside observer for at least some of the team meetings; establish criteria for measuring the team's effectiveness; be accountable to a group outside the team; plan extended periods away from the parish, both for the team and for individuals; and put a limit on each person's length of involvement on the team.

CHAPTER THREE

Part 1: The Hispanic Parish

St. Anthony's parish goes back to the beginning of this century when Italian immigrants flooded into the city. A new church was built, only blocks from the territorial church, to minister to their spiritual, physical, and social needs. St. Anthony's had no boundaries; its ministry reached out to all those of Italian background. Over the years the Italian population has dwindled, and in the last few decades immigrants from Latin America and the Caribbean have been taking up residence in the area. These people are Puerto Ricans and Mexicans primarily, but other countries in Central and South America are represented as well. At the moment, Italians amount to about a quarter of the parishioners; Mexicans make up about half; other Hispanic groups, primarily Puerto Ricans, make up the rest. About five hundred families are now considered members of the parish community, a third what the parish had in its heyday.

People from other parts of the city still remember coming to St. Anthony's on Columbus Day for the gala Mass and parade. But in recent years the parish has become so split among various groups that it has become hard to gather people for any occasion or feast day. It looked like an impossible situation. The pastor, who had been there during the transition, had tried to cope with the changes taking place in the neighborhood, but it seemed he could never do anything with one subgroup without the others complaining about unequal treatment. He invited a religious order priest who could speak Spanish to say first one, and then two, Masses for the Hispanics each Sunday. When he did this, however, the English-speaking parishioners complained about "giving away" the best Masses to the "Latins." His decision to close the school and consolidate with the territorial parish school just three blocks away threw the parish into an uproar for months. He finally threw in the towel and asked for a new assignment. The parish had become too diverse and confusing for him to deal with.

The diocesan personnel board had difficulty finding a replacement. Finally a priest was found, one who had been studying Spanish and wanted to serve in a predominantly Hispanic parish. Two laywomen who taught in the neighboring parish school agreed to spend six hours a week as part-time staff members of the parish. They were familiar with many of the parishioners, since they had taught their children in the parochial school. The visiting religious order priest, who had been saying the Masses in Spanish and ministering to the Hispanics in the parish, agreed to move into the rectory to help the pastor get started and to give him support. He made it clear, however, that his commitment to the parish could be only part-time, since he already had a full-time teaching position, and that his stay in the rectory would be limited to one year.

The new staff of four came together one evening to map out the strategy for the parish. What could be done at St. Anthony's to put some order into the chaos? The discussion went long into the night. All four were aware that this was a significant moment in the life of the parish. The three who knew the area—the religious order priest and the two women—talked about their impressions of the parishioners. They described the situation in the following way: The Italians are older people who own homes in the neighborhood. Their children have grown up and moved away, but the parents cannot leave because they will lose all the equity they have built up over the years. Many run small businesses in the area, such as restaurants, bakeries, and laundries. But their heart is no longer in their work or in their neighborhood. They don't feel attached to their neighbors or to their parish anymore. Many feel caught in a situation over which they have no control. Much of their time is spent talking about what it used to be like and about their present fears. They can't talk to the newcomers who have "taken over the neighborhood," as they put it, because many of these new people don't speak English, much less Italian. These "old-timers" live from one holiday to the next and look forward to the times when their children come back to the neighborhood to celebrate Christmas, Easter, and the Feast of St. Anthony. These are the days that give the people a reprieve from their fears and enough new energy to keep going until the next family celebration.

The situation for the "newcomers," the Hispanic parishioners, is different. They now make up the majority of the parish membership. They are part of a larger group of people in the area who call themselves Catholic but who no longer attend Mass. Many, instead, are attending storefront and "home" churches that have sprung up in the neighborhood. These more spontaneous religious gatherings seem better able to serve the spiritual and social needs of the Hispanic people.

It is important not to lump all the Hispanic groups into a single culture, for the people come from many different countries and have different customs. Some common threads, however, do bind the groups together. First, no native clergy have accompanied the people in their migration north. This means that the people are without spiritual leaders who can understand and relate to their tradition and culture. The people, therefore, feel estranged from a religious heritage that has been very much a part of their upbringing. Consequently they are attracted to the small, intimate, and devotional rituals of the storefront churches that relate better to their backgrounds than does the parish.

Also, these parishioners—whether of Mexican, Puerto Rican, or other Hispanic origin—do not have their hearts and souls in this country. They think they are going to be back in their "own" country next year, or certainly the year after next. "Once I get enough money, I'm going back home." Few ever see this dream realized, but it provides a mindset that has implications for the future of the parish. It fosters a lack of permanent commitment to the area and to the parish among the Hispanics and also a lack of concern about improving the neighborhood or getting involved in the parish. It makes the formation of an American-Hispanic parish difficult because the pull is always to the mother country. The original Italian immigrants must have felt this way when they first came to

St. Anthony's, but they did not have the luxury of considering a return to Italy. It was too far away and the mode of travel was too difficult. The present jet transportation and the proximity of Mexico and the Caribbean Islands makes that dream more realistic for many of the Hispanic parishioners, and so even many of the second- and third-generation Hispanics feel attracted to the homeland in a way that was impossible for previous immigrant groups.

Another common thread among the Hispanics is their deep piety and love for religious ritual. The Mexicans are devoted to Our Lady of Guadalupe, the Puerto Ricans to the rosary and St. John the Baptist. Many of their religious practices, grounded in ancient Indian rituals, have roots in the dim past before the Spaniards visited their lands. This religious heritage is evident in their songs, prayers, fiestas, and vigils. The Hispanic Masses in the parish reveal some of this piety, but there is still something missing. The young people are bored and the parents confused. Yet this piety and this love for religious ritual are vital forces among the people. If these are nurtured and given outlet in the parish, they can provide new life for the community.

Each Hispanic group has its own cultural and religious traits. For instance, the Mexicans find confrontation difficult; they don't want to offend by saying no or disagreeing. If asked to come to a meeting or a Mass, they will say that they will make every effort to attend, but in effect it may be a "no" answer. Many of the Puerto Rican parishioners, on the other hand, will come to meetings and talk long into the night. But many Mexicans need encouragement and support to come to a meeting. Once they have overcome their hesitancy, however, they will come and their warmth adds much to the meeting.

A significant number of the Mexicans do not have documents that give them official status as residents or as visitors in the United States, and so they live in fear of deportation to Mexico. This is a fear that the Puerto Ricans do not have. As a result, the Puerto Ricans may appear more sure of themselves than the Mexicans.

Much more was said that eventful evening when the four staff members came together to discuss the parish. The new pastor learned about the parish and about the people he had come to serve. In the weeks that followed, the pastor, along with his part-time staff, began looking at the operation of the parish with a critical eye. The buildings were in reasonably good repair. Even the school building was in good shape, despite having been vacant for a few years. The pastor made plans to rent the school building to the city for continuing adult education in the area. Without the financial burden of a school, the pastor did not have to initiate fund-raising events such as Bingo. It was a relief to him, nonetheless, to know that there was still a Catholic school three blocks away that served the needs of the people, and he encouraged the parishioners to support the school and accept it as their own.

He discovered that the weekend liturgies left much to be desired. The early Mass on Sunday was in English and attracted the Italian parishioners. He had the feeling that many of these people had given up on the parish and attended Mass only out of habit and a sense of obligation. Any attempt to introduce congregational singing met with little success. The other two Sunday Masses were in Spanish and were livelier, but there was no carryover into the people's lives, no expression of their own heritage, no celebration of their own piety and deep faith.

The new pastor decided to invite the people into the rectory after the Sunday Masses to talk about how they felt. He had intensified his study of Spanish and knew that if the Spanish-speaking parishioners talked slowly enough he could understand them a little. Slowly he became aware of in-groups among the Hispanics—not only among different cultures, but within each cultural group as well. He was able to identify leaders in each group, and he tried to become acquainted with these influential people. The others on the staff helped him to learn who were the natural leaders in the parish. Many of these were not frequent Mass-goers.

The pastor began to realize that the place to begin renewing the parish was not at the weekend liturgies. This was a departure from his previous parish experience. He called another meeting of the part-time staff to share his observations with them and to start making plans for the future of the parish.

The staff set aside a full day for their deliberations. The pastor has been reading about *Comunidades de Base*—Basic Christian Communities—and he wondered whether this might be the best approach for the renewal of the parish.

The staff met long into the night and again on the following day. They talked about the prejudices and the in-fighting they had noticed among the different subgroups in the parish, about the weekend liturgies that did not seem to inspire the parishioners, and about the possibilities of starting small groups or "Christian communities." Perhaps this would be a way of tapping the religious faith and piety of the people. Each staff member decided to spend time reading about the small-group concept for the parish and to come up with ideas on putting this approach into practice at St. Anthony's. (As the pastor now looks back on that meeting, almost five years later, he is struck at how naive they were and how much they have learned in the meantime.)

After their reading and reflection, the staff members committed themselves to forming four groups of ten persons each in the parish. The groups would meet one night a week for six weeks during September-October and again during Lent. The staff would invite the natural leaders to be members of the small groups. One of the groups would be English-speaking and the other three Spanish-speaking. The structure of the groups would be informal. Meetings would begin with a Scripture reading from the previous Sunday's liturgy, followed by discussion of how the Scripture readings might apply to the parishioners' everyday problems. The purpose of the small groups would be to provide people with an experience of community and to train parishioners to lead other small groups in the parish.

After the first six weeks, the staff got together to discuss the results and to decide what future there might be for this approach to parish renewal. Reactions were mixed. On the positive side, the staff felt that both the Hispanic and Italian people had enjoyed coming together. As proof of this, they reported that most of the people had stayed with the groups throughout the six sessions. On the negative side, the groups were too loosely structured, and too much depended on the staff member to lead the discussion. The staff decided to go ahead with the second set of small-group meetings during Lent, but they knew that some changes would have to be made for the coming year. About that time a word new to most Catholics became popular in the Church—*evangelization*. The staff began to reflect among themselves on how forming small groups might fit the new emphasis on evangelization. The staff members prayed and reflected together on Jesus' way of evangelizing: gathering a few people together and setting their hearts on fire with his presence and the promise of the Kingdom and then charging them with the work of keeping the new Church alive. With this in mind, the staff began making plans for the next year's small groups. Rather than forming the groups themselves, the staff decided to involve the parishioners in this process. The staff had so many other obligations that they had little time available for gathering people into groups. If parish groups were to be formed and maintained, much of the work would have to come from the people.

In May the staff asked one person from each of the first four groups to meet with the staff in order to prepare topics for the new set of small-group meetings. The staff wanted to know what neighborhood problems or concerns were on people's minds. Questions surfaced concerning food. How many times had people heard the word spoken in the past week, and what meaning did it have? People mentioned hearing food spoken of in connection with rising prices, sales, shortages, food stamps, ethnic foods, and special recipes. Then the people were asked to think of all the times Jesus had mentioned food: "My food is to do the will of my Father," "I myself am the bread of life," "A farmer went out to sow seed. . . ." What meaning did the word have for Jesus? The group members were then asked to reflect on whether a neighborhood response or action was needed to help people deal with the problems they might have in relation to food.

Food was one of six topics the four staff members and the four lay leaders prepared for the small-group discussions of the second year. Each group was to be led by the lay leaders with the support of the staff. The lay leaders invited more people into the groups so that each group would have fifteen to twenty.

This approach worked so well that new groups had to be formed in the spring to accommodate the extra people who asked to take part.

That was four years ago, and the groups are still in operation. The pastor and staff have learned a great deal since the original attempt was made to form "Christian communities" in the parish. For example, the preparation and running of the small groups is now handled by the parishioners. Each August and January, groups of four come together to plan topics and choose Scripture passages for the next session of small groups. This year there are ten such groups. Each group of four is responsible for one topic or theme. A coordinating group then takes the ten topics, edits them, and types up a program for the coming sessions. The themes for last year's groups were weakness, temptations, television, spirits, planting, journeys, rules, speed limits, men-women, recipes.

After the topics are agreed upon, the ten groups of four seek out new members to join them in the small groups. Most will be the same members as in the previous sessions, but new ones are sought out and encouraged to attend. These are people who may not be active Catholics but are interested in becoming part of the group discussions. The "Christian communities" average sixteen members each. An effort is made to include people from different cultures. A few of the Spanish-speaking groups include both Mexican and Puerto Rican members, and a few of the English-speaking have both Italians and Hispanics. The majority of the groups have a single cultural identity, though, and are composed of people who are at least acquainted with each other.

Each group has its own name, such as *Guadalupe, San Juan, Santa Maria.* The group members make a commitment at the start of each series to meet once a week for ten weeks. They meet in a different home each week, and the four original planners take turns leading each meeting while the other three lend their support. A staff member is often present but takes no role in running the meetings. He or she is just another member of the group.

The small groups spend time talking about the topic for that session and its religious significance, using the scriptural passages provided. The leaders encourage members to reflect on problems and experiences associated with the themes and how these problems might be dealt with from a Christian perspective. Occasionally the group reflection may result in an attempt to solve personal and neighborhood problems, but this seems to meet with limited success. The people find it a help just to come together to talk over their frustrations and concerns. This is one way they are able to deal with their loneliness, fears, and feelings of helplessness. This past year the ten groups met during the fall and again during the spring. After each series of meetings the original group of forty, composed of the four leaders from each of the ten groups, met with the staff to evaluate the meetings and to talk about improvements for next year's meetings.

Once a month one of the small groups plans a Mass and social in the parish. The Mass is attended by all the groups, both English- and Spanish-speaking. It is followed by a potluck supper in the basement of the church. In June the whole parish plans a fiesta. Each small group sponsors a booth featuring its unique contribution to the parish. The booth has the name of the sponsoring group across the front—"St. Anthony's Pizza," "Teresa's Tortillas," "Ring-toss by Francisco."

The change that these groups have produced in the parish during the past five years has surprised the pastor. The old-timers have reinvested in the parish; it feels like "home" again. They have a chance to come together now and share common concerns, to talk over the old days, and to meet the newcomers with less apprehension. They discover that many of their concerns and problems are shared by both new and old parishioners, whatever their background and culture.

The Mexicans and Puerto Ricans, young as well as old, seem to be getting to know each other better. The parish Masses are reflecting the changing mood in the parish. Last December's celebration of Our Lady of Guadalupe was attended by both English- and Spanish-speaking parishioners. Two choirs provided the music, in both languages, and a mariachi band played at the breakfast following the Mass. The fiesta and other celebrations during the year, such as the Mother's Day and Columbus Day dances, raise enough money for the upkeep of the parish and for community projects such as finding jobs for the newcomers and challenging the city to maintain public services in the area. These are outgrowths of one or more of the small-group projects.

The question now is where this small-group movement is heading. Where will the parish be five years from now because of these communities? The staff will probably be smaller then, since the religious-order priest plans to leave the parish. One of the women on the staff expects to move to another part of the city. That would leave only the pastor and one part-time staff member. Two of the core-group leaders appear interested in joining the parish staff, and this would help ease the burden. But they both have full-time jobs, so their commitment to the parish and the staff will be limited. This is a concern to the pastor because he realizes he cannot operate the parish by himself. Although the small groups function well with the people's leadership, it is still the pastor and staff who provide the motivation, impetus, and even the legitimacy for the groups to continue to function. At times like this the pastor feels it is unfortunate that a few of the core lay leaders could not receive training and be ordained priests. They could then help with the sacramental ministry of the parish. The formation of small groups is becoming known in the diocese, however, and other priests are showing interest in St. Anthony's small-group approach. They may be willing to help out in the parish for short periods so they can learn how to form "Christian communities" in their own parishes. This possibility gives the pastor hope that priests will ask to become part of the parish staff at least on a part-time basis when the religious-order priest leaves.

In the next five years the parish will have a higher proportion of Hispanic parishioners as many of the old-time parishioners die and more immigrants move in. More of the Hispanics will be second-generation English-speaking parishioners and will want to be considered Americans as much as Mexicans or Puerto Ricans. St. Anthony's might eventually become an American Hispanic parish in which the people are proud of both their own heritage and their identity as American Catholics. The pastor hopes that, in the process, the people will learn to respect one another's background and culture and will find a common identity in their care for one another and in their struggle to overcome the oppressive conditions that many have to endure. If this becomes a reality, it will be primarily because of the life and vitality supplied to the parish by the presence of the small "Christian communities."

Part 2: Forming Basic Communities

The "Basic Communities" concept has been most successful among Hispanics who have felt oppressed by their surroundings. They have felt the need for support and strength from others and for this reason are attracted by the chance to share their experiences in small groups. The small-group approach also works well among people who are neither sophisticated nor overburdened with numerous group activities. The people at St. Anthony's, for instance, considered the base communities a welcome relief from the monotony of their lives and work. It also helped the Hispanics deal with a new and strange environment.

The question is whether small groups can be a useful tool in other, more "typical" parishes where people have other commitments and many groups are vying for their attention and involvement. To answer this question I will discuss the *Comunidades de Base* (Basic Christian Communities) and see how they can apply to English-speaking American Catholic parishes.

The roots of the Basic Christian Communities are in South and Central America. In the 1950s, priests and sisters and other concerned people there thought the best way to educate the people was to bring them together in groups small enough to get to know one another and to speak freely about their feelings, problems, and needs. As these groups began to form, the organizers came to realize that the groups were communities rooted in a common faith.

The participants talked about their frustrations and feelings of helplessness. The group leaders helped the people see how this was related to God's Word in the Scriptures, and how God favored the poor and the oppressed. This experience gave the people strength and a feeling of self-worth. It also encouraged them to seek changes in their oppressive living conditions. To this extent these Basic Christian Communities had social justice implications. The communities concentrated on the present, trying to deal with immediate problems. They did this by talking about their problems, by listening to others who had similar difficulties, by providing support and hope to one another, and by seeking solutions to their problems. All this was done from a Christian perspective as they reflected on the significance of the Word of God in each one's life.

It is reflection by a supportive group on common problems and on the Word of Scripture that makes this approach so appealing to Hispanic groups in Latin America and in the United States. The groups deal with immediate situations rather than with long-range goals. For people who think of their stay in the United States as temporary, as many of the Hispanics do, this emphasis on the present moment is very attractive.

Small groups offer a direct and simple spirituality through a reflection on God's Word in the Scripture. For example, in St. Anthony's parish the groups reflected on how Jesus' words relate to common problems such as food, jobs, housing, and crime. This approach does not demand sophistication. As groups developed, they acquired more structure and complexity, but the root experience is simple: sharing common concerns in the context of the Scriptures with a view to overcoming fears and frustration. This approach appeals to people who do not have many other outlets for discussing their problems or for sharing significant aspects of their lives with other people. It also appeals to people who feel intimidated and used by others who have more money, prestige, or influence. The question arises whether such an approach can work in parishes where the population is not Hispanic. Certainly small groups can work in such parishes if they include large groups of people who feel oppressed by their environment and who do not have opportunities for voicing their complaints or for experiencing any hope that some change for the better is possible. That is why this model worked at St. Anthony's and would work at St. Joseph's, our parish in Chapter Two. But what about a parish that serves a middle- or upper-middle-class community? Will small groups work there?

This poses a problem. Unlike the predominantly Hispanic parish, the typical middle-class Catholic parish is composed of people who have many—perhaps too many—other outlets for group activity. They belong to voluntary organizations both within and outside the parish; their commitments fill whatever time is left over from work and family involvement. For some people these commitments revolve around the parish, so that the same people come to a number of meetings and belong to many parish organizations. For the majority of the parishioners, though, their commitment to the parish is limited to regular participation in the weekend Masses and an occasional appearance at a parish function. This is unlike St. Anthony's, where attendance at Mass did not have as high a priority for the people. They were more likely to attend other parish functions, but only if they felt comfortable and accepted.

Another difference is that the parishioners in a middle- or upper-middle-class Catholic parish do not feel that they are low persons on the cultural ladder. They may feel oppressed by the "system," especially as prices rise and fuel grows scarce, but they are part of that system and have some hope of being able to influence change. This is the difference; they have influence. These parishioners have adapted to the secular American culture to such an extent that they do not feel drawn to groups that provide a means to voice frustration or offer help in coping with an oppressive environment. That does not mean that people cannot be led to an experience of sharing with others and of gaining insight from Scripture into the meaning of their lives and current situation. The popularity of Marriage Encounter, Genesis II, Charismatic Renewal, and divorced-separated groups shows this is possible.

But the formation of small groups will encounter passive resistance from the majority of the parishioners in a middle-class parish. Only a small percentage of the parishioners is likely to become involved, at least in the beginning. The people need a positive emotional experience through direct involvement in small groups in order to overcome their initial resistance. This positive experience will have to be strong enough to compete with the overcrowded schedule of events that fill their lives.

In looking closer at the groups that are thriving, we find some common threads, many of the same ones that we found in the groups that became so successful at St. Anthony's. What keeps the people coming back to the group is some vital issue or personal concern. In the Hispanic and Black communities it is a common heritage, together with a sense of Christian support, that the group provides each person in the face of the frustration and fear they experience in their daily lives. In the middle-class parish, some groups thrive because of some neighborhood, parish, or family concern that touches each member of the group deeply enough to stir up interest. This interest creates a desire to keep coming to group meetings. It is the support and acceptance during a time of loneliness and pain that holds divorced-separated groups together. Concern for their children will bring a group of parents together. Others come together to talk over neighborhood problems or to talk about God's role in their lives. The chance to discuss some vital aspect of people's lives keeps drawing them back together. Without this, a group has no reason to continue to meet.

Small groups that stay together do so because participants—though not all thinking alike—share not only a common concern but a common viewpoint about that concern. The group members have many of the same values and are able to accept and respect one another's opinions. This is why artificial groupings of people who live in the same region do not usually succeed. At St. Anthony's each small group was formed by the core group of four who went around the neighborhood inviting people they knew, their own friends and friends of friends. This same element is present in parish subgroups that have continued to meet: The participants agree on a basic understanding of Church, liturgy, social involvement, and Christian education.

A closer look at groups that succeed reveals that the group members share a common goal or purpose. No one may be able to articulate the goal, but members know they come together to achieve a desired end. The goal of the "Christian communities" at St. Anthony's was to achieve a solidarity that would give the people a feeling of belonging and hope. The participants overcame their isolation from one another and helped one another gain confidence that they could improve their own condition.

Sometimes this solidarity would result in action, such as challenging local officials to put up a stop sign, collect garbage more often, or repair the streets. Other times the goal would be less obvious, such as helping each person understand his or her faith better, caring for one another, or reaching out to others with love and concern. This sense of direction is a necessary ingredient of a successful group. In the typical parish the goal might be to improve some aspect of the parish, such as congregational singing at the liturgies, educating the young, or visiting the sick in the parish. Whatever the focus, the group must be goal-oriented to have a future. Traditional parish organizations have continued to exist because of a well-focused goal or purpose. The Altar Society's goal is to care for the church building, the St. Vincent de Paul Society to collect food for the needy, the Holy Name Society to run parish benefits, and the choir or folk group to provide music at the parish Masses. This same sense of purpose must be built into the formation of any small group or "Christian community" in the parish.

Finally, the groups that stay together do so because of the demands *the group members* make on one another: demands to be faithful about coming to meetings, demands to keep the commitment alive between meetings (perhaps through prayer and concern for one another), demands to prepare for the next meeting, demands to participate in activities stemming from decisions made in the group, demands to support each person in the group and encourage everyone to take an active part. In other words, it is not the work of the parish staff to keep groups meeting; parish small groups must be self-initiating and self-sufficient.

Dividing the parish into geographical regions usually is *not* the way to form successful small communities. It is more realistic to study the parish carefully and try to discover what natural groupings already exist and build on these. Some natural groupings may be concentrated in geographical regions. Others will cross regional boundaries and even reach out to areas beyond the parish. Many divorced-separated or Charismatic Renewal or Cursillo groups are like this. Groups also form around a common task or ministry in the parish, such as the grammar school, the choir, reading or ushering at Mass, or visiting the sick and lonely. These are the groups on which to focus to see how they can be supported, encouraged, and given direction.*

Because the formation of small parish communities is difficult, only a limited number of them are likely to catch on or thrive. Too many other commitments get in the way, both in the lives of the parishioners and in the time that the parish staff can devote to the formation of small groups. Nevertheless, the demand for small parish groups does not go away. People need the companionship and support these groups provide if they are going to remain a part of the parish—or of the Church, for that matter. To make the formation of small parish communities a reality, I offer the following suggestions.

Suggestions for Forming Small Groups

Keeping in mind that Catholics are exercising more freedom of choice and that self-interest is the primary motivator, planners should *allow small groups to develop naturally.* The staff's job is to provide the framework, the invitation, the right environment and the best occasion for the small groups to get started, but it is not the role of the staff to sustain or prop up the groups that are flagging. The formation of groups takes time, even years. They never develop exactly as the planners had hoped or expected. Often the result is better than what the staff expected, but it is seldom the same as originally envisioned. The groups will be less tidy, less focused than the organizers might have wished. That may be a sign of success, however, because group members who grow close and form deep, lasting ties may not be concerned about following an agenda or ending on time.

*For a discussion on the ingredients of community-building, see Evelyn Whitehead's chapter in Whitehead's *The Parish in Community and Ministry* entitled "The Structure of Community: Toward forming the parish as a community of faith" (New York: Paulist, 1978), pp. 35-51. See also Evelyn Eaton Whitehead and James D. Whitehead, *Community of Faith* (New York: The Seabury Press, 1982).

Planners should *start small*. They should not try to restructure the entire parish into small groups at one time. A few solid groups to begin with, perhaps only one, is enough. These groups will provide the impetus for other groups to form later on. Also it is better to *have a number of people responsible for the planning and the running of the group* so that no one person feels overworked or becomes burned out in the process. Although many people in such a parish may be capable of leading groups, these people usually have a number of other commitments. To be given the responsibility of planning, conducting, and sustaining a parish small community is often too heavy a burden for one person. (See Davis Killian, cited in the bibliography.)

It helps to *gather the group leaders together for training and mutual support*. At St. Anthony's this was done before each set of group meetings. Although the purpose was to suggest topics for the groups to discuss, the planners gave support to one another and in the process learned how to run better meetings. In a large parish, where the staff is already overextended, these planning sessions for group leaders are the occasions for the staff to train and support the groups. The groups then function on their own. In this way, the success or failure of the group depends on the leaders of the group, not on the staff. The leaders, whether two or more per group, are usually the critical ingredients of a successful small group. This is why calling group leaders together is important, both to plan good meetings and to evaluate the operation of each group. Here a critique can be done on the groups that have not functioned well or have failed altogether. Such an evaluation helps other groups from making the same mistakes.

Another help is to *encourage each group to have its own identity, its own reason for existing*, and its own area of outreach or ministry beyond itself. Naming each group is one way to give it a sense of identity. A name, however, is not enough; many of the "named" groups in a parish have no life to them. If small groups are to remain alive, they must have a purpose or a focus for their energy. In the *Comunidades de Base* this sense of purpose flows from the desire to come to grips with and solve personal and neighborhood problems. In middle-class parishes the sense of direction and purpose can come from a common ministry or mission for the small group, such as seeking out and welcoming newcomers, or raising consciousness on social justice issues in the parish. In these areas the members of the group challenge one another and call the group to accountability to live up to the commitment of the Gospels that the members share.

Finally, the small groups need a faith component, one that is revealed and supported through reflection on the Scriptures. Otherwise the small groups deteriorate into Rotary Clubs or human-potential groups. At St. Anthony's the topics chosen for discussion included passages from Scripture as a way of focusing attention on the Christian response associated with each topic. This same effort of *including God's Word in the discussion of common concerns* must be an integral part of any small "Christian community" in a parish. Without this scriptural emphasis, the heart and soul of the group is lost.

These, then, are my suggestions for successfully forming small parish groups: allow groups to develop naturally; start small; provide training and support for leaders; give each group an identity and a ministry; and emphasize the place of Scripture in the faith life of members.

CHAPTER FOUR

Part 1: The City Parish

Immaculate Conception parish had its centennial celebration two years ago. It was a gala affair with a commemorative booklet that contained pictures of the first wooden church built at the intersection of two muddy streets, the old school building put up at the turn of the century, the half-finished Gothic structure that is now the church building, and the three pastors who directed the parish for most of the hundred years of its illustrious history. (The first two pastors lasted over twenty years each, and Father McKenney—loved by some and feared by others, but remembered by all—was pastor from 1927 to 1965!) The centennial celebration included special Masses, dinners, a dance, picnics, and even a parade. People came from great distances to be part of their former parish's celebration. Two years later, the parishioners are still talking about the celebration. They seem to feel a need to talk about the past since there is little to look forward to in the future.

The parish is located on the fringe of the city—neither inner city nor suburbia. The parish plant is elaborate, including a church that seats eighteen hundred, a rectory for five, a convent for twenty-two, two school buildings with a total of twenty-four classrooms and a recreation center that has a gym, auditorium, and cafeteria. The rectory now has only two priests and the convent four sisters. At one time plans were made to add a swimming pool to the recreation center, but these were never realized. Father McKenney had a reputation as a builder. The parish is now paying the price. At the moment, one year's heating bills come to more than the original cost of building both the rectory and the convent.

The average age of the adult parishioners is forty-five. The school enrollment, which peaked at 1,350, is down to 350, and many of the students come from families who are not part of the parish. The parish rolls, which once showed over 2,500 families, now show 950. But only about 300 families return envelopes in the collection.

The present pastor is becoming worried. The Sunday collection is not enough to pay operating expenses. The buildings are paid for, and there is a reserve account to draw from; but according to the latest projections, this reserve will be depleted in the next four years. Something must be done both to improve the financial outlook of the parish and to lift the low morale among the parishioners. Also, in the last two years the section of the parish nearest the city's core has been changing. Some parishioners are moving out and are being replaced by Hispanic and Black families. This has caused apprehension in the parish even though the new homeowners seem to be improving the area. Parishioners wonder whether the entire parish will undergo a change of membership, and if so, when. Many of the younger people have left the area, anticipating the change. Many of the older parishioners who would like to move have too much invested in their homes and too little income to think of changing.

Over a year ago the pastor called together his staff to think and talk about the future of the parish. Up to that point the only planning the staff had done was to deal with immediate crises, such as the fire in the choir loft or preparations for the centennial celebration or the diocesan assessment for inner-city schools. The staff then consisted of the pastor, the priest associate, the sister principal of the grammar school, and the religious education coordinator, who took care of the religious education program for public school children as well as the liturgical music program in the parish. Primarily because of her creative organizational skills, the principal of the parish school had managed against all odds to keep the school open over the last four years. And it was she who insisted that the staff deal with the future of the parish.

The staff spent a full day trying to figure out the present situation and possible options, given the limited resources available. They decided to look at the history of the parish for the last eight years—the time of the present pastor's tenure—

to see if the events of the recent past could shed light on the present situation. The principal drew a line across the blackboard. The line represented the life of the parish over the previous eight years. She asked everyone on the staff to tell her what each one thought were significant events in the lifeline of the parish, both positive events and negative ones. As the staff members remembered events, she put these on the board together with the approximate time they had occurred.

When no one could remember any more significant events, the staff of four looked at their composite history of the parish. They discovered that many organizations had at one time flourished but that now only a few groups remained. These organizations were the Holy Name Society, the Altar-Rosary Society, the Ushers' Club, and the choir. Even the parish council was a shadow of what it had been three years ago, when it was involved in the planning of the parish centennial.

The centennial had been a significant event—a lift for the parish. At the time, the parishioners had pulled together. But now they were back into their own little groups and cliques, especially in reaction to the new arrivals in the parish—the Blacks and Hispanics. The older parishioners did not show much openness to these newcomers.

As the staff looked at the history of the parish, they agreed that in recent years the people were less involved in weekend Masses. People were not interested in serving as lectors, and it was difficult to find families to bring up the gifts. So many people had moved that the staff were not even sure who were members of the parish. The construction of the parish historyline had forced the staff to realize how critical the present situation was. They wondered if the parishioners shared their own assessment of the parish so they decided to ask existing parish organizations for their impressions. Since the historyline had been such a help to the staff members, they decided to ask each parish group to go through the same experience.

Each staff member took two organizations to work with and helped each group draw up its own history-line. When the staff's and organizations' history-lines were compared, the staff discovered that the people had better memories than they themselves did, especially in remembering those events that revealed the amount of change in recent years. For instance, the people were more aware of the time when four times as many sisters taught in the parish school, when the altar rail was removed, when the early and late Sunday Masses were dropped, when the youth group began providing music at the 11:30 Mass, when there was standing room only at most of the Masses, and when violins played at the Christmas Midnight Mass. And of course the people all remembered the centennial celebration as the most significant event that had happened in the parish.

At the conclusion of the exercise the members of the organizations agreed with the staff's assessment that the parish needed new life and plans to keep people from losing hope. It was indeed a critical time for the parish. Actually, they had already turned the corner on the way to new life, though they had not been aware of it at the time. The turning point was the parish census.

The pastor mentioned at the parish council's history-line session that the census cards were almost worthless because they were so out of date. He asked the council if they had any ideas, and from this simple question came the birth of a new parish spirit. The staff and council put their heads together and came up with a scheme for finding out who were and who were not still members of the parish. First, a new census card was designed, and during the month of September the cards were put in the pews during the weekend Masses. One member of each family unit was asked to fill out the census card and put it in the collection basket or in a box in the back of the church. These new cards were put in the parish file to replace the outdated ones. The new cards included not only census information but also whether people needed assistance from the parish such as visiting, information about parish groups, or a Communion call. This simple procedure updated over half of the census cards.

But four hundred old cards remained in the file. Were these people still living in the parish, and if so, why didn't they come to Mass? Were there other Catholics in the parish about whom the leaders knew nothing? The staff and council decided to find out. The six council members and the four (already overworked) staff members could not do the job by themselves; volunteers were needed. The six council members divided the parish into six regions and each took responsibility for one region. They had to find twelve volunteers for each region to help take the census. An announcement was made at all the weekend Masses asking people to volunteer for a limited amount of time—three hours on Saturday morning and enough time to cover one city block door-to-door. In return they would receive a free lunch on Saturday and a dinner after Mass the following Sunday evening. It was meant to be a good time as well as a help to the parish.

The response surprised everyone. The council needed seventy-two persons, but over a hundred volunteered, both old and young. Many who volunteered said they had been waiting for an opportunity to become involved in the parish, but none of the existing groups or activities had attracted them. This project was appealing because it would take only a few hours of their time and did not require much skill or experience.

The volunteers were asked to come to an orientation meeting on the following Saturday. In the meantime the staff, with the help of the council, prepared a flyer describing the parish's long history in the neighborhood, existing parish organizations and activities, and the schedule of parish Masses. They also made up an instruction sheet for the census-takers, indicating that those parishioners who had filled out a census card at the parish Masses did not have to be visited. The canvassers could still pay them a friendly call, however, and would contact everyone else on the block. If an individual or family showed interest in joining the parish, a census card was filled out for them. The people visited would be given the opportunity to ask for help of any kind from the parish or to suggest ways of improving the parish. Everyone was to be given a flyer describing the parish and its operation.

On Saturday morning almost all the people who had volunteered came to the meeting, and they were grouped according to the six parish regions, each group led by one council member. The volunteers were asked to choose as a partner someone they did not know well, perhaps someone older or younger than themselves. (Many new friendships stemmed from that morning's pairing up.) The pairs received enough census cards and parish flyers for the block they were to cover. Because so many volunteers showed up, and because they did not have to visit the families already listed in the updated parish file, each pair had to knock on only about forty doors.

The leaders told the volunteers what to do if no Catholics lived in the home (leave a flyer, answer questions, ask for ideas) or if the home included Catholics not registered in the parish (ask if they would like to register, if they have any complaints about the parish, if they would like a member of the staff to visit them, and if they are in need of any assistance such as Communion, transportation, or counseling). If no one was home they were to leave a flyer with a note saying they would be back later. The pairs were encouraged to start immediately; they were to complete the canvassing before the next Sunday. The meeting concluded with a prayer service centered around the theme of Jesus choosing seventy-two disciples and sending them out in pairs. After lunch the volunteers set off with enthusiasm to canvass the parish.

The census concluded with a Sunday evening Mass and dinner. Before Mass the volunteers gathered to deliver their census cards and tell stories about their adventures—barking dogs, people talking through locked doors, discovering a long-lost acquaintance, returning to a home seven times before finding anyone in. Their experiences provided the theme for the Mass and lively conversation during dinner. The Altar and Rosary Society prepared the food, just like old times.

That evening became a key moment in the life of the "new" parish. Besides the two hundred new census cards that were added to the file, many requests came in to help a sick person, to visit a shut-in, or to talk over problems with a staff member. As a result of the door-to-door canvass the final tally for the parish membership was 550 family units, many of them single or widowed persons living alone. Over half of the parishioners were more than fifty years of age. Many of the new census cards, however, came from younger couples with large families who had recently moved into the area. This information provided a better picture of the type of parish the staff and lay leaders were trying to serve. Of greater importance, however, was the new life the census-taking instilled into the council. They had had a job to do, and they had done it well. The experience also gave hope to the many volunteers. The hundred-plus census-takers so enjoyed the experience that many asked when they could take part in another project. At the same time they made it clear that they would come so long as it did not require a lot of meetings and the task was easy to manage. The good food also served as an attraction.

The staff was surprised to see so many requests for assistance from the parish but could not hope to accommodate all of them. The pastor thought that another staff person might be needed, someone who could minister to the sick, shut-ins, and the needy of the parish. He knew it would be an extra expense, but he hoped that the position would provide a boost to the parish and would eventually pay for itself. When he brought up the matter to both the staff and council, he was surprised to learn that they had reached the same conclusion and were waiting for the right moment to bring it to his attention.

The Catholic Charities office of the diocese helped him locate a laywoman with a master's degree in social work and background in hospital ministry. The pastor and staff were encouraged when she described how she envisioned her own contribution to the parish. Rather than undertake the home visiting herself, she hoped to train others to do it. She, along with the staff, would coordinate and direct the parish visiting and act as a resource for difficult situations. She hoped to use existing parish organizations rather than create new ones. She would enlist the St. Vincent de Paul, Holy Name, and Altar-Rosary Societies along with those census-takers who were looking for another opportunity to get involved in the parish.

The match was perfect and she was hired. She began by talking to the staff and parish groups about their impressions of the parish and what they thought the visiting program should be. She also studied the new information available from the updated parish census and the many requests for help received in the door-to-door canvass. She visited a few people in the parish who at one time had been sick or living alone; she wanted to find out what they would have liked from the parish when they were convalescing, in critical need, or lonely.

From this informal research she constructed a profile of the kinds of persons who requested help from the parish and what kinds of help they were looking for. She put together a short course on how to care for the sick, lonely, and needy. The course would last five weeks—one evening each week. She took the staff through an abbreviated version of the course and asked for their evaluation and impressions. They were delighted and remarked that they had learned more about caring for the sick and needy in that short course than in any previous reading or instruction on the subject. She was now ready to ask for volunteers.

She began with the census workers and the St. Vincent de Paul Society, which consisted of five elderly gentlemen. Those who wanted to participate would be required to attend the five-week course, with no exceptions. After that initial commitment, the requirement would be to visit only one person or family who asked for help, for as long as help is required.

Since the appeal for volunteers was well planned and had the enthusiastic support of the pastor, many people agreed to help. Seventy-five people began the five-week session, and sixty-three graduated as certified parish visitors. The Sunday after Easter was Commissioning Sunday. At the ten o'clock Mass each graduate was given a commission of one person or family to visit. The commission included a commitment to get to know the person or family and to establish a genuine relationship. The understanding was that the visitors would benefit from the interchange as much as would the people visited. Those visiting the sick, shut-ins, and needy were encouraged to spend an hour a week visiting, to provide occasional rides to the doctor, or to help with the shopping if necessary. For some families the assistance would come in the form of babysitting, learning how to manage on a limited budget, or caring for a problem child. The visitors were also trained and commissioned as Communion ministers, should the need ever arise.

After the commissioning Mass and a few weeks of visiting, the volunteers were formed into support groups that met once a month. These groups gave the volunteers a chance to talk over common experiences, deal with problems that had arisen, and provide support for one another. Staff members attended these meetings only if requested by the group.

The program has been in operation for almost a year, and already the change in parish spirit is noticeable. A second short course for new parish visitors is being planned because both the requests for visits and the response from volunteers have been so great. Every parish organization is encouraging its members to take part in the visiting program, because they have seen how the people who have already taken part have brought new life to the organizations as a whole. This is especially true of the St. Vincent de Paul Society, which now coordinates the visiting of needy families. Its members visit people in order to provide help with money management, marriage counseling, dealing with government agencies or landlords, or whatever the need might be. The Society has grown from the original five to twenty, and includes both men and women. Even younger people belong, and just last month, to the delight of everyone, a young woman was elected the new chairperson.

The weekend Masses also have more life, and more people have begun to come to the Masses since the door-to-door census. On the census cards many people had suggested ways for improving the liturgy, and these improvements have made a difference in the way people respond during the Masses. The commissioning of the parish visitors just after Easter seems to have set the tone. The Masses now include both old favorites and specially prepared new music so that more people are singing during Mass. The parish visitors who take Communion to their "friends" ask for extra hosts at Mass. They then bring the Eucharist to the sick and shut-ins they visit later that day. This is setting the tone for a new understanding of lay ministry, as well as drawing people to a new sense of intimacy with their Lord. Parishioners are showing interest in learning more about the Church, about the changes since Vatican II, and about different ways to pray.

As people take more interest in the parish, they assume more responsibility in contributing to its programs (and to the Sunday collection). The newcomers, consisting primarily of

Black and Hispanic families, are sending their children to the parish school and those children are replacing the children of families who have moved out of the area. The school board and the parish council are considering plans to convert one of the two school buildings into a Day Care Center to help working parents in the area. The staff and council are also thinking about converting the convent into a parish center that will serve as a meeting place for senior citizens and will be planned and run by the elderly of the parish. Some of the retired parishioners are talking about a seniors' fair, in which their own handcrafted works would be sold to help finance the renovation of the convent.

This is something new in the parish: people making plans for the future. Until the census and the parish visiting began there were no plans—only memories. The pastor and staff are pleased with the change. It all seems so simple, and yet so profound—people caring for people on a one-to-one basis. This has turned the parish around. Now it is time to plan for the future. The staff came together recently to do that. They constructed a history-line of the last two years, just as they had done two years ago when they looked at the significant parish events of the previous eight years. The current history-line contains key moments, such as the first staff meeting that led to parish organizations constructing their own history-lines, the council's decision to take a parish census, the call for volunteers and the week of canvassing, the hiring of the parish ministry coordinator, the commissioning Mass after Easter, the new life in parish Masses and organizations. No longer does the parish look back to the centennial as the only significant moment in the last five years at Immaculate Conception.

As the staff members looked at the significant events of the last two years, they realized that parish groups were interacting with one another. The staff described it as a linking of groups: linking in the sense that no longer was the parish a collection of groups cut off from one another and working independently, sometimes even against one another. The centennial celebration had shown that the people could work together on a project; the census and parish visiting confirmed it. Some of the pairs who did the door-to-door canvass were made up of people forty years apart in age. A few partners did not even speak the same language. Most of the volunteers had not known each other or worked together before that week. But they did work together on the census, they did it again in the visiting program, and they want to continue doing so. People are experiencing a new sense of community at the parish Masses. The Greeting of Peace is no longer a perfunctory exercise. It now has symbolic value as a sign of deep feeling and caring among the people. This linking of groups gives the staff hope for the future of the parish. The challenge now is to keep this spirit of unity alive and to give it new support and encouragement.

The continuing influx of new groups into the parish—Blacks and Hispanics mostly—will make the breaking down of barriers among people even more necessary in the next few years. But if this community spirit can be fostered among the parishioners now, it will help provide the right environment for welcoming and integrating all newcomers into the parish.

Part 2: Linking Groups

One important part of the recovery process at Immaculate Conception, which has application in other parishes, was the effort to link together subgroups. Most parishes are composed of many groups that do not have the chance or the desire to interact. A parish becomes a collection of polarities: old-timers and newcomers, Catholic school and public school students, folk group and choir, traditionalists and progressives, singers and non-singers, joiners and loners, families and singles, old and young and in-between.

Subgroups form for many reasons; some are conducive to the life of the parish, and others are not. For example, the existence of small groups in a parish can be a positive influence in giving people a sense of worth, belonging, and ministry. The parish "Christian communities" described in the previous chapter are proof of this. But parish subgroups can hinder parish life if they become completely self-sufficient and too close-knit. Outsiders feel excluded and find it difficult to break into these groups. This can happen with traditional parish organizations such as the Holy Name Society or Women's Club, but it can also happen with newer groups such as Marriage Encounter, folk choir, or Bible Study. When the members of a group discover that they enjoy one another and experience success in dealing with personal, group, and parish concerns, then new members who have not experienced the struggles and joys of the "regulars" feel left out and unwelcome. This is true no matter how hard the group members try to keep the group open and to invite new members.

Size also makes a difference. Parish groups form so that parishioners can get to know one another. This is true even when the group's purpose is to perform a service, such as singing at parish Masses, teaching religion classes, or counting the collection. If the group becomes too large—thirty members or more—then it is too large for personal interchange.

When members see their group getting too large, they try to limit the number of new people joining. This effort is usually not explicit, but "outsiders" soon know whether the group is open to their involvement.

This attempt to control the size of a group creates cliques, in-groups, and competition among groups and thus hinders community spirit. On the other hand, these same groups can foster parish spirit by providing people with a sense of belonging and involvement. But because of the possible harmful aspects of parish subgroups, the effort to link groups—to build bridges between them—becomes important.

People come together for many reasons. Groups of parishioners form around different types of Masses because they like to worship and pray in the same way. They form groups around different approaches to religious education or around different types of parish organizations because they share the same understanding of parish or are attracted by the same priest or staff member, or because they share the same needs.

Parish groups often include people who are similar in age, ethnic or racial background, or who have similar occupations or educational level. People also come together when they share the same fear or insecurity, such as the fear of going out at night, of losing a job, of living on a fixed income, or of being a newcomer. The task of parish leaders is to provide opportunities for people in different groups to come in contact with one another. In this way the parish becomes a network of interacting subgroups, not just a collection of isolated cells. Linking groups is an important responsibility of the leadership.

Fortunately for parish leaders, many helps and resources already exist to encourage them in this task. There are the Gospels and Jesus' promise of the Holy Spirit, who will stand by us. Jesus himself prayed "that they may be one, as we are one . . . that their unity may be complete" (John 17:22-23). The Catholic Church, furthermore, has a long tradition of struggling to keep its doors open to all comers and believers, even though it sometimes experiences more success than at other times. Recent efforts at reducing the distance between the Orthodox and the Roman Catholic churches are proof of this desire to bridge the gap that separates these two Christian groups.

The experience of the American Catholic Church is encouraging because the many ethnic groups that migrated to this country have found room to develop while still belonging to the same Church. These groups have drawn closer together and have bridged the gaps between them. The result is not a uniform Catholic Church in this country where all groups worship and function in the same way, but rather a Church that allows for a rich cultural unity-in-diversity.

These experiences of the larger Church provide support and encouragement to the local parish in its attempt to draw subgroups closer together and form a unified parish community. I will suggest four steps to help in this unifying process.

Steps Toward Unifying Subgroups

The first step is to *look for the best occasion or most suitable environment for linking parish groups.* At Immaculate Conception the parish centennial provided the occasion for all ages and interest groups to become involved in planning and celebrating the anniversary. Then the census provided another suitable occasion when all the subgroups could "belong" to an activity without sacrificing their own group's identity or allegiance. The same was true for the parish visiting program. It was a new experience in which many parish groups could participate and still maintain their own character and interests.

Immaculate Conception parish also tried to bring different liturgical tastes together by joining the choir and folk group for an occasional liturgy. The Mass provides a good occasion for linking groups together because each group can express its own identity by contributing different types of music, providing lectors, and by bringing gifts to the altar. This is especially true for Masses on feast days and important holidays. At St. Anthony's, the Hispanic parish of the previous chapter, each small Christian community sponsored a Mass and invited other groups to join with it in the celebration.

Parish events and joint projects sponsored by a number of parish organizations provide occasions for drawing different groups together: parish bazaars, socials, picnics, dances, census-taking, anniversaries, dedications, graduations, ordinations—any occasion that appeals to more than one age group or interest group. Unfortunately, these opportunities often come and go without the publicity or creative planning they deserve.

Sometimes it helps to emphasize the differences among groups and cultures to display the rich diversity in the parish. Such occasions might include an ethnic fair, a dance with a number of bands who play different types of music, a dinner or picnic with a variety of ethnic dishes. The crafts fair being planned at Immaculate Conception is one such occasion. Providing these occasions is especially important when a parish is experiencing a change in membership. Rather than ignore the change, accentuate it and use it to the advantage of the parish and its people.

Religious education programs for adults and children can provide opportunities for drawing groups together. At Immaculate Conception the school is beginning to attract children from the new Hispanic and Black families. The children provide entree to the parents. School open houses, socials and fund raisers, plays and recitals draw people from different backgrounds and interests and provide the opportunity for various subgroups to interact.

Parish sacramental preparation programs, in which parents are encouraged to participate, provide occasions not only for instructing the children and updating the parents, but also for drawing the parish subgroups together. Family catechesis programs, which provide educational experiences for the whole family rather than for adults and children separately, can be occasions for families of different backgrounds and educational levels to interact and enjoy one another. The families are drawn together by common concerns about how to raise children, how to give them a desire to learn about and practice their faith, how to deal with conflicts and crises, how to provide a supportive home environment, and how to face the prospect of a divorce or of raising a family as a single parent. These concerns cross cultural, economic, and educational lines and are shared by all parents.

Parish ministry programs also provide a means for different groups to come in contact with one another. At Immaculate Conception the parish visiting program broke through the walls separating parish groups. Other forms of shared ministry draw different groups together, such as ministers of Communion, teachers of religion, volunteer drivers, baby-sitters, letter-writers, church cleaners, singers, collection counters. These areas of shared ministry are open to all adult parishioners.

Some parishes begin the school year by commissioning the parish ministers at a special Mass. This gives the people a sense of mission, as well as recognition and visibility. It's a way of saying we're all in this together, no matter what our talents, interests, or inclinations. It sets the tone for the coming school year in which all groups work together for the good of the parish as a whole.

Another important step toward helping parish groups interact is to *encourage person-to-person contacts*. Groups must be small enough so that people have a chance to interact and to discover what they share and how they differ. As I have mentioned, the door-to-door census at Immaculate Conception was done in pairs. The people were encouraged to pair up with a person they did not know well, perhaps someone of a different age or a different neighborhood. This approach can apply to other situations, but "pairing" must be done with gentleness and sensitivity. It becomes easier if it is an accepted practice. In effect this gives the people permission to mix with others they don't know well.

The effort to keep the interacting groups small is important when attempting to draw subgroups together. Large gatherings make dialogue and exchange of ideas difficult. If the turnout for a parish gathering is larger than expected, an alternative approach of breaking into smaller groups should be planned. This also holds true for some parish Masses. Large Masses are important to provide a feeling of solidarity and belonging, and to help people realize that they belong to a parish larger than their own subgroup. But small-group liturgies are also important to stress community and give people a chance to share prayers, concerns, and petitions with more freedom and less formality.

At the core of this personal interchange must be an openness that accepts the other person as important even though one disagrees with that person's outlook on life, the Church, or world situation. It requires the ability to separate the worth of the individual from the positions that person may hold. This acceptance demands time for personal give-and-take. Nor can this sharing of viewpoints and opinions be fabricated. It is up to parish leaders and planners to look for the best opportunities for people to come together naturally and without pressure to listen and learn from one another and to build respect for one another. A simple, non-threatening experience is best, such as working side by side at a bake sale, bingo game, raffle, or fund drive.

Another step in the process of linking groups is to *ground the process in prayer and shared faith.* We are, after all, attempting to do the impossible, for people's natural inclinations are toward forming groups with their own kind. This tendency was prevalent in the history of the American Catholic Church. Different ethnic churches were built within a few blocks of each other, each with its own customs, feast days, and rituals. It is a natural tendency, but Jesus sought to overcome it by choosing apostles and disciples from a variety of backgrounds and temperaments and by inviting all people—Jews, Samaritans, Romans—to be members of his Church. We have no choice as followers of this Jesus but to try to break down the barriers that separate us.

We could never hope to accomplish this on our own. We need the Holy Spirit in our midst. We need to call on the Spirit continually to overcome the divisions among us. We must keep emphasizing our need for the Spirit's help in our intergroup activities and moments of interaction. Immaculate Conception parish did this when they sent out the census-takers after prayer and reflection on Scripture and celebrated their return with a Mass and a meal together. This is also the reason parish visiting began with a training program that included prayer and spiritual reflection and continued with group meetings in which the visitors shared their experiences in a prayerful and celebrative atmosphere. If the linking of parish groups and individuals remains *only* a human experience and fails to include this prayerful, transcendent reality, there is no hope of lasting success. Too many natural, human factors are working against it.

The fourth step in the process of linking parish groups is to *provide a structure for interaction*. The occasions for group interaction need planning, direction, structuring, encouragement, and support from the pastor, staff, and lay leaders of the parish. Many parish organizations, small groups, and projects can function on their own without much assistance from the staff. But the occasions for intergroup exchange are not so easily handled. Parish leaders must plan the right moments and create the right environment for parish subgroups to come together. These moments must be scheduled into the regular calendar of events and emphasized as key moments of community-building. Once scheduled, they need the combined encouragement and support of the staff and council. At Immaculate Conception, for instance, the large number of volunteers that turned out for the census was due, in great part, to the enthusiastic appeal from the pastor and the combined support of staff and parish council.

The people who respond to the invitation to interact with other groups or to join special projects need recognition, support, and encouragement. Staff can provide that through parish publications, announcements, and appreciation notices. I emphasize support because it takes more courage and demands great personal risk from people to step beyond the boundaries of their own groups and venture out to meet people they don't know well. They need encouragement to establish rapport with other people and to work on joint projects with them. This is especially true for newcomers in the parish who are not only strange to the area but may be from a different culture or background or speak a language different from the majority of the parishioners.

In addition to these four steps, I see four *imperatives* for parish leaders who are trying to link subgroups.

First, *be honest*. Parish leaders, first of all, and then the parishioners themselves, need to be honest about their feelings toward other groups and peoples in the parish. They need to articulate the prejudices, misgivings, lack of trust, or fears of failure they feel. Parish leaders—staff and council and committee heads—have to be honest about how much they really want to draw different groups together. The parishioners have to be honest about how much they want to interact with other parish groups. Once people are honest about their feelings and about their own expectations, it becomes clear how much preparation is needed by way of conversion and reconciliation among the staff and lay leaders themselves, and among the people, before any linking of parish groups is possible.

Next, *be realistic*. The parish leadership is attempting not only to change patterns of parish interaction but to change people's attitudes and behavior as well. This takes a long time. The staff and lay organizers need to be realistic about how difficult a task they are setting for themselves and to be satisfied with only limited success. Usually they are working against a long history of parish cliques and in-groups. This takes time to break down. That is why Immaculate Conception started simply and slowly. They were delightfully surprised that so much did happen in such a short time. But they also realized that much more had to be done.

Be sensitive. People give off many signals and non-verbal messages. The signals say, "Don't push or rush us. Don't dominate us. Give us room to maneuver." But the signals might also be saying, "Don't underestimate us. Don't give up so easily." People who strive to unify the parish or bring groups together must be attentive to many levels of communication. They must try to put themselves in the other person's shoes. They must be aware of the pressures people face, the demands on their time, the need for space to move in, the risks people are taking by agreeing to participate.

Finally, *be creative*. The parish has only limited resources of time, money, talent, and facilities. Using these resources to best advantage demands a creative approach to planning. The best way to link groups is to build on the lived experience of the parishioners. The leaders must know what these experiences are and how they can be used for drawing the parish closer together. Many parishioners encounter similar pushes toward linking diverse groups in their businesses, clubs, and schools. How can these experiences be used in the parish?

How can existing parish groups and organizations be used for building bridges between peoples? The opportunities are limitless to those who know how to use them.

Whatever methods are used, a parish has no choice but to keep seeking ways to unite different groups and peoples. This gives people the chance to share a rich diversity in a common belief of the Lord as members of the same Catholic Church.

CHAPTER FIVE

Part 1: The Young, Suburban Parish

Mary Queen of Heaven is a young, vibrant, middle-class, suburban parish. It was established in the 1950s as the people moved from the city into a new subdivision. The school was built first because that seemed to be needed more than a church. The Sunday Masses were celebrated in the school auditorium. As it turned out, the church building was never built. The parish still gathers for liturgy in the school auditorium, although everyone now thinks of it as the church.

Space has been a problem from the beginning. When the parish began there were 200 families. In five years it had reached 800, and by 1970 the membership leveled off at 1200, with 900 students in the parish grammar school. In the last ten years the school enrollment has dropped to 600, but the need for meeting rooms and storage space is still critical. Most of the seven Masses on the weekend are crowded, and for special feasts, such as the midnight Mass on Christmas and the Easter Vigil, admission tickets are distributed on a first-come-first-served basis.

In 1978 the proposal to build a new church was a hotly debated issue. It was finally decided, over the opposition of a significant minority, to remodel the existing structure. Rumblings are still heard from a few, but most parishioners seem satisfied with the present environment for liturgy. The altar stands near the longer wall, and chairs (the pews have been removed) are arranged in a semicircle around the altar. The new arrangement is flexible, allowing for other cultural and social events to be held in the church-auditorium. The remodeled church has added to the space problem, however, because now the church cannot hold as many people as when there were pews and people could squeeze closer together.

Since the crisis over the remodeling of the church, the parish has been moving at an even pace. The only difficulty is that each year seems to bring more and more activities and projects. The staff and council are feeling overwhelmed. The new projects are good in themselves, and they respond to the needs of a variety of groups and individuals in the parish, but together they have become a bewildering blur to those who are supposed to plan, direct, and facilitate these projects. The very scheduling of events and the conflicts over space and meeting times are getting out of hand. The staff and the council are using up all their meeting time dealing with scheduling difficulties. This leaves them little time for direct ministry.

Last year, in exasperation, the pastor asked that the regular agenda for the week's staff meeting be put aside and the entire meeting be dedicated to the airing of feelings about the confusing array of activities now going on in the parish. At that time the full-time staff consisted of two priests, two religious education coordinators, and the sister principal. There were three other part-time staff members who came to the one evening meeting each month. These included the permanent deacon, the music director, and the youth minister. All eight were present when the pastor made his plea. They now look back on that meeting as a "blessed event" for themselves and the parish as a whole.

The pastor asked each staff member to write down all the parish activities, ministries, or liturgies in which he or she was involved or was responsible for planning or running. The composite list, constructed from the combination of each one's contribution, came to a total of sixty-four activities going on at once in the parish. These included long-standing organizations, newer groups, educational programs, and special liturgical functions. The list seemed endless. It frightened all present when they saw for the first time all that was going on in the parish and all that the staff and lay leaders were asked to manage. No wonder there was a problem of burnout among the people and frequent turnover on the staff. Something had to be done.

In the effort to come up with alternatives, two extremes were quickly eliminated: to continue at the present pace, with each group fighting for time and recognition, or to stop everything, except perhaps the weekend Masses. Of the two, the second option looked more appealing to the staff. But they decided to look for other options that lay somewhere between these two extremes.

The staff scheduled another meeting for the following month in order to come up with alternatives to the present situation, and the pastor asked a consultant from the diocesan planning office to facilitate the meeting. The staff members looked forward to this meeting as a way of gaining relief from the pressures they were experiencing. After spending the month gathering ideas from the groups they worked with, they discovered that many of the active parishioners shared their own frustrations about the bewildering array of activities. The people were often confused about where the many activities fitted into the purpose and direction of the parish as a whole. Some parishioners asked if they could attend the next staff meeting, and it soon became clear that a much larger group would be involved in this next meeting for seeking options to the present situation.

The meeting was held on a Sunday afternoon and evening and consisted of thirty people, including the staff, most of the council, and a few of the overworked active parishioners. The facilitator helped the staff restate the problem for the newcomers: There were too many activities in the parish with too limited facilities or staff time to accommodate the activities. What to do? It didn't seem feasible to stop offering activities, because people needed outlets for parish identity and involvement. But if the present situation continued, the parish.community, pastor, and staff might give up in exhaustion.

The facilitator asked the group to spend time praying to the Spirit for light about how best to proceed. Each person was to spend time alone in prayer and reflection, jot down any insights or inspirations, and come back to share these with the others. After forty-five minutes the people came together in groups of five to list the ideas produced in the individual reflection period. Each small group was then asked to choose the two best ideas from its list. After a potluck supper, the whole group reassembled to see what options had come out of the small groups.

The groups all agreed that the parish must begin by setting up a list of priorities so that existing organizations and programs could be put into an overall framework. Each group or activity would not exist for itself but would fit into the larger picture and would help the parish achieve its goals or purpose. Some groups offered suggestions on how this list of priorities might be drawn up, but one idea seemed to catch the imagination of everyone.

The suggestion was to spend the coming year focusing on twelve key aspects of the parish, one per month. Existing groups would continue to meet, but the staff and council would spend their own time preparing for and giving direction to each one of the twelve areas. At the end of the year, the parish leaders would ask for feedback from the people and would then construct a list of parish priorities for the following year. The idea was received enthusiastically by the people at the meeting. A group of three staff members and two parishioners volunteered to work out the details and present the plan at a second meeting of the group one month later.

The committee worked hard throughout the month. They told the parish at the weekend Masses about the recent meeting, the suggestion, and their special committee. Prayers were offered at all Masses for the success of the committee's work. When the second meeting came, the staff was surprised that another twenty interested parishioners came as well as the original thirty, partly to hear what would be proposed and partly to be sure that their own priorities would not be lost in the reshuffle.

The committee presented its plan, and the overall reaction was favorable. A few refinements were made in the choice of monthly emphases, and then the plan was accepted by a unanimous vote. At the next weekend's liturgies the committee presented the idea to the parishioners for their acceptance and support. The celebrants cut short their homilies so as to leave time at the end of Mass to explain the proposal. The coffee-and-donuts time after Mass gave people a chance to react. The response from the parishioners was more enthusiastic than the staff and council had expected. It was settled that weekend that the plan would go into effect the following August. What follows is a description of the plan as it was put into action over the twelve months of August through July.

August was the month to emphasize *leisure* in the parish. The annual parish picnic was rescheduled from its regular time earlier in the summer to coincide with the emphasis on play and relaxation. The liturgies stressed the need for people to relax, to get to know one another, to take a look at their own lives and their hectic pace. Families were encouraged to take outings together and to set aside time during the coming year for family get-togethers and celebrations. The parish sponsored a few socials during the month, including neighborhood block parties and a crafts bazaar in which all ages and parish groups became involved. A few parishioners made up a booklet listing nearby places to visit and explore. The response from the parishioners to these "at-home" socials and outings went far beyond anyone's expectations. In most other years nothing was going on in the parish during the summer months, but this August the parish became the focal point of leisure and fun.

September was the month for *adult enrichment*. All the staff and parish leaders focused their attention on adult religious education. They met at the beginning of the month to coordinate an attractive program that would continue over the entire school year. The Masses focused on the need for renewal and updating of one's faith. The homilies included explanations of what topics were going to be offered during the coming year. A table laden with books and magazines for purchase or borrowing was set up in the church vestibule. The after Mass coffee-and-donuts time gave people a chance to talk over their reaction to the proposed topics for adult education outlined in the homilies. During the four Sundays of the month a special adult enrichment series was held in the cafeteria after the 10:30 Mass. Guest speakers were invited to speak on various areas of adult enrichment, such as stages of adult development, intimacy with loved ones and with God, the role of women (and men) in the Church, authority in the Church, and personal conscience-formation. The parishioners received a calendar of coming attractions listing special sessions for different age groups so that they would be aware of what would be offered during the coming year. An adult Enrichment Committee was organized to direct the program during the year.

The best outcome of the month was that the parishioners came to realize that religious education does not stop at graduation from Catholic school or from a CCD program. Many people mentioned that this had been the first time they had reflected on their faith development since they were teenagers.

October was *ministries* month. The emphasis was on providing outlets for people's desire to share in the ministry of the Church. In the past the same few people had volunteered to be ministers of Communion, visit the sick, or serve on committees. This pattern changed during that October. It seemed that emphasis on ministries was a natural sequel to the new consciousness of faith development gained in the previous month. As in September, all the people who were responsible for the various aspects of ministry met to make a list of the opportunities for sharing the ministries of the parish. The list included liturgical ministers such as ushers, lectors, singers, babysitters, Communion ministers. It included administrative ministries such as typing, phone answering, cleaning, preparing the newsletter, running the parish council or school board— anything having to do with communicating and keeping the parish running smoothly. Outreach ministries included welcoming newcomers, visiting the sick and shut-ins, seeking out and inviting back inactive and alienated Catholics, becoming aware of social moral issues, and raising the consciousness of parishioners and political leaders. Other ministries included teaching CCD classes, running the bingo, leading adult enrichment discussions, and planning parish socials.

Once the list had been constructed, the Mass themes focused on the idea that ministry belongs not just to priests and parish staffs but to all baptized Catholics. A sheet explaining the opportunities for ministry and the number of hours per month that would be required to perform them was mailed to every adult parishioner. Indicating the amount of time required was important, as many people had refrained from volunteering because they did not want to commit themselves to something they had no time to do.

The people were also encouraged to look at their personal lives in a new way and to reflect on what aspects might be considered ministry. It was made clear that every Christian is called to be a minister to others, whether at home, at work, in school, or in the neighborhood, and that the parish was not in competition with the call people had to be ministers in their daily lives. Rather, it was to act as a challenge and support so that people would come to realize that every aspect of their lives was an opportunity to minister to the needs of others.

The parish, however, could become an outlet for people to exercise their call to ministry in areas of need that lay beyond one's individual or family life. On the third Sunday of October the people were given the chance to choose one area of ministry sponsored by the parish for the coming year. These commitments were then coordinated by the Ministries Committee.

The last Sunday of the month was Commitment Sunday. Persons who volunteered for ministry received a commission to carry out the work of Christ and the Church in whatever area of ministry they felt called to fulfill. Care was taken to include those who felt called to be ministers in their personal lives, whether at home or in their occupations. Those who did volunteer to participate in the ministries of the parish were asked to limit their commitment to one, or at most, two areas so as not to become overburdened.

One outcome of the Commitment Sunday was that people began to feel that the parish belonged to them. They felt the parish provided both a support to their efforts to be ministers in their personal lives and an opportunity to take responsibility for the needs of the parish and the larger community. The ministries committee spent the month of October working out the details of the program for the year so that not too much would be required from any one group or individual. They made sure that the people involved in each kind of ministry had a chance to meet so as to gain support and to share the experience of ministry. They also gave the volunteers frequent praise and recognition for the time and effort spent in ministering.

November was the month for *music*. The purpose of the month's focus on music was to help people see the link between singing and the celebration of the Eucharist, and to establish an atmosphere in which the people would willingly join in the communal song of praise and worship.

Music had been a forgotten part of parish life at Queen of Heaven. Although there were four singing groups—a senior choir, a children's choir, singers for weddings and funerals, and the folk group—congregational singing left much to be desired. The overworked part-time music director felt discouraged and unsupported in her efforts to improve the music program.

At the beginning of the month the music director visited the singing groups, the accompanists, the liturgy committee, and the staff to gather ideas about what could be done to improve the music program. She told the parishioners on the first Sunday of the month that this was to be music month, and she asked if they had suggestions for improving the music, particularly the congregational singing. Cards for suggestions were provided; they were to be filled out and put in the boxes at the doors of the church. In addition, all those involved with music in the parish focused their attention on how to improve the congregational singing. The weekend Masses stressed the role of music in liturgy as a means of praising God and of setting the tone or emphasizing the theme of the Mass.

Toward the end of the month a concert of liturgical music featured all the singing groups and instruments used in the parish music program. Parishioners are still talking about how beautiful and inspiring that concert was. Also, representatives from all the singing groups met with the music director and the liturgy committee to work out a program for congregational singing for the rest of the school year. The program that resulted included a variety of music that fitted each type of Mass congregation and season of the year. It allowed ample time for learning new songs and for singing old favorites.

On the second and third Sundays of November a call went out for "congregational singers." This group of singers was to learn new songs and then situate themselves throughout the congregation to provide an atmosphere of strong and enthusiastic singing. This helped people to feel that it was all right to sing out loudly and not to feel intimidated in their efforts at singing. These "congregational singers" needed no experience; they were not in any choir or singing group. Nothing more would be asked of them except to meet fifteen minutes before one Mass every other month. This provided a core of about fifty people who helped create an atmosphere conducive to congregational singing. They were also able to learn new songs, and this eliminated the need for a special song practice for the whole congregation before the Masses.

The Masses did include quiet time for reflection as well as music by singing groups, which served to enhance the celebration of the Mass and the prayerfulness of the people. As a result of that month's emphasis on music, the parish has since become a model in the diocese of liturgical music and congregational singing.

December became the month for *building community spirit* in the parish. The focus for Advent was preparing for the Lord's coming as a Christian community and not as a collection of individuals who happen to attend the same church. The community-building committee prepared suggestions for the parishioners that would help them celebrate the holidays and would foster family traditions. Those who lived alone were encouraged to join Advent groups in which they shared with one another some of the family traditions of the past as a way of preparing for Christmas. The parish Masses stressed the Christmas customs of a variety of cultures and the common bonds that draw people together. The staff and council encouraged parishioners to put the buying of gifts and the writing of Christmas cards into a Christian perspective. Parishioners young and old volunteered to write cards to people who were alone and forgotten, to go caroling in nursing homes, hospitals, and neighborhoods, to put together food baskets and contributions for needy families, to sponsor neighborhood parties and get-togethers. By avoiding the usual frantic rush to get everything done, many people were finding that they had more time for relaxation, get-togethers, prayerful reflection, and thinking about the needs of others. The liturgy committee planned not to stress the midnight Mass as much as in the past but to make all the Christmas Masses an expression of joy and community. Tickets for the Midnight Mass were no longer necessary. Thus the month of community-building appropriately culminated in a more serene, balanced, and genuine celebration of the feast of Christmas.

January was the month of *youth education*. Both the school and the religious education program had been going on since the fall, but during January they received special attention. Soon after the beginning of the new year and before school classes began again, all those involved in the education of the youth in the parish came together for a weekend of reflection and discernment about their role as educators. For the first time, the school and religious education teachers had a chance to share their experiences, difficulties, and insights. One outcome of this workshop was a joint presentation at all the Masses explaining the month's emphasis on religious education. All in the parish, especially those who did not have children in the religious education programs, were able to hear about both the school and CCD and were able to ask questions of the teachers and staff at the coffee-and-donuts get-together after Mass. Special student drawings and projects from all levels of religious education were on display in the cafeteria and hallways for the parishioners to see.

During this month, those involved in teaching drew up topic outlines for the rest of the school year and made tentative plans for the next school year. The pastor, school board, and teachers met together to evaluate teacher performance, negotiate salaries, and write up contracts. For the first time in the parish both administrators and teachers knew well in advance what changes would be necessary for the next school year. The religious education committee recruited volunteers for its classes so that the new teachers could sit in on classes during spring and thus prepare their own classes for the fall. The staff began making plans for a family catechesis program for a pilot group of ten families. The families agreed to one meeting each month over the next five months to see how feasible this approach to religious education might be in the parish. Those who had become active in the adult enrichment program last September were encouraged to relate their experience to the education of their children in January. This linking of the adult and the youth religious experience provided a shot in the arm for both the adult and youth education programs in the parish.

February was *administration* month. The focus during this month was on finances. Everyone involved in the leadership of the parish, both paid staff and volunteers, had a chance to provide input so that the financial responsibility for the parish did not fall on just a few people. The pastor was especially happy to see this topic addressed. These were two emphases for the month—putting together a budget for the next fiscal year and asking the people to increase their contributions. The diocese offered to help with both of these efforts.

At the beginning of the month those in charge of each area of parish life submitted a budget to the parish council. The finance committee worked out the details and submitted the revised budget to the council for discussion and approval. The council then prayed over the task, realizing that a budget is a reflection of parish priorities. They tried to keep a larger perspective in mind and not to get caught up in minutiae. The council was surprised at how much easier it was to settle on the budget than it had been in previous years.

The weekend Masses included a description of parish expenses and the use of parish money as well as an explanation of the responsibility all parishioners had to share with others the gifts received from God. The pastor urged people to give two percent of their gross income to the parish, either through a yearly payment or through weekly envelopes that could be mailed or put into the collection box at the entrance to the church. The pastor promised that, as of that Sunday, there would be no more collections during Mass or any other special collections during the year.

The pastor explained that one quarter of the parish income would go to causes like diocesan or mission appeals, to·poorer parishes in the diocese, or for crises such as storms, floods, or accidents. Many parishioners now look back on the month of February as a freeing experience because everyone learned where money was being spent. As a result, the financial response from the people was much more generous than anyone could have predicted.

March was the month for *prayer*, a theme especially appropriate for Lent. All parish groups and gatherings focused on prayer during that time. The staff and council began with their own weekend of prayer. The people were given many opportunities for closed retreats and days of recollection reserved for the parish at the retreat center not far away. The homilies were devoted to explaining different approaches and methods of praying. The parishioners became aware of different prayer groups and opportunities for shared prayer in the area: Life in the Spirit seminars, novenas and rosary devotions, Praying the Hours, Cursillo, Praying the Scriptures, Home Retreats. During this month Scripture reflection groups started, which still meet every other week in the parish. Each parish organization was encouraged to spend a large part of its meeting time in prayer and reflection on Scripture. The month ended with a "mission" for the whole parish, with one staff member leading each of the sessions that introduced participants to different styles and experiences of prayer and reflection on Scripture. In a way, prayer was the simplest of all the months' emphases, but many people remarked that it was the emphasis that helped them the most in their own lives.

April was centered on *liturgy*, especially on the liturgies of Holy Week and the Easter season. All that had gone on before in adult enrichment, ministry, music, education, administration, and prayer found its expression in these paschal celebrations. The liturgy committee and music planners focused their energies on preparing for this event. All levels of the parish were invited to participate in the liturgical life of the Church. Once again the planners attempted to make all the Easter liturgies equal celebrations of joy, so that the church would not be crowded at the Easter Vigil. Following Easter the Masses included explanations of the Mass, its historical context, the reasons for the recent changes, and practices since Vatican II.

During the month the staff and liturgy committee mapped out the liturgical program for the rest of the year in order to plan the seasonal liturgies better and to prepare the people better for liturgical celebrations. As a result, more people volunteered to be ministers of Communion, more began taking Communion under both species, and more started receiving

Communion frequently. Some of the older people came to understand that they did not have to go to confession before receiving Communion. The staff realized that they had wrongly assumed that parishioners understood the meaning of the Mass. They found that many of the newer changes had not been explained well when introduced, so that the people had never had a chance to catch up with the new approaches to the Mass. The month of April helped to alleviate that problem. At the end of the month people commented that they then had a much better idea of what the Mass was all about and of the reason for the newer forms.

May was *outreach* month. On the first Sunday of the month the pastor urged that during the month each parishioner should contact one person who was no longer active in the church and to invite that person to consider becoming active again. For some it was their own child or relative; for others it was a person in a second marriage that had never been rectified. Whoever the inactive persons might be, the parishioners were encouraged to contact them, listen to their complaints, and ask them to give the Church or parish another try. If parishioners did not feel comfortable approaching someone, then they were encouraged to put the names of the inactive people in the collection box so that others could contact them later in the month.

On the second weekend of the month one person from each family was asked to fill out a census update card for the new parish files. During the following week the administration committee updated the files and started putting them into the computer system. At the same time the outreach committee put out a call for volunteers to help conduct a door-to-door census of the area. The volunteers were told that the parish would be divided into sections and that pairs of volunteers would be asked to cover one block of one section. The turnout of over 200 persons impressed everyone. The purpose of this census was to seek out inactive Catholics living in the parish who were perhaps waiting to be asked back. The census would also help to spread the word about Queen of Heaven to other people living in the area who did not belong to the parish. The census-takers were delighted at the warm reception they received from their own neighbors, people they had never had the chance to meet.

Once the results of the census were in, the outreach committee worked out plans to stay in contact with the less active members of the parish and the newcomers and to respond to those who had requested assistance from the parish.

The last Sunday of May was ecumenical Sunday. Clergy from other denominations in the area preached at the Sunday Masses. A traveling potluck supper was held that began with soup and salad at Queen of Heaven and went on to other churches for the rest of the meal.

The outreach committee also sponsored four discussion-talks during the month, each centered on a different area of the world—South America, Africa, the Orient, and Eastern Europe. The intent was to help parishioners reach out beyond the limits of the parish and country and to come in contact with the needs and concerns of other parts of the world.

June was the month for Catholic *traditions*. The elderly of the parish were the celebrities during this month. They were encouraged to talk during the Masses about their own experience of God, of the Church, and of the parish. The traditions committee planned novenas and devotions during the month. One of the novenas was in preparation for the feast of the Sacred Heart, which came in the middle of the month. Members of the traditions committee led the rosary each morning after Mass; the Saturdays of the month were dedicated to Mary, the patron of the parish. Parishioners were invited to a holy hour on Wednesday evenings for prayer and reflection. The music at parish Masses recalled "old favorites"—including some in Latin—which had not been heard for some time in the parish. Benediction followed the holy hour each Wednesday evening during the month. The traditions committee also sponsored discussions on how changes had taken place over the years and which customs had endured and which had been replaced by other traditions. As part of a special "parish town-hall day," the people who had been members of the parish since its beginning in the fifties constructed a history-line of the parish, so that all could see what had been significant events in the life of the parish since its beginnings. That history-line is still displayed in the vestibule of the church. The school and the religious education classes stressed continuity with Catholic traditions as the foundation for present Catholic teachings. The family religious education program highlighted family customs: People described how they celebrated special days such as Christmas or birthdays. It was interesting to see which family customs were still practiced after many years and which were not. This demonstration of how change happens and how customs come and go helped people understand the process of change in the Church.

The emphasis on traditions served to bridge gaps that had built up over the years—gaps between old and young, traditional and progressive, old Church and new. Many people commented at the end of the month that this accent on Catholic traditions had been too long in coming. They had come to realize how rich are Catholic traditions and history and how little they are used for the benefit and growth of all.

The month of July was the month for *youth activities*. Right after the Fourth of July the children of the parish spent two weeks in a "backyard" summer camp, having fun together and learning about the Bible. The teenagers ran the program for the younger ones. The parish school rooms were converted into meeting places for youth groups of different ages, and a youth committee (one had to be under nineteen to qualify) planned both recreational and service projects for the month. The service projects included not only the running of the Bible school but also mowing lawns for the elderly, putting on skits in nursing homes, and babysitting for working mothers. Some money came in as a result, and the youth group decided to put it into a common fund in order to sponsor more youth activities for the summer and the coming year. One Mass each Sunday became the young people's Mass. These Masses were planned and coordinated by youth of various ages. The youth group spent hours figuring out how to keep the summer projects alive during the school year; they decided to have at least one activity for the junior high and one for the senior high each month during the next school year. July ended with a retreat designed for each secondary grade level; it was held during the weekend at a camp on a lake not far from the parish.

That was the year of monthly emphases when Mary Queen of Heaven first tried out short-range planning. It is now the third year that this approach has been used, and each year has brought refinement to the process. Twelve committees take care of parish programs during the year. The people know what to expect each month and have learned to center their attention and energies on that area. At the end of the first year, a survey was distributed to a sampling of the parishioners to find out how they reacted to this new approach. The response was enthusiastic. The survey also produced many ideas on how to refine and improve the approach.

Ninety-five percent of the people, of all ages, liked the plan. It became obvious from the survey and other comments made to the parish leaders that some months had been more difficult than others. The people's glowing reaction to other months' topics surprised the leaders, especially to November's emphasis on music.

The leaders and staff are in the process of setting up next year's program, and much of the work has already been done by the twelve committees. These committees work well because members know they will be required to work hard during only *one* month of the year. During the other months their responsibility will be simply to keep their area of ministry in operation.

In a recent meeting the pastor asked for the staff's reactions after three years' experience. The following is a summary of their comments:

Parishioners now appear to be more aware of the general direction of the parish and of its more important works and ministries. More parishioners are involved in parish functions so that the same few people no longer do all the work. People now know that they will be required to make only a short-time commitment rather than one lasting the whole year. Because parishioners are taking on more ownership of the parish, they are singing better, giving more money, and providing more ideas for the running of the parish.

Much is being accomplished in the parish, but people do not seem to feel as drained or worn out as they were before the present plan was put into effect. The monthly emphasis keeps the parish Masses and activities fresh and alive. Each month sees a new facet of parish functions, new banners, new flyers, and new people in charge. The parish year is planned a little at a time rather than all at once. As a result, planning is easier to handle and not a burden to be carried by just a few.

The staff and leaders feel better about the use of parish resources and about their own use of time and energy. They know what is happening in the parish, why it is happening, and what is coming up next, so they can get ready for it. They have more time to do long-range planning, that is, to spend more time thinking about where the parish might or should be five or ten years from now. Further, they are aware that they are working more closely with the council and parish leaders and are sharing their leadership role among themselves better.

All of this does not mean that there is no room for further improvement. As the staff looked forward to next year's monthly themes, they pinpointed the following as important needs to be addressed:

- the need for a better long-range planning process, with explicit goals for the future, along with time-commitments and role definitions for the staff, the council, and the twelve committees
- the need for a full-time parish administrator. This person could handle the running of the parish. In this way the pastor and other staff members would be free to concentrate on the spiritual life in the parish and not spend time on maintenance and parish structure
- the need to establish criteria for a "good" parish, to see if Queen of Heaven is coming closer to the ideal. These criteria might eventually mean a change in the monthly emphases in years to come

Despite these concerns, all the staff agreed on one point: that incorporating planning into a well-ordered, predictable framework is far better than what was happening in the parish just a few years ago. Whether the parish will continue to focus its energies on one area each month is not clear. This structure did provide an alternative to the haphazard approach of the past. The staff and council agree that it is now time to focus on the purpose and future direction of Mary Queen of Heaven parish. The pastor has asked all staff, council, and committee members to participate in a special weekend retreat to reflect on the purpose of the parish and on what type of structure and organization are best in light of that purpose and direction.

Part 2: Parish Planning

Planning is a newcomer to Catholic parishes. Until the mid-1960s, parishes followed the predicted model of Masses on Sunday morning, pastor in charge, Holy Name Society, Women's Club, and Scouts. Then came a change. The Second Vatican Council gave parishes the freedom to be different, to offer more than one model or approach to being parish. Along with the freedom came the struggle to figure out what were the essentials of a Catholic parish and what were its reasons for existing. The result of this struggle was an attempt to better organize the efforts and energies of parishioners. This process has led to an emphasis on parish planning.

Unfortunately, many Catholic parishes today have no planning process whatever. Instead, they use the "response-to-crisis" approach. The parish leaders run the parish as if it will continue to operate that same way forever. They see no need to establish a different future direction for the parish. This mode continues until a crisis arises, such as no longer being able to pay for the parish school, or not having a replacement for the departing associate pastor, or the sanctuary becoming too small for the weekend Masses. When the crisis arises, all the energies of the staff and parish leaders are spent dealing with it. Once a solution has been found, it is "back to normal" until the next crisis comes along.

Somehow the parish continues to function, but this approach takes its toll on parish leaders. No one person can withstand the pressure it produces for very long. This was the approach that was operating at Mary Queen of Heaven when we began the story of the parish. It was the "whatever-seems-best" approach. The parish continued to expand in all directions at once. No one agreed on the purpose or focus of the parish or how best to use the people's many talents and interests. Eventually the level of frustration and confusion got to such a point that the pastor blew the whistle. Everyone was grateful because they realized that the resources of the parish were not being used well.

It is an important moment in the life of a parish when the leaders realize that the parish needs help and that some form of planning is necessary. At this point many pastors and parish leaders look around for an acceptable model of parish planning. They usually begin by asking the diocese or neighboring parishes for ideas. One method often suggested is goal-setting. This approach tries to help leaders formulate what they think is the purpose of the parish. This formulation is usually called the "mission statement." Using the mission statement as a basis, the leaders spell out a number of goals for various aspects of parish life. These goals provide a direction and a focus to the parish for the next three to five years. In order to reach these goals, a number of concrete objectives are determined that give direction to the parish for the next year or so in such areas as worship, education, leadership, community-building, and outreach.

This method of reaching goals by establishing concrete objectives is called the Management-by-Objectives approach, and it has been used in many parishes with great success. This method has its pitfalls, however, and parish leaders should keep these in mind if they are thinking of using this approach. For example, goals can fail if they belong to the leadership but not to the people; the result will be apathy. Many times the pastor, staff, and council can spend hours, even months, establishing goals for the parish and then have their hopes dashed because the majority of the parishioners do not accept or "own" these goals.

This pitfall can be avoided by including many people— members of parish organizations or committees, Mass-goers, inactive persons—in the formulation of parish goals and objectives, or at the very least, in the critique and eventual approval of parish goals.

A second danger is to accept the Management-by-Objectives process but forget that a parish is *not* a business or management. A successful parish demands good organization and management skills, but it is also a faith community that exists in response to the Lord's call. Therefore, a parish could go

through a process of writing a mission statement and formu-
lating goals and still not be in touch with the Gospels or be
attentive to the urgings of the Holy Spirit. A parish could
establish its goals for the coming year and miss the whole area
of social justice because the majority of parishioners, or at least
the more articulate ones, do not feel that this is an important
aspect of being a parish community. In an instance such as
this the Spirit may disrupt the process through a vocal minority
in the parish or a conscientious staff or council member. This
disruption can send the whole process into chaos and bring
"progress" to a halt.

One of two things can happen at this point. Either the
majority can choose to disregard or silence the disrupting elements and proceed with the original goals, or they can listen
and take to heart the complaints of the disruptive parties and
change parish goals in light of the new information. If the first
course is followed, the parish will fail, at least for the time
being, in its mission of becoming a reflection of Christ's Church
on the local level. The prophetic groups or individuals become
alienated and marginal to the parish and are no longer heard
from. If the second course is followed, the parish has a chance
of staying in touch with the gospel imperatives and of becoming
the type of faith community it was called to be. Planning is
for the parish and not the other way around.

Even though pitfalls do exist, the goal-setting method of
planning can be a great help to a parish if done with sensitivity
to the needs of the parishioners and to the promptings of the
Holy Spirit. When the pastor and staff at Queen of Heaven
parish, for instance, realized they could no longer cope with
the parish as it was, they went to both the diocese and the
parishioners for help. The parishioners were kept informed
about meetings and were invited to attend. When a course of
action was decided upon—that of focusing on one topic each
month—the plan was tried out for only one year. The people
had the opportunity of responding, both while the plan was
in process and more formally at the end of the year by means
of the parish survey. Only *then* did the parish leaders work on
goal-setting or long-range planning.

Having related the experience of Queen of Heaven parish as an example, I will suggest one approach to planning that uses the goal-setting method but also leaves room for the promptings of the Spirit and the involvement of the people.

Parish leaders, and especially the pastor, must realize the need for long-range planning as a means for using the resources of the parish to better advantage than the haphazard approach of responding to each successive crisis. The staff and lay leaders must be willing to commit themselves to some form of organized, predictable, and understandable planning process. Parish planning must be *organized* so that it provides a framework for the work of parish leaders. It must be *predictable* so that it can provide direction to the parish and can suggest alternatives for crises that are likely to occur in the future. It must be *understandable* so that parishioners become aware of and can accept the planning process.

The Planning Process

Once the leaders are committed to parish planning, their first task is to *listen*. Parish leaders must first listen to one another in order to learn each one's expectations for the parish, and to discover consensus and opposing views among the staff and council members. Next, the leaders must listen to the parish as a whole. This can be done through informal discussions, individual conferences, phone calls, townhall meetings, or written surveys. Listening to the promptings of the Holy Spirit to learn what the Lord desires for the parish is also part of the listening process. This is done through individual prayer and group discernment.

After listening to the people and to the Spirit, the next step is to *respond* to what is heard. If leaders are serious about listening, they will hear much more than they can act upon at one time. The staff and leaders will have to put the results of the listening phase into an order of priorities. The items at the top of the list should be taken care of immediately, and the items further down will have to wait for a later time. Constructing the list of parish priorities is not a task for the staff, council, or planning committee alone. It is important to include the parishioners in this as well, at least in critiquing or approving the list. Writing this list of priorities takes both time and prayerful reflection; but it respects the desires of the people and attends to the promptings of the Spirit.

The next step is to *work on a few of the more pressing items* on the top of the priorities list. Even small successes can stir a parish to new action and vitality. If people notice that something is happening in an area they think important, they are more likely to become interested and take part in the parish as a whole; they will begin to view it as their own. The action could be something as simple as toning down the organ during Masses, improving the church public address system, or getting a new parish answering service. Or the action could be a larger matter such as deciding whether to build a new church or parish center, hire a new staff person, or close out some of the grades in the parish school. Whatever the area, people become aware that someone is listening to them and, what's more, that someone is acting on a suggestion they felt was important. Even if the decision does not agree with the person's own views, that person is more likely to accept the decision if she or he realizes that someone has been listening and is trying to do whatever is best for the parish community.

The next step is to *set goals* for the parish. Only after the parish has dealt with a few of the more pressing issues can it begin to look at some of the longer-range, less-pressing issues. At Queen of Heaven, for instance, after the first year of focusing on twelve key areas, one per month, the leaders could think about hiring an administrator who would take charge of coordinating parish programs and who would free the priests and staff members to work on specific areas of parish ministry. The time to set goals for the parish, in other words, is after the listening and responding process has taken place. Parish goals are then more likely to reflect the needs and desires of the membership as a whole and not represent the views of only a few people who happen to be in positions of leadership at that time. This is a good time to examine prayerfully the list of parish priorities to be sure that whatever direction the parish might take in the next few years is in response to the Gospels, the traditions of the Catholic Church, and the needs and expectations of the people.

A parish goal is meant to be a guide to action or a statement of a desired outcome in the parish. A goal for worship might be that people will participate in the congregational singing to such an extent that they enjoy singing and come to the weekend Masses wanting to worship the Lord in song. Such a goal is challenging; it calls for investment and involvement by the people; and it is long-range. The parish is not likely to achieve this goal within one year, but it does give those involved in liturgical planning a goal to work toward and a focus for their energies.

Similar goals can be written for other areas of parish life, always keeping in mind the interests of the people and the ideals of the gospel message. A goal to increase parishioners' awareness of the parish's role in social justice issues may not be a response to the actual interests of the people, but it may be a reminder of the Lord's call to all Christians to care for the oppressed and the needy.

Committees or special groups—for instance, those working on liturgy education, community-building, outreach, or leadership—usually write their own goals. Goals give focus and direction to the parish over the next several years. They are tentative, however, until they are critiqued by the parish leadership—staff, council, and other leaders—and ratified by the parish membership, perhaps through a parish-wide meeting or special liturgy.

Reflecting on these various sets of goals can help leaders see a focus, direction, purpose, or mission for the whole parish. They can then draw up a brief statement on why the parish exists and what it is trying to become. The statement of purpose is then publicized. It becomes part of each Sunday's bulletin along with other important information such as the times for Masses. It can also be printed on the parish stationery and made visible at liturgies through banners or posters.

Once the goals have been agreed upon and the purpose of the parish established, it is up to the people who are responsible for each area of parish life to create an environment in which the goals and overall purpose can be achieved. One way to do this is to make up a number of "action contracts." These contracts spell out details of what will be done over the coming year to achieve the goals and purpose of the parish: what concrete action will take place, toward what group of people it is directed, when, how often, and where the action will happen, what parish facilities will be used, what groups or individuals will be responsible for planning and carrying out the action, how the action will start and stay in operation, and how the people planning it will measure its effectiveness.

At Queen of Heaven parish, for example, the group responsible for parish liturgies and music decided to form a "congregational choir" in which volunteer singers sat at random among the people during Mass and created an atmosphere of enthusiastic and prayerful singing.

When the year is completed, those working on the "action contracts" evaluate the year's work in order to determine whether the actions planned were achieved, and whether the parish is closer now than last year in attaining its goals for each area of parish life.

An important step in the planning process is to *expand and strengthen leadership.* Too often planning depends upon an individual or a small group, such as the pastor or the staff. Sometimes a parish comes to life and takes on new enthusiasm because of the talents or initiative of the pastor or a staff person, only to be sent back into depression and apathy once that person leaves. Any model of effective parish planning must have a process for transferring leadership to those who will remain. In a parish community, those who provide this continuity are obviously the parishioners. In the parishes I have surveyed in recent years, over half of the professional staff come or go every four years, but only seventeen percent of the parishioners move in or out of the parish during the same time. The parishioners must be given encouragement, support, and training to keep the momentum of parish planning going. This is done by including the people in the planning process from the beginning and by encouraging them to take the initiative and to assume responsibility for the parish's continuation and growth. It is true that a new pastor sets the tone, but if the parish is known to have an effective model of planning, this can influence the type of pastor that will come and will help determine his approach to ministry and mode of operation.

Another step in the planning model I propose is to *get feedback* from the people, both from the active and inactive members. This is necessary in order to find out to what extent the parishioners are aware of the goals and direction of the parish, whether they like what is happening, whether the parish furthers their relationship with the Lord, and truly helps them to care for others. A written survey is one way to get this information (see Appendix).

Mary Queen of Heaven parish used this method as a means of refining the monthly-emphasis process. People can be surveyed through small-group or parish-wide meetings, through telephone interviews or informal discussions. Whatever method is used, it is important to check with the people after a new emphasis or program has been operating for a few years in order to see how well it is getting across, how the people feel about it, and what changes or refinements may be necessary. In this way the process of listening and responding to specific issues, of putting these issues into a larger context or plan for the future, and of expanding the leadership to include the parishioners becomes an ongoing one of renewal and revitalization. It is never a once-and-for-all process, although sampling people's opinions may receive more attention at a particular moment as the need arises.

Although the process of listening to the people, forming goals, developing lay leadership, and getting feedback will vary with the size, background, and needs of the parish and local community, this model could be used in all seven types of parishes mentioned in this book. It is a way in which the parish can better minister to the needs of the people it serves and respond to the call of the Spirit in its midst. Parish planning is worthwhile only insofar as it accomplishes these two ends.

CHAPTER SIX

Part 1: The Well-established Parish

A few years ago parishioners described this parish as the "Status Quo Vadis parish; it looks like it's going somewhere, but it's actually standing still." Its real name is St. Michael's, and most of its parishioners are upper-middle-class Catholics who moved out of the city into this prestigious suburb. The parish plant is an impressive set of buildings, most of which were built in the late 1950s. The school was the first to be built, and it still serves 600 students. This is down from the peak enrollment of the 1960s, since many of the children are now beyond elementary school age. Then came the rectory and convent, both built to hold three times the number that now live in them. The church, a commanding stone structure of American Colonial style, was the last to be built. In the 1970s it was remodeled, and the altar was brought closer to the people. No expense was spared, and most people like the combination of warmth and majesty. The present pastor was responsible for the remodeling, and the people feel lucky to have him. He is a good manager of parish affairs and well liked by his people. He also started the parish council and considers it to be invaluable. He especially likes the advice they give him on making up the budget and on spending priorities in the parish.

Most of the adults are in their forties and fifties. The large homes attracted them because most had large families or were planning them. These people were anxious to provide a good environment for their children. This area seemed ideal, as did the parish.

For many, their homes are now too large because their children have grown and moved away. But the people like the area. They feel "settled" and are not considering moving into smaller homes. Many, however, spend extended vacation periods away from the area. Money does not appear to be a problem, although inflation, the rising cost of energy, tuition rates, and high taxes are frequently topics of conversation.

The people also talk about how pleased they are with the liturgical celebrations, the choir, the sisters in the school, the pastor and associates. Belonging to St. Michael's is an important part of living in the area, and attending Mass on Sundays is a matter of pride, almost a status symbol.

The staff wonders, however, whether this highly positive response from the people is a way of remaining aloof and uninvolved. "You're doing a great job over there, Father. No, I'm sorry I can't make it to that talk tomorrow night. But I'll be sending you a check for that Cuban family the parish is sponsoring." The majority of the people seem to be high on satisfaction but low on participation other than the weekend liturgies. It's always the same few people who show up when the call goes out for volunteers or to fill vacancies in organizations.

Father Flynn, the pastor, says it has always been this way and nothing can be done. "The people are generous," he says, "but they're busy in so many other groups and organizations they can't be expected to spend much extra time with the parish."

This was the picture of St. Michael's a few years ago. It is no longer that way. Recently the staff and council compiled a list of events of the past three years so they could better understand what had happened. It was a period of conversion for the parish. It was as if the Spirit had taken hold of St. Michael's and shaken it. A few pieces are still flying about, but the parish has come together as never before. How did this happen?

The pastor admitted that before the foundations were shaken, his own as well as the parish's, he had been satisfied with the direction of the parish and with his own style of leadership. All the newer church practices had been introduced, such as a parish council, Communion in the hand, women ministers of Communion, Communion under both species, neighborhood study groups. None of these experiences had touched his life, however. The rectory was a confortable place to live. The people were supportive. He had a good staff. The parish had a good reputation in the diocese.

Then Father Tom Plank, the first associate who had served the parish for over ten years and who also described himself as "satisfied" and "not anxious to make waves," got involved in a "Think and Drink" group. It was composed of priests and staff members from two parishes in the neighboring suburbs. A group of eight, four priests and four women staff members, met once every three weeks to discuss parish ministry. For each meeting a different person chose the topic, led the prayer, and brought the refreshments. The refreshments were sometimes exotic, but the questions were down to earth: What is the ideal parish? What should be its priorities? How can we help people cope with life? How well are we coping?

Tom Plank could feel his treasured categories of "Church," "parish," and "priesthood" being challenged and destroyed as he tried to defend his views. What surprised him was that he was glad it was happening. The people's support and love for him were far more important. He asked if he could bring the pastor along sometime. That prompted much discussion and ambiguous feelings, but finally the "Think-and-Drinkers" agreed.

The next meeting was a disaster. Neither the pastor nor the group felt comfortable. No one was at ease or was willing to share. The topic for the evening was leadership, and it was obvious that the group's view of leadership was a long way from that of the pastor. Everyone was relieved when it was over. The associate felt terrible about the whole experience.

But then a strange thing happened. The pastor asked if he could come again, and after some hesitation, the group agreed. Why the group did agree, no one can say. It was from that moment, however, that the story of St. Michael's conversion begins, because it was the start of the pastor's own conversion experience.

Father Flynn did return with the associate three weeks later, and he brought the drinks, Harvey Wallbangers. His topic was the meaning of "spirituality." After a few Wallbangers, the suspicion and animosity in the group lessened. The discussion went later than usual, but no one seemed to mind. It was obvious to all, except perhaps to the pastor himself, that he was a different person at the second meeting, less quick with all the answers and more willing to listen. He talked about his own narrow life in the parish and his fear of being a hypocrite, of talking about spiritual growth but not experiencing it himself. The result of the evening was a surprise to everyone. The group agreed to take off from their own parish commitments and go on a three-day retreat together, with no leader or agenda—just time apart to grapple with the topic of spirituality. They wanted to spend time discussing how each tried to live (but failed to live) a spiritual life.

The rest of the staff at St. Michael's could not believe what they were hearing—that the pastor and associate were going off for a retreat *together*. (It was common knowledge that the two didn't always get along.) The staff members were both pleased and anxious, wondering what impact this retreat might have on future staff meetings. The staff's next shock came after the two priests returned from the retreat and announced that there would be a day-long staff meeting. This had never happened before. The staff day was to be held at the pastor's vacation home on the river. This was indeed a departure; that had been off limits for all but a few select parishioners and personal friends.

The two priests spent most of the day relating to the staff their own experience of conversion, and they suggested that the staff as a whole could benefit from a change as well. The only business discussed during the day was setting up times for regular staff meetings that would include prayer and personal feedback as well as the regular parish business. The pastor wanted to hear any gripes or frustrations or insights they might have about what was needed in the parish. He also announced that he was going to ask for a four-month sabbatical away from the parish that would include spiritual direction as well as updating in theology, pastoral care, and training in parish ministry. At that point most of the staff members were trying to climb back onto their chairs, having been knocked over with the shock. Father Tom Plank continued to beam appreciatively.

The pastor lost no time making arrangements for his leave. He was off within three weeks, feeling it was long overdue and that there was no reason to delay. In his absence, Father Tom was in charge, but both the pastor and the temporary pastor assured the staff that a new approach to decision-making would be initiated, one that would include more sharing of parish plans, more emphasis on group prayer, and more time devoted to finding ways of spreading this experience of conversion throughout the parish.

Most of the parishioners were not aware of any change in the staff or the parish—only that the pastor was taking off for a much-deserved vacation. The council, though, had some inkling that something had happened when the pastor told them before leaving that upon his return he would like more of each council meeting devoted to prayer and reflection and less to the budget and parish maintenance.

The pastor was gone from June to November, and in his absence the staff met each week not only to take care of necessary business but also to improve their own communication and interaction. Up to this point the members of the staff—which consisted of the pastor, two associates, the principal, two religious education coordinators, and the music director—had worked independently of one another. The monthly staff meetings had consisted of hearing reports on what each member was doing and then working over the calendar for the coming month so that each one's projects and programs would not get in the way of the others'.

The conversion of the pastor changed all that because it took the lid off the staff meetings. It encouraged all the members to work more closely together on projects, to share ideas about the direction of the parish, to pray in common, and to begin to enjoy one another's company.

One result of this new cohesiveness was a growing awareness that the parish needed new life, a shaking up, a change of heart. Everything was too comfortable, too convenient, too satisfying. What was needed was a simpler parish life-style, a deeper faith experience, a challenge to commit oneself to the Lord. The staff agreed about these things, but they hesitated to make any plans until the pastor returned.

Return he did. It was now nine months since his first experience in the "Think and Drink" group. The staff and council were anxiously awaiting his first moves to see what had happened during his sabbatical. His first move was to describe during the weekend liturgies his conversion experience and what had happened during his time away. He talked about how he had made a retreat for thirty days, had learned for the first time how *really* to pray, how to let go and allow the Lord to lead, how to sort out different choices and directions as he moved through a process of discernment. And after the retreat he had gone back to school to learn about new directions in the Church, in liturgy, counseling, pastoral ministry, adult education, and lay spirituality.

The parishioners were not sure this was the same man who had been their pastor for twelve years. For one thing, he was twenty pounds lighter and enjoying it. The staff was delighted, the council apprehensive, and the parishioners confused. What was going to happen to their safe, secure, predictable parish? Deep down, however, they were excited. The foundations were beginning to quiver.

The staff's first meeting with the pastor was a celebration and an affirmation of everything the staff had worked on. After the celebrating, the staff got down to serious talk about the next steps to be taken. They all agreed that the council would be the place to begin, so they invited the council members to participate in a mission-retreat experience. It would consist of one evening session a week for four weeks and a two-day weekend retreat. All fifteen of the council members agreed to give it a try, though not without some unvoiced but noticeable apprehension. The council decided that Lent would be the best time to try the program because everyone would be in the parish and not on vacation. Many of the council were unenthusiastic, but when they saw how important it was to the pastor they decided to go along with it.

Each of the four evening sessions was run by two staff members, although all the staff participated in the meetings. At the first session the pastor and staff shared their own conversion experiences and invited the council members to talk about similar experiences of God's intervention in their own lives—perhaps during the birth of a child, a family crisis, or a moment of insight.

At the second session the staff and council shared Bible readings. Each one spent half an hour looking through the Bible and finding a passage he or she liked that seemed to fit the occasion. Some of the council members had never used the Bible before and were not sure where to look. When the group reassembled and everyone was asked to read a short passage and tell why he or she had chosen it, many of the council members were not sure they had found anything worthwhile. In the sharing that followed, however, staff and council members were amazed at how the readings built on one another and worked toward a composite whole. All of them became aware that the Holy Spirit was alive and working in their midst.

At the third session the two staff members leading the group asked each one to write on index cards what he or she thought were the five best aspects of the parish at the present time and what were five of its greatest needs. Some of the plusses they mentioned were the choir, the confirmation program, the visitors to the sick, and even the recent change in the pastor. Some of the needs they listed included getting more people involved in activities, establishing a senior citizens' group, and emphasizing adult spiritual renewal. The lists from individuals were compared so that the staff and council could see what positive aspects they all agreed on and what they all saw as needs in the parish. The combined list of parish needs set the stage for the two-day weekend retreat.

The focus for the fourth evening session was leadership. The staff members introduced and discussed various alternatives to decision-making other than voting or using Robert's Rules of Order. The alternatives, they said, included forming a group consensus on issues. In this approach to decision-making the discussion of an issue continues until everyone can accept the final result. The discussion usually takes longer than when a vote is taken; everyone must be willing to compromise and let go of his or her first choice, but the decision has a better chance of being carried into action since it is supported and accepted by all.

Another alternative used for making an important decision is one that demands much deliberation. Parish leaders use a process of discernment in which people spend time praying over the matter to be decided. After a period of prayer everyone makes a list of all the reasons why a proposal should *not* be followed. These reasons are shared with the whole group. Once again the people spend time in prayer and then make up a list of all the reasons a proposal *should* be followed. The intention is to allow room for the Spirit to move people and influence the decision. In this way the leaders can learn what the Lord desires and so come to a final decision.

As the time for the weekend retreat approached, the council and staff members had begun to come together as a community, experiencing themselves as parish co-leaders whose one desire was the good of the parish. Any suspicion or apprehension that may have been present at the beginning was left behind. The task at the retreat was to decide what should be done to stir up the parish and bring it to life; so far only the staff and council had been affected. But how go to the people? They would be a hard group to move, because many were over-committed to various clubs, organizations, and projects. Furthermore, many had withdrawn from parish involvement because of divided homes, shallow experiences with religion, and alienating encounters with church leaders.

The staff and pastor prepared for the retreat by looking through the many programs available for parish renewal. All these materials proved helpful as they searched for the right vehicle to help the parishioners examine their faith and respond to it.

The staff and council began the weekend with little idea of what would happen or what plan they would settle upon. They began by praying for light and then looking over the alternatives available. Then they talked about the essentials of "being a parish community" and about what they could do to create a spirit of community. They reflected on their own experience and how each one's conversion had happened. They made up a list of elements that had been a part of each one's experience.

Each one, for instance, had become aware of a need, a thirst or desire for a deeper and more meaningful life. Without this longing the conversion experience would have passed them by. Then came an opportunity or special occasion, and something told them that this was an important moment, one not to be ignored. It was a chance to make a choice, to take a risk, to get into deeper water. This invitation usually came from another person or group of people. For example, the associate had invited the pastor to attend the "Think and Drink" group. The staff had invited the council to be part of the retreat sessions. Next came the elation that went with the willingness to say yes. Many council members had experienced this in the emotional moment when all were sharing the Bible readings; they were swept up in the surprise and thrill of the moment. Then came a feeling of unworthiness, but along with it a delight to be given a chance for a new, closer relationship with the Lord. Next came a firm decision to allow the Lord to work within them and a decision to make changes in their lives to strengthen the initial conversion experience. Along with this firm decision to say yes came a desire to share the new commitment with others. The change could not be kept to themselves; it had to be shared. It was a responsibility rather than a privilege. Finally, the people had a feeling of commitment to others, a realization that the conversion was not an individual but a group experience. It must flow into action with and for others.

After identifying these common threads, the question now for the staff and council was how best to offer the rest of the parish the same opportunity for conversion. First, they decided the parishioners had to experience a longing for a deeper spiritual life, an ache for a life-style that lies beyond material possessions, country club memberships, and the endless round of projects, meetings, and parties. The council members were sure that the parishioners did have this desire; their own experience proved it. Next, the people must be given the opportunity for a change of heart, the chance to risk and take the plunge. To provide that opportunity was the work of the staff and council. But what would it be?

While the staff and council were trying to figure out the best route to follow, one of the priests hit upon something that everyone responded to immediately. He had been studying the

Rite of Christian Initiation for Adults, the restored Rite of the Catechumenate. He was thinking of using it in the parish for people who were interested in joining the Catholic Church. Perhaps it could be adapted for people who were already Catholics but who would like to make a deeper commitment. "It might be the answer to our prayers of providing an opportunity for parish conversion," the pastor remarked, "a way of reinitiating the adults of our parish into the Church. Many of our parishioners have never made a commitment to the faith. They were born into it or fell into it without much thought or conviction."

During the rest of their time together the staff and council excitedly made plans for the adult re-initiation of the parish. They decided to follow, with some adaptation, the four steps of the Rite of Christian Initiation for Adults: becoming catechumens, the election and enrolling of names, the celebration of initiation, and the living of one's faith after Baptism. The description that follows is the story of conversion at' St. Michael's parish.

The first step was to offer the people a choice, to invite them to a re-initiation into a deeper understanding of the Church, of prayer, of their own role as Christians. This was done in October. The priests, along with the staff and council, gave a series of sermons on all four Sundays of the month, relating their own stories of conversion and the new insights they had gained in the process. They invited anyone else in the parish to share in the experience.

. A huge banner was made for the occasion. It showed only a large circle, to signify the simplicity of conversion, its wholeness, its communal aspect, and the feeling of dedication and completeness that comes as a result. The staff and council explained that the invitation to re-initiation was for those who had a thirst for a deeper understanding of their faith and of their God. They would have to commit themselves to weekly meetings during Advent and Lent, and to two full days of retreat in January and February. This invitation was open to all adults seventeen years of age and over and to persons at any level of parish involvement, even to those unhappy with the Church or parish. But it was restricted to those who would stay with it; no part-time commitment would be allowed. The pastor promised that no one would be the same after the experience. He himself was living proof.

On the last Sunday of October there was a special evening liturgy for those who wanted to give the re-initiation a try. The Mass, the first step in the process, would be the people's acceptance of the invitation to conversion. The staff and council had made bets with one another on expected attendance, but all bets were off when the Mass began. One hundred fifty-two people showed up, young and old, women and men, singles, widowed, husbands and wives, active and inactive. That was twenty-five more than the highest estimate.

The Mass was a celebration of joy and expectation. One of the readings was from the Introduction to the Rite of Christian Initiation for Adults. The reading, in part, said:

> The catechumens will learn to pray to God more easily, to witness to the faith, to be constant in the expectation of Christ in all things, to follow supernatural inspiration in their deeds, and to exercise charity toward their neighbors to the point of self-renunciation. (*Rites of the Catholic Church as Revised by the Second Vatican Ecumenical Council*, trans. International Commission on English in the Liturgy, New York: Pueblo Publishing Co., 1976.)

The pastor explained the meeting times, proposed the schedule of events, and called for questions. The group prayed together; then those who wished to sign up for the next step— one evening a week during November and another evening Mass the first Sunday of Advent—did so as they left the church. Almost everyone did sign the roster; only those who could not make all the meetings reluctantly refrained from joining.

The weekly evening meetings centered on themes of praying, witnessing (telling one's story of faith), being aware of inspiration (expecting the unexpected), and exercising charity (love of God and love of neighbor are the same). One staff person and one council member prepared each of the evening sessions, and all the council and staff acted as sponsors to the "circlers," as they began to call themselves. The banner used at the October Masses was hung in the meeting room with much ceremony at the beginning of each meeting.

The turnout remained high throughout the month of November, so that by the first Sunday of Advent there were still one hundred and thirty-nine in the "circle" group. The memories of the Mass and celebration that Sunday evening are still fresh in people's minds. The circlers experienced new life, hope, and expectation, something they had not felt in the parish before. The purpose of the Mass was to enroll the names of those who wanted to continue in the program. People were asked to make a deeper commitment, to take a greater risk, to "elect" to follow the call of Christ. The names of those who chose to continue were recorded in the circle book, and everyone was given a simple, adjustable ring that was of no monetary value but had great significance for those who received it.

Next the circlers spent two Saturdays, one in January and one in February, in prayer, reflection, and sharing. The Saturday in January was called the "day of scrutinies"; the focus was on the need for repentance and conversion, but the meeting also stressed an awareness of one's gifts and graces. The people were encouraged to take a look at all they had to offer the Church and others and at how they sometimes fail to use their gifts well. The day ended with a communal reconciliation service.

The Saturday in February was the "day of presentations." Everyone brought a Bible, and the group spent the day sharing Scripture readings. People learned how to use the Bible for prayer and reflection, and the staff was on hand for spiritual direction. The day ended with a communal prayer service, first in small groups with the council members acting as sponsors and group leaders, and then together in one large group.

After the two days of retreat, the people committed themselves to one evening session a week during Lent. These meetings were spent in preparation for the re-initiation ceremony to be held at the Easter Vigil. One hundred and twenty-five people were still involved in the program, to the amazement of all—even of the circlers themselves. Each week centered on a different aspect of the re-initiation rite: water, light, oil, white garment, and laying on of hands. The participants learned the significance of each of these symbols and what it called forth from each person's experience.

By the time Holy Week came, the parishioners were aware that something unique was about to happen. The parish had never before been the occasion of such expectation and excitement. The church was packed for the Easter Vigil. The circlers, along with the staff and council, who acted as sponsors, participated in the lighting of the new fire, the procession with the paschal candle, and the readings portraying God's involvement in human history. Then came the circlers' moment. The one hundred and twenty-five people formed a half circle in front of the altar, facing the congregation. First they were asked to wash their hands and faces in a basin, and one of their number explained to the people that this signified a new and cleansing experience to the participants. Then they each lit a candle, which they themselves had made, and another circler related a personal experience of the new life and insights she had gained in recent months. The sponsors then anointed each circler's forehead with oil, and the people heard another person speak about new strength and dedication. Then each person put on a homemade white cloth that looked like a wide stole or a scapular. One man told about how different he felt compared with six months before and said that he expected to be a permanently changed person. Finally, all the staff and council filed past each of the circlers and quietly laid their hands on each person. This was to signify the commitment each person had made to be a witness to Christ, to show that it was each one's responsibility to share the conversion experience with others and not hold onto it as a personal gift. Many tears of joy were shed that night, and not even the pastor could hold back his own tears of thanksgiving and exaltation.

But the participants knew that one further step was required of them: sharing the re-initiation experience with others. The circlers attended two more evening meetings, in April and May, to make plans for the coming year. Each person was to sponsor another one, who would go through the circle experience beginning the next October. During the summer the original circlers were to think and pray about who the new persons might be in September and to invite them to be part of the program for the next year.

This is where St. Michael's parish stands now. It is true that none of the circle people are the same as they were a year ago. Neither is the parish the same, for its foundations have been shaken. It contains one hundred and twenty-five adults, plus the staff and council, who have undergone a conversion: a new birth in the faith and a willingness to commit themselves to the Lord, to the parish, and to others. These people are now seeking out others to embark on their own journey of faith.

Next year at this time it is likely that there will be twice the number of circle people in the parish. The movement is reaching out beyond the parish boundaries: The circlers are looking for ways of witnessing and sharing their riches with their relatives and friends, people in need, those they work with, and with other parishes. It is too soon to tell where this might lead, but plainly it is no longer correct to call St. Michael's the "Status Quo Vadis" parish. Its people have come alive, and the parish is turning upward on its journey of faith.

Part 2: Adult Spirituality

The experience of St. Michael's speaks for itself. The parish had been content not to ask questions, content to live on the surface and be a respectable, efficient, convenient parish composed of respectable and contented parishioners. Then the change occurred. It began with the pastor. Little permanent change can come in a parish unless the staff, and above all the pastor, changes. The diocese had offered many opportunities in recent years for the continuing education of the clergy, but it took a personal invitation for the pastor at St. Michael's to risk exposing himself to updating and change. Then, of course, he had to decide to use the opportunity offered.

Often parish priests feel swamped by their duties and cannot find time for their own updating, renewal, and conversion. Nevertheless, adult spiritual growth is as indispensable to priests and staff as it is for parishioners. The people need models to look to. The staff and the parish council, or if there is no council, then the core leaders of the parish, must be those models.

Often people want to become involved in the parish but are not given the opportunity for spiritual growth. Too much time is devoted to parish maintenance—budgeting, hiring staff, planning renovation, building, or raising money—but too little time is spent on prayer, spiritual growth, or fostering community spirit. If leaders have an experience of adult spiritual growth, they may then become advocates for these programs. An example of this is the training of some men in preparation for ordination to the permanent diaconate. Much of the training includes insights into how to pray, introduction to recent trends in the Church, learning different stages of adult spiritual growth, and discovering how they as deacons fit into the ministry of the Church and parish. Sharing these new insights and knowledge is perhaps the most valuable ministry that deacons can perform.

I have come to believe that there is a spirituality unique to lay persons. It is different from the spirituality of the celibate priesthood or the religious life. I have experienced this with my own mother. When my father was alive, her spirituality was relational. Her relationship to God always included her relationship with her husband and, later, with her five children. Her prayer had this as its focus. Nothing "spiritual" was done without her husband: Mass, Sacraments, activities. She found God in and through her spouse. That was true for my father as well. His relationship to God—his prayer, repentance, and grace—was centered in his wife. Nothing else mattered. I am not sure that a celibate person can understand that kind of dedication and absorption.

When my father died, a new life opened up for my mother. She spent more time praying alone, reading the Scriptures, and attending courses on spiritual direction. Her spirituality became less relational, more direct, closer to that of a priest, religious, or unmarried person.

Much more study and thought needs to be done concerning this unique form of relational spirituality for married people. Too often they are given, as the only model, the spirituality followed by members of religious orders or congregations. But it does not fit their own life-style. As yet, we have only the lived experience of people who have found their way to God through devotion to a spouse or to their children. This lived experience must be fostered and reflected upon in parishes. Opportunities must be given people, old and young, to come together and tell their story of how they have discovered God working in their lives, in their marriages, in their relationships, in their families.

It should also be remembered that adult spirituality is more than just prayer. Too often the person who prays more is regarded as more "spiritual." But adult spirituality is a much broader concept. It includes not only prayer but a response to God's personal invitation to know him better, to become a friend of God, and to act out this relationship in service to his people, especially the poor, the lonely, the oppressed.

Authentic adult spirituality must also include a tendency toward simplicity—simplifying one's life-style by limiting one's possessions, engagements, and memberships. This was especially important for the people at St. Michael's who were caught in the endless round of benefits, clubs, socials, and projects. Simplifying one's life is important if one is to make room for the Lord's work. People must experience a thirst for a deeper relationship with the Lord. If one's life is filled with things—possessions, status, reputation—then growth in spiritual matters becomes difficult. The task of raising a family is, of course, hectic and unending, but it can include celebrations of simple moments and a seeking out of more modest, yet rich, family events.

Finally, the adaptation of the Rite of Christian Initiation for Adults at St. Michael's was only one of many possible routes to spiritual growth. Whatever path is used, it is essential to realize that we are en route to becoming Christians, to becoming community, and that we will never completely achieve these goals, at least not in this life. The Lord is always before us drawing us on to a deeper knowledge and love of him and his people.

It is possible, however, to identify common elements in this journey of faith, ones that can be anticipated, encouraged, and celebrated in the parish. They are the steps in a conversion process, a process that may be repeated many times in many forms during a person's lifetime.

Elements of the Conversion Process

A conversion experience becomes possible if a person is *aware of the need for change*. It seems that preceding every conversion there is an awareness of and a desire for something deeper and more meaningful. "There must be more to life than this," we find ourselves saying. Without this longing or need for a shaking of one's foundations, the opportunity for conversion will pass us by. This is why the same experience or crisis or special event may be a moment of conversion for one person, while for another it remains only an "interesting" moment to be enjoyed or lived through and endured.

Also, those who have experienced conversion can usually point to a *specific moment* which they can remember *as pivotal* in their lives. They see it as a moment in which something told them, "This is an important time; don't let it pass you by." It may be an opportunity for a choice, the chance to take a risk, the time to get into deeper water. The person *sees* it as a choice that will make a difference in what follows.

This opportunity for change often comes from another person or group of people. It might be an invitation to attend a meeting or prayer session, to go on a trip or spend time with others, or to share a unique experience. Sometimes the personal contact can be with some unseen person so that the individual feels he or she is being called by Jesus or by the Spirit. But even this spiritual encounter is often initiated or made possible through contact with another human being— a parent, relative, friend, or loved one.

If the invitation is accepted and the person decides to give a qualified yes to the moment of conversion, then the person usually *experiences a thrill* as he or she is willing to risk, to change, to let go of the past and seek out the unknown. The individual feels swept up in the surprise of being able to say yes, even in a halting and qualified way. It is this elation that stays with people as they look back on key moments of conversion, even if the experience is a painful one. They are grateful for being able to say yes even to pain since it led to change and new growth.

Close on the heels of this elation comes an *awareness of not being worthy*. "Why have I been given such an opportunity for growth, such a privilege to live life at a fuller, deeper level? Why me? I've done nothing to deserve this."

Once the person has opened up to the conversion and realizes how unworthy but fortunate he or she is to be given this opportunity, then comes a *stronger commitment* to let the conversion change the course of one's life. This decision implies making changes in one's life to support and strengthen that conversion. This decision may not always be lived up to in all its initial resolve, but if the conversion is authentic, the decision to *try* to live on a new level of understanding and commitment must be there.

Then the person often experiences a *desire to share this decision and new direction with others*, especially with those who can understand. The conversion process is too great a mystery and contains too much power to be contained. It must spill out into a community of persons who recognize the experience, who can share ideas about what it will mean for the person's future, and can provide encouragement and support for new directions in the person's life.

At this point symbols also become important. Many times the process of conversion cannot be expressed in words; the experience can only be described and shared indirectly through song, art, dance, poetry, or ritual.

Finally, the proof of an authentic conversion is in the *living out of the commitment:* in learning how to translate the change of heart into a greater love and sensitivity for others, a greater response to human needs, a greater commitment to service. In this way the converted person comes to realize that what has happened is not just a privilege but primarily a responsibility. This is the link between individual conversion and public service. The person who has changed becomes an agent of change for others.

The story in St. Luke's Gospel about the two disciples on the road to Emmaus (Luke 24:13-35) is a story of conversion. The two people are in need. They are dejected and depressed. All their hopes have been dashed. Life has lost its meaning. It is time to start over. They are, in other words, open to change.

Then a stranger joins them on their walk. This stranger becomes the unique experience for a conversion. As the three of them continue their walk, the two disciples pour out their sorrow and frustration, and the stranger listens. Then he gives them insight into the significance of recent events surrounding this Jesus person. What began as conversation has developed into a moment of conversion.

Then comes the choice. The disciples could let the moment pass, could continue feeling miserable, and could let the stranger continue his journey. But instead they decide to say yes to the moment and to invite the stranger in. They are willing to let this experience change them.

Along with the yes, the disciples must have felt humbled and unworthy of this conversation, of the time this person has taken with them, of the explanation he has given of the events leading up to and following the death of Jesus. But still they say yes to the moment. They take the risk of inviting the stranger in, and as a result their eyes are opened as they break bread together. They discover who the stranger is—the one their hearts long for.

As soon as they understand what has happened, he is gone. The moment has passed, but its impact and power remains. They are on fire! It is too much to contain, too much to keep to themselves. They *have* to run back immediately to Jerusalem and tell everyone what has happened. They need the support and solidarity of others who can understand what they have experienced.

The other disciples did understand and could share their joy because they too had experienced a conversion. "The Lord is alive!" St. Luke does not tell us what happened to the two disciples afterwards, but it is not difficult to trust that the conversion found expression in a decision to believe in this person Jesus and to translate this belief into service and care for others. If so, it was an authentic conversion experience, and it produced lasting results.

It is the task of the leaders of the parish to recognize these aspects of personal conversion, to foster a community of believing people who can help one another through these experiences, to reach out to others who are experiencing a desire for a deeper commitment to the Lord, and to give them support and encouragement on their journey of faith.

CHAPTER SEVEN

Part 1: The Small Town/Rural Parish

Saints Agnes and Boniface is a rural, small-town parish. The total membership is exactly two hundred seventy-five people. The town is just over a thousand. About half of the parishioners do not live in the town. Those who do are mostly older people who have moved in after turning over their farms to their children or renting their property out to tenants.

Sts. Agnes and Boniface has been a focal point of the town for many years. It is the only Catholic Church there now. Not so long ago there were two parishes, St. Agnes and St. Boniface. The former was for the Irish and the latter for the Germans. If there was a marriage that crossed parish "boundaries," and this happened only rarely, the new family belonged to the husband's parish.

In the early 1970s, the younger people of the community began moving into a city almost a hundred miles from the town, leaving the area with too few Catholics to support both parishes. It was at this time, too, that the shortage of priests became apparent. Combining the two parishes seemed a logical move, since only one priest could be spared for the area. The bishop did everything in his power to make the amalgamation as smooth and painless as possible. He visited the town, inspected both parish properties, interviewed parishioners, had long discussions with the priests and the lay leaders, and even talked to the town's mayor. (Although all this happened more than ten years ago, people talk about it as if it happened only last month!) A short time after his visit, the bishop announced his decision. The buildings of St. Agnes would be used, since they were in better condition, but the pastor from St. Boniface would become the pastor of the combined parish, now called Sts. Agnes and Boniface. (Most people now refer to the parish as St. A-B's, or Abby's, as it appears in the town's paper.)

Each parish community felt relieved that its parish had been preserved, either in the location or in the pastor. Pent-up frustrations and anger became apparent, however, when the decision was made about which statues would be kept and which would be removed. Compromises were made, but some parishioners still walk down only one side of the church and refuse to acknowledge the existence of the "other side" of the church with all those "foreign" saints.

Eventually the wounds caused by the merger were healed, and most of the parishioners, in their large-hearted way, accepted the new arrangement. They began to come together as a single parish community. Only now, however, after these many years, are the parish picnics a single event. At the time of the merger, each parish had its own set of socials at traditional times each year. When the socials were eventually combined, there were still two parish communities, identified by the two sets of hot dishes and the two seating areas. But slowly the people started trying out a new hot dish or chocolate cake or strudel. And now the divisions are only a memory, though well preserved in stories and jokes about the "good old days."

One of the unforeseen difficulties associated with the merger was that the pastor had no backup when he wanted to get away. The first pastor had no problem with this since he was used to living alone and was satisfied to stay in the parish year round. A few years ago, though, he retired. The new priest, a man in his forties, did feel the need to get away on occasion. But it meant finding a priest to come in from outside, and this had to be planned well in advance in order to fit the schedules of those teaching in the seminary or the diocesan high school, or to coincide with the schedules of the religious-order priests who were looking for a break from their own apostolates.

On one occasion a visiting priest who had volunteered for a two-week stint at St. Abby's cancelled at the last minute and left the pastor with his vacation plans made and no one to take his place.

Since it is difficult to keep a secret for more than ten minutes in a community this size, the parishioners were aware of the pastor's plight before he had time to hang up the phone and go back to his room to unpack. The parish communication system went into full swing, and in about two hours there was a knock at the front door. The president of the parish council was there with a suggestion.

"We heard the news about your having no replacement, Father." Father was not surprised that it was now common knowledge in the parish, but he was surprised at what came next. "We feel that you deserve your vacation and you've worked hard to get your time off. Now, if you can give us permission, we feel that we could have a Communion service on Sunday at the Mass times, and if a crisis comes up we could call for a priest from one of the other towns. But you should go on that vacation. We can manage for the two weeks you're away. Anyway, we'll appreciate you a lot more when you get back. What do you say?"

The pastor was tired and discouraged enough to take the people up on their suggestion. It was one of his best vacations, though the whole time he was away he kept wondering how the parish was getting along without a priest.

He returned to find the parish in better shape than when he had left. The people were so pleased with themselves! A spontaneous social happened after each of the Communion services while the pastor was gone. The feeling of community and pride ran high. No one died, and no tragedies occurred, but there was constant contact by phone among the parishioners just in case some need should go unattended. The pastor was so delighted at the people's initiative that he wondered if he should not have stayed away longer.

Before the vacation the pastor had been thinking of including more of the parishioners in the liturgy, but had hesitated; he was not sure they were ready. He now knew that they were not only ready but eager to take a more active role.

He asked a few members of the Altar Society to meet as the beginning of a new liturgy planning committee. The new committee met with the pastor for a number of months. The members learned how to train others who wanted to help out. Their next job was to find people to do the reading at Mass, to help with Communion, and to bring up the offerings.

Each member of the liturgy group took charge of a different area. One met with the new readers each month to give them support and confidence in reading. Another started training the extraordinary ministers for taking Communion to the sick and shut-ins. Another worked with the persons who brought up the offering at Mass and helped them think of other gifts that could be brought up as a way of emphasizing the theme for each Sunday's Mass. Another was responsible for the servers, a group long neglected in the parish. The pastor asked one man to join the liturgy committee and to work with the ushers and suggest a change of emphasis for them. In addition to their regular duties of taking up the collection and handing out bulletins, they would welcome people to church and help create an atmosphere of friendliness at Mass. The sixth member of the committee spent time with the organist, trying to find music that people knew and enjoyed singing. One committee member even suggested using guitars at a few of the Masses, a departure for St. Abby's. The committee decided to give it a try.

The pastor was delighted to see the people assuming so much ownership of the parish. Parishioners who had never volunteered before were showing up at meetings and volunteering to read, distribute Communion, or bring up the gifts. The people were leaving behind their biases and were drawing closer together. This was especially true for the German and Irish communities that had always been friendly but had never pulled together as one team.

After a few months the pastor asked the new liturgy committee to evaluate his sermons and suggest ideas for the coming weeks. At first the group held back. They all said they liked his sermons and thought he was doing a good job. But the pastor insisted, and after a few months the discussion over the sermons became the most enjoyable part of their meetings.

The pastor also concentrated on the parish council. Before his vacation the council had been little help to him; they met four times a year to discuss the budget and to give suggestions on needed repairs to the buildings. When the council president suggested that the pastor take that vacation, the council was the body that assumed "command" of the parish. After returning, the pastor made a mental note of this and made plans not to let it lose this initiative.

He suggested to the council president that he think about becoming a permanent deacon so that he could get some training in ministry and assume a larger role in the parish. The president, after some thought and encouragement from the council (and his wife), agreed. The council as a whole revamped its constitution so that it would become responsible not only for maintaining the parish but for coordinating all its functions: socials, educational programs, and liturgies. The council was enlarged to include a member from the liturgy committee, a person to represent the parish socials, and the religious education coordinator. The coordinator was a volunteer who had been handling the education programs for the past few years. She was delighted at being invited to be part of the council because she felt it was a sign of acceptance and support of her work in the parish.

The formation of the new council showed the pastor that he was not equipped to deal with this new direction in the parish. He needed new ideas and further training. Nothing in his seminary formation, now twenty years in the past, had prepared him for this emphasis on lay involvement in parish ministry.

Fortunately, an opportunity presented itself. The bishop was offering a summer of retreat, study, and pastoral updating, all expenses paid, to the first twenty priests who applied. The bishop had himself experienced such a summer the year before and had found it so helpful that he wanted the priests to have the same chance. But he also realized that it would mean a sacrifice for the parishes involved, since he did not have twenty priest-replacements to fill the positions left vacant for the two-and-a-half months. A few places would have to go without a resident priest for the duration.

The pastor at St. Abby's reflected on how well the people had filled in during his absence and how well they had responded to the new emphasis on shared ministry over the year. He not only applied to be one of the twenty but told the bishop that he was sure his parish would survive his absence during the summer without a replacement.

This suggestion to the bishop became public knowledge in the parish in a short time. The people were excited not only that the pastor would have what he desired—time away for updating and renewal, and hopefully a little rest—but that they would be singled out by the bishop for the special experiment of being without a pastor for almost three months. The bishop himself visited Sts. Agnes and Boniface in May for the Confirmations, and he explained to the congregation what would be expected of them.

There would be no daily Mass, but the liturgy committee would arrange for a Communion Service every morning at 7 o'clock. Every other Sunday a priest from a neighboring town would come and offer a Mass at 1 P.M.. The bishop did not feel he could impose on the already-overworked priests in the neighboring towns to come every week, since it meant three hours of travel on top of their own Sunday Mass schedule. Of the two closest parishes, one had an elderly priest who was not in good health, and the other had a priest who was part-time in the parish and had a full-time job in the Chancery. That would mean that it would be up to the parishioners to conduct their own Sunday service on the alternate Sundays. Before he left for the summer, the pastor would work out with the deacon-in-training and the liturgy committee the services for those alternate Sundays.

Then there was the matter of emergencies. In the case of a death or accident, the council could call in one of the priests from the nearby towns to provide the Mass and sacraments. The parishioners would have to help out in these situations so that no one would be left unattended or unsupported.

On the feast of Corpus Christi there was a farewell for the pastor amid cheers and songs and raised toasts. The pastor was moved and flattered by the people's response and heartened by how far the parish had come since he had arrived just a few years ago.

During the summer, the pastor received many letters from the parishioners. It appeared that the parish was doing better than he had thought possible. His own work, while meeting his needs, was not so easy. The program began with a retreat, one on one, with a retreat director. The experience seemed to uncover issues that he had never adequately addressed before. The classes on spirituality, Scripture, and pastoral ministry only served to heighten his questioning. Getting away from the pressures of the parish was at once freeing and frightening. He began to realize that one summer would not be enough. He needed more time to learn about new directions, both in the Church and in himself.

The upshot of his renewal program was that the pastor decided to take off a year for more study and reflection, perhaps even get a master's degree. He knew that if he did not take this time for himself now, he might not get another chance. He decided to ask for a sabbatical and to begin it the following January.

The pastor was peaceful once he had made the choice, but he was worried about his dear people at St. Abby's. How would they receive the news? What would they do without him? It was likely that there would be no one to take his place as pastor. What, then, would happen to the parish? He talked to the bishop about his decision and received a great deal of personal support but no assurance that a priest would be available to take his place.

Summer came to an end, and his return to the parish was nothing short of triumph. The people were overjoyed to have their pastor back again and proud of how well they had done in his absence. Everyone was full of stories about what had happened during the summer. Many different versions were told of the same stories—such as how the deacon got laryngitis and did the whole service with actions and his wife's words, or about how the visiting priest's car got bogged down in the mud just outside of town and had to be pulled with Jake's (or was it Sam's?) four-wheel-drive pickup. There was even a tractor-pull benefit to raise money for some of the migrant workers in the area. On and on the stories went. It was obvious the people were pleased with themselves, and rightly so.

The pastor waited a few weeks before telling the parishioners about his plans to take a sabbatical. He had to work hard at not revealing his hand before he felt it was time—the people were so adept at picking up on any little clues. But this time his news fooled them all. The church was silent when he announced his decision and spelled out what it could mean for the parish. He gave them all the alternatives he could think of. There were only three.

The first option was the simplest but the least likely. The bishop would assign a priest to fill the pastor's vacancy. The only trouble was that no such person was available. The town is too far from the diocesan chancery and the diocesan schools to allow for a part-time priest, and there had been no applications for placement from priests outside the diocese. So the people should not count on finding a priest to take his place.

The second alternative was that the parish would continue to operate during the year as it had done during the summer. An administrator would be hired to help manage it. It would be hard to find the right person, but perhaps someone could be found.

The third option was to close down the parish for the year. The parishioners would be obliged to attend St. Charles parish in the next town. There was a noticeable groan in the congregation when the pastor presented this last alternative. St. Charles parish is pastored by an older priest, and there is very little room for lay initiative and participation in parish liturgies and parish life.

The response from the parishioners was what the pastor had expected. The people tried to understand and support his decision to take a leave of absence, but they could not hide their hurt and their feelings of being abandoned. Such a reaction did not make it easier for the pastor in the few months that remained before January. He had an intuitive feeling that this might be a final departure and that he would not return to St. Abby's. He wanted to prepare the people for the future as best he could, whatever that future might hold.

Within a few weeks of his announcement he received confirmation from the bishop that there would be no priest replacing him. The bishop said he felt that he had no alternative but to close the parish for the year. The pastor read the letter with sadness and anxiety. There had to be another way. He called the council president and two other trusted parish leaders and asked them if they would be willing to go with him to the bishop and present a plan for keeping the parish open.

A meeting was arranged, and the four from St. Abby's prepared their case. The deacon's wife, who had been active in the parish council and religious education program, agreed to become the acting parish administrator until a full-time person could be found. The two priests who had filled in during the summer agreed to continue their visits if they could cut them down to once every *other* month. Travel during the winter months would be difficult and would take more time. That would mean that a priest would be in the parish only one Sunday a month. All regular sacramental ministry—Masses, anointings, reconciliation, weddings—would have to take place then. The council president, due to be ordained deacon in February, could handle the baptisms and the funerals. The regular operation of the parish—maintenance, activities, socials, budget, religious education, sick calls—would be handled by the council and the parish administrator. The devotions and Communion services would be directed by the liturgy committee, headed by the deacon. Two other men in the parish had agreed to begin preparation for the diaconate in order to take the load off the present deacon. The permanent parish administrator would live in the rectory, and the parishioners promised to increase their contributions to the parish in order to assure a salary of at least $15,000 a year, in addition to free rent. If someone was hired who had a family, the people felt they could raise more money. It was that important to them to keep their parish open.

The bishop listened with much interest to the plan. He knew that many other parishes would be confronted with the same crisis—a priest leaving, retiring, or dying, and no one to take his place. He needed a model as an alternative to simply closing parishes; this might provide just such a model. At least it should be given a try. After talking to the pastor and leaders and making sure that the pastoral and spiritual needs of the people would be taken care of, he gave his blessing to the venture. In fact, he promised to help find a suitable administrator and to come there for a special Mass and celebration when the administrator moved into the parish. The parish representatives returned to St. Abby's full of the news—the parish would stay open!

On December first of last year the pastor took leave of the parish. The people gave him a gift of a month's vacation before he started his studies. He wanted to make his departure a simple affair, but he knew that would be impossible, so he gave in to the wishes of the people and agreed to a party in his honor. It was joyous and it was sad. There was hope as people looked forward to new beginnings and opportunities for both the pastor and the parishioners. Many of the people did not understand why all this had to happen, but they courageously accepted the fact and even celebrated it. They were used to dealing with the mystery of God's actions in the unpredictable changes of weather and crops. This was another example of how God worked out strange patterns in their lives.

Christmas was not an easy time for the parish. No midnight Mass was celebrated there, although all were invited to St. Charles. Most stayed home for the 1 P.M. Mass on Christmas Day, and it turned out better than expected. The music was lovely, the spirit was uplifting, and the people rejoiced that it was *their* liturgy. But they also felt uncertain about the future of the parish, and the priest who celebrated the Mass was in a sense a stranger to them. It just wasn't the same as having their own pastor.

In February a religious sister agreed to come live in the rectory and act as administrator for the year. She asked that the job be only two-thirds time so that she could spend at least two days a week with a group of her own sisters who taught in a school about fifty miles from St. Abby's.

The bishop came to install the new administrator. The parish presented her with a new car, and the diocesan newspaper did a front-page story on the parish. Sister Carol made it clear from the start that she was there only as a resource to the people; it was still up to them to keep the parish alive and growing.

She has been living in the parish for only half a year now, but already the people are accepting her as one of their own. What of the future? In a word, hopeful. The monthly Mass is prepared for and celebrated with more feeling and involvement than ever before. The Communion services on the other three Sundays of the month are pulling in other townspeople who are curious to see what is happening in this Catholic church without a pastor.

The organizations are thriving, and the socials and picnics are well-attended. Sister Carol is now exploring the possibility of finding permanent housing for the migrant workers in the area, and the parishioners are providing her with many ideas on how this might be done.

The letters received from the pastor become community property and are worn thin in the many readings. His studies are now almost completed, and the parishioners pray each Sunday for his safe and speedy return. Whether he will in fact return is not certain. The bishop has suggested that the pastor think about setting up a training center for shared ministry in the diocese once his studies are completed. The pastor himself is not sure what will follow this sabbatical as other options apart from St. Abby's begin to surface. If the pastor does not return, though, the parish is likely to continue, even without a resident pastor, because the people trust their God and are willing to own the parish and continue ministering to one another and to others in need.

Part 2: Shared Ministry

What happened at St. Abby's is not a common occurrence, but it might be in a short time, because there are simply not enough priests to fill vacancies. Fewer men are being ordained, and the average age of priests in the country keeps rising. All of this points to a sharing of ministerial duties with people who are not priests. I consider this the most significant change in the American Catholic Church since Vatican II, more significant than the English liturgy or shifts in theological emphases. Ministry is no longer the sole responsibility or duty of the priest: It belongs to any baptized person—man or woman—who is willing to assume the commitment and can fulfill the requirements of ministry. As a result, lay persons like the parishioners at St. Abby's are assuming the responsibility for leading worship services, bringing the Eucharist to the sick and shut-ins, directing religious education programs for the young and adults, administering the parish, reaching out to the marginal and disfranchised Catholics, caring for those who are in need of support, friendship, or counseling, speaking out against injustices, directing retreats. The job of the pastor and staff is to help others carry out those ministries.

The increase of shared ministry in recent years becomes obvious when we consider the groups that are involved in ministry. These include parish staffs, permanent deacons, council members, parish boards, religious education directors, various commissions, subcommittees and planning groups, teachers, parish visitors, musicians, readers, Communion distributors, counselors, and many more.

But with any sudden shift or change of emphasis come confusion, problems of adjustment, and a disruption of the routine. I will concentrate on two areas of adjustment: the priest's own identity and the problems of recruiting ministers. At St. Abby's, the pastor had wanted parishioners to take a more active part in the ministry of the parish, but he was not sure how to get started. His vacation and the people's response in assuming responsibility for the parish in his absence gave the pastor the occasion he was waiting for. He gathered a group together and began training them to become leaders and recruitors of others who would minister in the parish. From then until his departure, the pastor and leaders worked together as co-leaders and co-ministers.

In some parishes, however, shared ministry has had a difficult time gaining a foothold. Some pastors (and associate pastors) are reluctant to share their duties and responsibilities with those who are not priests. Sometimes the pastor is forced to let go because of sickness, the large size of the parish, or a shortage of priests, staff, or finances. But he does so not because he is committed to shared ministry but because he has no other choice. Unfortunately, when this happens, people are not usually trained for their new responsibilities, and the attempt at shared ministry has only limited success. This reinforces the pastor's suspicions about the people's inability to assume ministerial positions, and he terminates the experiment. As a result, areas of ministry that the priests or staff are not able to maintain are left unattended.

In other parishes, though, as at St. Abby's, the pastor may want people to assume a greater role in parish ministry, but he does not know how to begin or how to motivate them and give them direction and freedom to perform a certain ministry. He might even be afraid to try, since it might threaten his own position in the parish. This may have been true for the pastor at Sts. Agnes and Boniface. Rather than the people, it was perhaps the pastor who was not ready for shared ministry. Then came his vacation, when the people rallied to his support and arranged for his two-week absence without a substitute priest.

At some time after returning from his vacation and seeing what a good job the people had done in ministering to one another, it must have occurred to him, "I wonder if I'm needed. Maybe they can do a better job without me." That can come as a shock as the reality of that question sinks in. And then he may have asked himself the deeper questions, "What are the essentials of my priestly ministry? What is my role in the parish?"

Many tasks considered essential to a pastor's role twenty years ago are now being done by others. "The deacon is doing the baptisms most Sundays, and his sermons are improving a great deal. The people pay as much attention to him as to me," the pastor at St. Abby's might think to himself. "The liturgy committee is training the servers and the readers, is choosing the themes and prayers for Mass, and even critiques my sermon afterwards—in a supportive way, of course. The deacon's wife is getting enough experience training teachers so that I don't have to do much there either. I wonder what I do that is important or that someone else couldn't do better." That's a tough question to answer, and if a person does not feel confident in his own priesthood or have a positive self-image, a question like that can be devastating.

Yet the influence of the parish priest, especially of the pastor, on the atmosphere of a parish is far-reaching. This often becomes apparent when a parish experiences a change of pastors. The tone of the liturgy may change, the parish priorities shift, a new set of leaders emerges. The impact of a change in pastors is lessening as more people participate in the decision-making and running of the parish, but the pastor is still the most influential person in setting future directions and priorities. To a lesser extent, the other priests who serve in the parish also have an influence in setting priorities.

So what is the role of the pastor (and the associate pastors) in light of the increase in shared ministry? Obviously, the unique contribution a priest makes to parish ministry, one that no one else can perform, is crucial: presiding at the Eucharist, proclaiming the Word, administering the sacraments. But the role of the priest is broader than that. It has to do with setting the tone or spirit of the parish, providing the climate for people to assume their responsibilities of ministering to one another, creating the kind of environment where people can celebrate the Lord's Presence and spread the Good News. And yet, it is just this capacity for facilitating spiritual leadership that many priests find difficult. They really *want* to share their ministry with others, and they even begin the process of including others in the running of the parish; but then people start taking the new approach to heart and begin to believe that they are co-ministers with the priests. Some of the people might even challenge the way the parish is being run or the way the priests perform their own ministerial duties.

Conflicts and bad feelings can then arise between the priests and people. At this point the priests, and especially the pastor, may become worried about what will happen to the parish. He loses his nerve and faith in the process and may withdraw his support of the shared-ministry experiment. He does this because he is not trained in this new style of leadership which demands skills in conflict management, in creating an atmosphere of mutual trust, and in allowing others to share in the "ownership" of the parish. When he becomes frightened, he withdraws his support, and the whole process comes to a halt. As a result, the people become frustrated, confused, and angry. They had been led to think *they* are the parish and that they, along with the priests and staff, are responsible for its growth. Then they realized that if the pastor is not part of the shared ministry process there is little chance for lasting success. What to do in such a situation?

Easing the Transition to Shared Ministry

It is important to realize that we are experiencing a new phenomenon in the Church. Not all pastors are equipped to deal with the new approach to parish leadership that stresses shared ministry. We cannot expect miracles from people who are not able to handle new—and to them frightening—ways of leading the parish. Therefore, *patience and understanding are the first requirements* for parish ministers who find themselves in parishes where the pastor is not at ease with the shared ministry approach.

The second requirement is support—support to the priests and especially to the pastor. Too often pastors get loaded down with worries and fears about their ability to cope with the new situation. They get "dumped on" by the very people who should be offering help—their staff and parish leaders. A pastor has many pressures to deal with. Fending off his co-workers should not be one of them. Persons involved in shared ministry should realize that one important area is ministering to one another. This is a ministry of support and affirmation as well as one of challenge and evaluation. The pastor who feels accepted and supported by his co-workers might feel more inclined to take risks and allow others to assume a greater share in the ministry of the parish.

A *third requirement* to help the pastor and priests *is to be in touch with outside resources* that are available for helping leaders deal with the demands of a modern parish. Many dioceses now have a number of offices that offer training courses, individual direction, and group facilitation as helps to parishes in the area of shared ministry. Other Church-related groups, those not connected with a specific diocese, offer resources on how to foster shared ministry in the parish. Some of these groups are associated with universities or seminaries and offer degree programs in the field of pastoral ministry. Others are national organizations or publishers who provide specialized services and materials geared toward fostering parish shared ministry. Ten years ago there were few such resources available to parishes, but now a wide variety of options exists. The only complaint is that many parishes are not using the talents, experiences, and creativity of these resource groups.

Mutual responsibility, then, is an issue that must be dealt with in encouraging shared ministry in a parish. Understanding, support, and outside resources are needed to help the priests cope with a new way of being pastor or associate.

Ministers should also try to *make the parishioners aware that they can minister* in the parish *and encourage them to get involved* in an area of ministry. The complaint I hear most often is that the same few people always volunteer. "How can we get others beside these same few 'faithful' ministers to volunteer?"

To answer this question it is important to realize that our American culture, especially its religious aspects, is built on voluntarism. We are a nation of joiners, but "free" joiners in that people feel free to choose what will occupy their lives and satisfy their interests. As a result, people are flooded with many possible alternatives to fill the time left over after work. Parish ministry programs are just one of many possible avenues of voluntary participation. The reason so few show up when the call for volunteers goes out is that these parish programs are low on the list of possible options available to persons above and beyond the demands of their jobs and family. How then can the parish move its programs up higher on the parishioners' priority lists?

Solving the Recruiting Problem

The first step is to *choose "high interest" topics.* A parish must offer areas of ministry that appeal to people, that are exciting. Sts. Agnes and Boniface had no trouble getting people to come to a meeting to decide which statues should be kept and which removed because this issue touched people's self-interest. Persons also responded well to the call for ministers to help out at Mass when the pastor left for the summer because liturgy was an important part of their lives. It meant a great deal to them that the Masses, or at least a Communion service, continue over the summer.

The areas of ministry that thrive in a parish, then, are the ones related to the desires and interests of the people. The ministry of singing (choir or folk group) will attract plenty of volunteers if people like the music they sing, if it is directed well, if they take pride in how well it is performed, and if they enjoy doing it. The ministry of education will thrive if the parents feel they are cooperating in passing on the essentials of their faith and of the Catholic traditions. The ministry of leadership (council and committees) will have enough candidates each year if the members feel the parish is doing something worthwhile, and that it is worthwhile because of their efforts. They not only feel proud of the parish but are aware that the parishioners and staff appreciate the work they are doing.

Once interesting areas are identified, the next step toward recruiting persons is to *have a clear description of the ministry to be performed.* Persons become suspicious of participating in another parish project if the last time they agreed to do something, it turned out to be a much larger commitment of time and energy than they had expected. There is no better way to turn people away than to coax them into volunteering with the impression that little will be required, when in reality much will be expected of them. To overcome this suspicion and reluctance to participate, the amount of time and energy, preparation and experience required for a task must be made known to perspective volunteers and then adhered to. If possible, *limit the time required of people* to only a few hours a month or even to a single appearance. For example, the parish census referred to in Chapter Four was a success because the volunteers realized it would be a one-shot ministry lasting only a few hours. They knew what had to be done and knew no more would be required of them.

Along with clear definitions of those requirements, giving persons a sense of owning the ministry they are performing will encourage them to stay with it. Owning the ministry means that *volunteers are included in the planning and running of the programs.* It may be necessary for the staff to do the preliminary planning and training when introducing a new type of ministry. But if the staff wants people to stay with the project, the parishioners should be included in as many of the decisions connected with the new ministry as possible. The resulting program may not be as "tight" or as well organized as the staff would have liked, but it will assure more involvement because it belongs to more people than just the staff. This helps reinforce the belief that the ministry comes out of the lives of the people rather than out of the experience of the professionals such as the pastor or other staff members.

Our American culture is pragmatic; we enjoy *doing* things more than just talking about them. That relish for getting something done helps in encouraging more persons to participate in parish ministries.

Many persons are not attracted by talks or classes but do respond well when asked to volunteer to help in a project such as fixing up the church, helping with a benefit, or baby-sitting during Mass. *Projects are especially successful if the parishioners discover an area of need on their own and set up a project to take care of it.* "That school hall needs painting. We should get some people together the next few Saturdays and get that done" (ministry of maintenance). "The storm we had this weekend didn't hurt people around here much, but the migrant workers' trailers were badly damaged. We should give them a hand" (social ministry). "So many of the mothers are working these days, and many can't find people to take care of their children. I wonder if we could set up a network of people to help them out" (child care). Once people become involved in an area of ministry and come in touch with problem cases, they begin to seek the best ways of dealing with those situations. Then is the time to bring together those ministers working in the same area to talk over common problems and to give them a chance to share their experiences.

Finally, a word should be said on the problem of *burnout* in relation to solving the recruiting problem. Some people are so good at ministering and so generous with their time that they take on too much, become overextended, and eventually collapse in exhaustion. This is hardly the desired outcome for parish ministry, but it happens all too often. When the pastor or staff member "discovers" a new worker who can handle a given parish ministry, apparently with ease and desire, it's difficult not to keep calling on that person whenever a volunteer doesn't show or special expertise is required. This happens often enough that the minister's other commitments— family, spouse, job, and self—suffer. The person eventually gives up *all* parish involvement, never to be heard from again. It is unfortunate that all that good will and talent is used up in such a short time.

What is the way out of this? One way is through *rotation*. Those persons who have a tendency to become overextended are given a limited term of service and limited areas of ministry. They are also given time off with no parish responsibilities. This not only gives them a rest but allows room for fresh blood in the ministries. Sometimes the only reason a talented newcomer does not volunteer is that the position is already filled with a "veteran." When the veteran sits on the sidelines and makes room for the "rookies," the whole parish is the winner.

These are only a few suggestions for solving the recruiting problem in parish ministry: focus on high-interest areas, make job descriptions clear, ask only a limited term of service, involve volunteers in planning and running the ministries, begin with activity and then encourage reflection on the experience, and finally, rotate the most involved people in and out of the ministries.

Key Individuals and Groups

One important figure at St. Abby's was the *council president-turned-deacon*. Until the crisis of having no priest to take the pastor's place arose, the deacon's role did not appear necessary. Once the pastor realized the situation, however, the need to empower a permanent deacon became evident. Too often this process has been reversed. A man is ordained deacon and then looks around for some ministry to perform. Then he often does the work the priests or other parish ministers do—preaching, baptizing, giving Communion, visiting the sick. But at St. Abby's the need for a coordinator and organizer of parish liturgies arose, and a person was trained and ordained to handle that need. This seems to be a more productive way to proceed. Of course, it might happen that the need for which the deacon was ordained would no longer exist and the deacon would be without a ministry for a while. I see no problem with that. When another need does arise the deacon will be there to respond and provide leadership.

Another important figure at St. Abby's was the *deacon's wife*. Often during the training of deacons, their wives are involved in the program and become qualified and dedicated to ministry like their husbands. They become "deacons," at least by association. Perhaps someday the Church will legitimate their calling to service with ordination. At St. Abby's the deacon's wife came forward when the parish needed a temporary administrator who would handle the day-to-day operation of the parish. She was relieved when a full-time administrator was hired, but she was equal to the task when the need arose. In the parishes I have worked with, women are more likely to be active in parish ministry than the men and are just as likely to be leaders in the parish, either as members of the staff or of the council. Care must be taken that women not become alienated from Church ministry or even Church membership because they are not given recognition as co-ministers.

Another important parish group for fostering shared ministry at St. Abby's was the *council*. Persons who serve on some parish councils discover after a few months of service that the council is powerless: The pastor and the staff do as they please regardless of what the council proposes. The feeling of powerlessness leads first to frustration, then to anger, and finally to apathy. Because of this experience it is difficult to get people to run for the parish council or to volunteer for council commissions or committees. This was not the situation at St. Abby's in the last few years. There, the council members saw themselves as helping to shape parish policies and to give direction to the parish. They felt they were fulfilling a necessary function and that without the council the parish would not be as well run or as successful in dealing with its crises. The congregation saw the council as an important ingredient in the parish, and the people grew to trust its direction and decisions. It became an effective voice in its own right and not just the mouthpiece of the pastor, or later, of the parish administrator.

The *parishioners themselves* were key elements in the growth of shared ministry at St. Abby's. As mentioned in the first chapter, one of the most effective methods of this approach is peer ministry, in which persons of the same age, education, interest, or occupation minister to one another. This is not easy to accomplish because people within the same group often do not trust one another to be ministers—they know too much about one another. This is especially true in a rural community where prejudices have been built up over generations. To break out of those predetermined expectations is difficult. But it did happen at St. Abby's when the crisis of not having a pastor arose. The people learned to put aside their prejudgments and to minister to one another. They did this by planning the liturgies, participating in the worship service as singers, readers, distributors of Communion, and by sharing their reflections on the readings. They ministered to one another through their concern about crises that arose in their community, rallying to the support of those who were sick, dying, involved in an accident, or even stuck in the mud. They ministered by participating in the education program, sharing the responsibility of passing on to their children the essentials of the faith. Once that tradition of shared peer ministry was established, the parish rose to a new level of vitality and service.

Finally, the *administrator* became an important individual because she did not "take over" the ministries the people had initiated, but created an environment in which their ministries could continue to grow. This is a new kind of parish ministry but one that will become more common as the shortage of priests becomes more acute. Only a small proportion of American Catholic parishes now have lay administrators, but they are providing alternatives for the future. Not only do these administrators (both men and women) take care of the administration of the parish (budgeting, salaries, contracts, maintenance), but many of them also oversee the parish education programs (the school and religious education for adults, youth, and families) and facilitate staff interaction and parish communication. The administrator frees the pastor so he can be the spiritual leader. The pastor and associates are then able to spend more time preparing for and leading liturgical celebrations, counseling, giving spiritual direction, and visiting people in need of pastoral care. At St. Abby's the sister who became parish administrator had to take care of much of the spiritual leadership because there was no resident pastor. But she deliberately downplayed this role. She spent her time fostering peer ministry among the people and making arrangements for the best use of the limited time the visiting priests spent in the parish. The role of parish administrator is still too new to know what will eventually be included in the role description. But the need will soon be so great that parish administrators or pastoral leaders will be much sought after in the years to come.

Our discussion of shared ministry touches the larger truth that all Christians are called to a life of service and ministry. Not only should a parish provide occasions for people to respond to a call to ministry in specific areas sponsored by the parish; it should also be a support and challenge to parishioners to be ministers in their individual and family lives. We referred to this wider concept of ministry in Chapter Five when discussing Queen of Heaven parish and its emphasis on ministry during the month of October. An excellent resource for this broader notion of shared ministry is a booklet published by the Andover Newton Laity Project called *Empowering Laity for their Full Ministry* (Newton Centre, Mass.: Broholm and Hoffman, 1981. Used with permission.)

Challenging All to Minister

The booklet describes a nine-step process that a parish could use to help people understand how all are called to be ministers in their everyday lives. The steps do not have to be in this order, but some steps do follow logically from others.

The first step in the process is to *raise the consciousness of both leaders and people* so that they will see that *everyone* is called to be a minister, not just the relatively few who are now leaders in the parish or who participate in ministerial programs. The pastor and staff must start with their own presuppositions to be sure they accept this broader view of shared ministry.

The second step is to *realize that each person has unique gifts and talents* that can be used in ministering. No one is exempt from full-time ministry, because everyone has something to offer for the spread of the Gospel and for serving others. The parish needs "gift-evokers," people who are good at helping others see how gifted they are and how they can use their gifts in ministry.

The next step is to *support people who are trying to be ministers in their daily lives.* This is especially important for those who experience little encouragement from persons with whom they live or work. This is done best through groups small enough that people can talk about their personal lives, can explore with others what aspects of their lives might be considered ministry, and can gain help and support from others who are in similar situations.

Step four is *spiritual formation.* This approach to full-time ministry demands a close relationship with Jesus. People must have the opportunity to discuss their faith and prayer life with another or others who can understand and give direction about how to pray, how to use Scripture, how to be open to the workings of the Spirit. A parish should be the place for this spiritual direction, either through prayer groups, staff counseling, or Scripture classes.

The *liturgy* is the next important step in the process. Parish Masses and other liturgical rituals must relate to the lived experience of the people. People must become aware that the Mass is a way of symbolizing, in the presence of the community, one's daily life before God. This can happen only if parishioners are involved in planning and executing parish liturgies. Otherwise the liturgies will not be an expression of the ministry they exercise in their individual and family lives.

Step six is *validation*. Parish leaders must look for ways of giving public recognition and support to persons who are trying to live their lives in a ministerial fashion. Special liturgical ceremonies should be planned to acknowledge the service performed by individuals and groups in the parish. Many parishes single out those who participate in ministries sponsored by the parish in liturgical, educational, pastoral care or leadership areas. But few parishes recognize anyone for extraordinary service as a parent, shopkeeper, laborer, civil servant, or professional. This takes much more creative thought and planning.

The next step is an organizational one. A parish that is committed to the notion that everyone is called to full-time ministry must *look at its own structures and modes of operation to see what changes might be necessary.* Is it realistic to expect large numbers of people to volunteer for parish projects? Perhaps many do not participate because of a commitment to ministry in their personal lives. Are there opportunities for people to gather in groups to talk about personal experiences and to discover which of these relate to a call to ministry? Are there people on the staff or in positions of leadership who are good as initiators and who could empower parishioners in their full exercise of ministry? Do present committees and organizations help foster this wider understanding of ministry, or do they get in the way by making unrealistic demands on people?

Step eight is *education*. Those who are willing to accept the call to be full-time ministers will need training and theological grounding in order to sustain their commitment. Through study groups, training sessions, and theological reflection, people come to understand how the call they experience is part of a larger mystery. Their efforts to be a more loving spouse or parent, a more honest and trustworthy worker, a more open and accepting neighbor, a more caring and concerned citizen, are linked to what it means to be a Christian. People need opportunities to voice their opinions, to share their difficulties and frustrations, to discover where their own experiences are reflected in Scripture and Church traditions. The parish is the place where this reflection and sharing can happen.

The last step is to *redefine the content of shared ministry.* If a parish accepts the challenge to broaden its understanding of ministry, it will discover a need to define the meaning of ministry. As parish leaders start applying this broader vision, they may find that their own categories are too limited. They may begin to ask, What is included in ministry? What are the limits to shared ministry? How many people are needed to participate in parish ministries? How many should be freed for ministries outside the parish?

In our stories about different types of parishes we have been concentrating on the life and operation of the parish. But the parish is not an end in itself. It should be the occasion and the framework for people to come together as community to worship the Lord, to support one another, and to send one another out as Christ's ministers. It is to this broader notion of full-time ministry that Christians are called. The role of the parish is to make sure that this happens.

CHAPTER EIGHT·

Part 1: The Nonterritorial Community

People still remember that "Welcome to Blessed Euphoria" banner stretched across the entrance to the gym. They laughed when they saw it, but it was a good way to introduce the contest for choosing a name for the Mass group. The group had started out simply enough: Thirteen friends gathered for a liturgy in the apartment of one of the couples. A priest who had just begun graduate school at the University agreed to offer Mass for the group one Sunday morning. The participants had no intention of making this a regular event.

Once the informal Mass was over, though, the people liked the experience so much that they started making plans for the next time. They did repeat it a month later, with a few of the original group missing and a few newcomers. The people talked, during the shared homily and during the coffee klatch afterward, about how little feeling of celebration they got from their own parish liturgies and how much more this smaller, informal liturgy meant to them. They asked Father Chuck if he would be willing to make a permanent commitment to the group, to celebrate Mass twice a month for the next seven months— that is, until the beginning of summer, when most of the group would scatter. He said he would be delighted. He had been hoping there might be a worshiping community somewhere near school that he could be part of, since he too found it difficult to fit into the typical parish scene. He didn't think he could join a parish and live in the rectory and still get his course work done. He knew from experience how absorbing parish ministry was, and he knew that eventually his degree work would suffer. On the other hand, if he were to come only to a parish on Sunday mornings to celebrate a couple of Masses, he would always be a stranger to the people. That functional definition of priesthood didn't suit him. But with this arrangement he would get to know people, and yet it would not make great demands on his time. He said he would be willing to offer Mass every Sunday, but most of the people were not ready for so regular a schedule. Perhaps later, after the group had more time and experience together, they would opt for weekly Mass.

The original thirteen were in their twenties or early thirties. Two of the couples had young children. Throughout that first year the group continued to meet, usually in the same place because it was conveniently located and was large enough for the group. A few times they met in another couple's home; and twice, once in December and again before Easter break, the group had an evening Mass and potluck supper to celebrate their time together. It was a congenial group. They looked forward to the times they spent together singing and praying and sharing their faith. It was a welcome contrast to the intervening weeks when they all attended Mass in their own parishes.

Then the summer came and with it, the group's first critical moment. Should they make plans for the summer or for the coming school year, for that matter? Would they stay in existence? As they look back on that decision and others like it, they realize that these moments were the most creative and growth-filled in the life of the community. But at the time it was hard going. Chuck would be back in his home diocese for the summer, leaving the people without a priest. Should they still meet? They decided not to have any get-togethers until the first Mass in September. A few did volunteer to meet over the summer and plan the themes of the Masses for the coming year. That settled it; they would be in existence for at least one more year.

It was fortunate that nothing was planned for the summer because everyone scattered, and it was hard for even the planners to find a time to meet. But meet they did, and they were pleased with the themes they came up with—the seven gifts and the twelve fruits of the Holy Spirit. (Someone had to call his mother to get the complete list. She could still rattle them off without any trouble.) Each liturgy for the coming year would center on the Sunday readings but from the perspective of such gifts of the Spirit as fortitude or piety or fear of the Lord.

When the community came together for its first liturgy of their second year, they were surprised to find not only the original thirteen (plus one newborn from the summer) but eight new people who had been invited by members of the core group. They hardly had room to breathe—and only one bathroom! But people did not seem to mind, because they were all so happy to see one another again and to talk over summer experiences and make plans for the coming year. They liked the idea of using the theme of the gifts and fruits of the Holy Spirit. It was something they had not reflected on for a long time.

One of the more practical minded in the group voiced the opinion that the group would have to find a larger meeting place; the present apartment was no longer adequate. Chuck suggested, somewhat timidly, because he was not sure it would work out, that they might be able to meet in the conference room in the building at the University in which his office was located. It would only be temporary and would mean paying the building maintenance crew a little extra, but it would relieve the crowding for a while. The conference room had a sink and a place to make coffee. It could accommodate up to thirty people and had a warm atmosphere. The people took him up on the offer.

For the rest of the year the Mass group met twice a month in the psychology department's conference room. The department chairperson was not sure how this group meeting fit into the guidelines of the school, but he felt it could do no harm so long as it didn't cause any trouble. After all, it was only temporary. So Chuck reserved the room for the Mass group on alternate Sunday mornings. The Mass group did create some friction with the Newman chapel staff on campus. When the staff got word of a "Mass-group" that was meeting on campus, one of the Newman chaplains confronted Chuck about it: "Why don't the people come to the Newman chapel for Mass? We have a warm atmosphere and good music and coffee afterward. What's wrong with our Masses?"

Chuck tried to explain that the people who came to "his" Mass did not attend the University. "They're mostly young couples who belong to other parishes but participate in this group because they like the informal, more communal aspects of the liturgy. They know one another. They're used to worshiping together and would like to maintain their own identity." Chuck knew that the chaplain was not convinced and that it might eventually mean the Mass group would have to move off campus. It was just too sticky an arrangement. He brought his concerns to the next Mass. It happened to be their pre-Easter celebration, and he felt apologetic about bringing difficulties into a festive occasion, but he did feel uncomfortable with the present arrangement.

He explained that his original intention had been to be one person among equals. True, he did happen to be ordained and therefore was the one to preside at the Eucharist. He was happy that others besides himself were planning the liturgies and taking responsibility for the group. He had expected his role to be a simple one, but that was no longer the case. He felt pressured by the Newman Center, who looked upon him as the head of this community. That was a position that he was not sure he wanted to have or that the Mass community wanted him to assume either. Something had to be done. His exams were coming up. He needed a relief from the burden the Mass-community had now become to him.

People were very quiet as they listened to Chuck. Most were not even aware there was a problem; they had just enjoyed coming to the liturgy every other week. They now began to realize that they had to seek a solution. So they incorporated the deliberations into the context of the Mass, praying for light and asking the Spirit for guidance.

The outcome of the pre-Easter liturgy was a quantum leap for the community. They decided not to keep the liturgy just for themselves but to open it up to a larger group. This decision surprised them all. They had thought they might disband or go back to the original small group in an apartment. Instead they decided to contribute money to pay rent for the use of a local public school's gym. One of the members worked for the school board, and she could arrange for the gym twice a month beginning the next September. Such a decision, while solving immediate problems, created a new set of obstacles, such as how to create an intimate atmosphere for liturgies in a large gym and how to deal with the possibilities of large numbers. As one person said, "Aren't we back to the parish problem again—large church, formal liturgies?" Chuck was asking how that relieved the pressures of the over-involvement he was feeling. Yet inside he knew it was the direction he wanted to go. He was excited. Perhaps the impossible could be achieved— a close, warm, worshiping community that was open to any and all who wished to join.

Chuck brought up the problem of gaining acceptance from the diocese. He had written a letter to the bishop when he arrived in the area and had mentioned that he planned to be working with a home-Mass community. After he had received faculties in the diocese, he received no further communication from the bishop.

Now it appeared it would be necessary to gain permission for this new gym Mass. It would be attracting more people and with it some notice and publicity. Eventually the bishop would hear about it and wonder what was going on. Someone suggested that perhaps they could find a parent parish to sponsor them. Rather than considering themselves a parish, they would become just another Mass group in an existing parish. Chuck wondered what a pastor would think if a group of thirty people, priest in hand, marched up and asked him to be their sponsor. But he responded, "One way to find out. Let's give it a try!"

The public school gym was located within the boundaries of a parish that had a reputation for openness but not for innovations in the liturgy. The pastor was close to retirement. He was loved by his people, a good person-to-person pastor, but not an organizer or innovator. A few of the Mass group went with Chuck as he met with the pastor to explain their plan. The group wanted permission to have a Mass in the parish but not in the church. All they needed was the pastor's permission. If he thought it necessary, he could tell the bishop about what was happening. Nothing else would be required of the pastor or the parish. It was not a weekly Mass, nor were there any other activities, just Mass. The older pastor listened, nodded, and said that he thought it would be all right, but he looked puzzled and did not seem to understand the plan very well.

The remaining Masses before the summer recess were filled with plans and the excitement of anticipation. None of the original group had dreamed that the community would continue for as much as three years, let alone grow to such proportions. They were much relieved to have the prospect of more room, though, because babies and active children were getting out of control as more couples with young children joined the community. Perhaps in the gym setup some provision could be made for babysitting during the liturgies.

Summer came, and a group of seven met every two weeks to set up the themes for the coming year. Chuck stayed in town that summer, partly to prepare his dissertation proposal and partly to stay in touch with the committee's planning for the coming year. He was hooked far more than he cared to admit.

That July the gym was secured for liturgies, and the local pastor sent a letter agreeing to sponsor the group. Everyone breathed a sigh of relief. Then someone mentioned the need for a name—so far it had just been the "Mass Group." Someone else suggested having a contest for the name, and a third person joked about the prize being an indulgence of "seven years and seven quarantines." At the end of the summer one of the planning committee made a banner "Welcome to Blessed Euphoria!" Even after the name was settled upon—the "Jesus is Lord" Community—they still used the Blessed Euphoria banner in their lighter moments and even in a few of their heavier ones.

The first few meetings were difficult. No one liked the atmosphere of the gym, and it took much more work than they had realized to set up all the chairs and banners beforehand and take them down afterward. The Mass itself was not satisfying, at least to Chuck and the original group. Yet the new people who came kept saying how pleased they were to discover this community; it was so much better than their own parishes. Eventually a routine was worked out that eased the frustration at least somewhat. A carpet was stored with the gym mats and rolled out before Mass. Everyone carried his or her own chair in from the storeroom, and people were encouraged to bring floor pillows. A simple table became the altar, and the people sat around on the pillows or chairs. There were banners and candles and flowers, depending on the season, so that after a few months the place felt just as homey as the previous places of worship. A few people volunteered to tell Bible stories to the children in the annex. After Mass and coffee, the setting-up process was reversed, with each person returning the chair or pillow, and by rolling up the rug for storing until the next Mass. A small group of volunteers stayed behind each week to take care of the details for the next liturgy: calling on people to prepare the readings, lining up babysitters, choosing symbols to fit the theme, and organizing people to bring bread and wine for the next Mass.

By now one hundred adults were showing up regularly, but new faces always appeared. They had heard about "Jesus Is Lord" via the grapevine and were curious to see what it was like. The "regulars" became aware that the complexion of the Jesus Is Lord community was changing. Nametags were needed because there were so many new faces. It was much more difficult to change the schedule for Masses because so many people had to be notified. Lists for volunteers had to be circulated to handle the details of bread bakers, wine suppliers, readers, sweepers before and after Mass. Someone mentioned during one of the Masses, "My worst fears are being realized. We're becoming a structured, organized parish all over again." Everyone laughed in a self-conscious sort of way. But then a much greater crisis struck that put the fear of overstructure far in the background.

Chuck received a letter from the bishop. The letter expressed concern over rumors about liberties that were taken at the Mass Chuck was saying every other week. The bishop had been informed about the gym Mass at the beginning of the school year and had not given it further thought. But recently he had received complaints he could not ignore. Was it true that the celebrant offered Mass while sitting at a table instead of standing at an altar? Did he use spontaneous prayers in place of the approved Eucharistic Prayers? Were lay people leading parts of the Mass such as the penitential rite, the Communion service, and were they giving homilies? The bishop concluded the letter by saying the liturgies were to be "discontinued as of this moment until these matters can be discussed and cleared up." The next scheduled liturgy never took place, although the community came together. They spent the time trying to decide on the best avenue to follow. The group discussed the matter and prayed for discernment. The two extremes were rejected—dissolving the community or continuing as if no letter had been received. Chuck breathed a sigh of relief, for had the people decided to continue as they were, he was not sure he would have been able to remain as their priest.

An appointment was made with the bishop to see if a middle position could be found. While Chuck and a few of the people met with the bishop, the rest of the community held a day of prayer asking the Spirit to bless the meeting and allow the community to continue. After the bishop got past his initial hurt about not being kept aware of what the community was doing—an error the people admitted—he did give them permission to continue for a year, provided they adhere to the requirements of the legitimate Roman liturgy, which included using vestments, unleavened bread, and approved Eucharistic Prayers. After a year they were to seek approval for continuance.

The delegation returned to where the community was gathered in prayer, not euphoric, but happy that they could stay in operation. One advantage of their Mass had been the freedom to experiment with new forms of liturgical expressions. Now they would have to do that experimenting within the confines of the approved Roman rite. This was a challenging restriction but one that proved in the long run to be beneficial.

The Sunday Masses that followed were remarkable in that all requirements of an approved liturgy were adhered to, but within that framework, many creative innovations were tried. For instance, at the Easter Mass vestments were worn not only by Chuck but by everyone else as well. Everyone came in a white garment to which were attached symbols of hope, new life, and resurrection. At another Mass the approved Eucharistic Prayer was interspersed with quiet prayer and explanation so that the Eucharistic Prayer took most of the Mass time. Some people mentioned afterward that this was the first time they had paid attention to or understood what was being said.

As a result of this experimenting with the Roman Rite, the people went back to their own parishes with new ideas for improving and enlivening the liturgies. Joining their own parish liturgy planning groups and providing fresh life to parish masses became one of the apostolates of the community's members. Now that the Jesus Is Lord Community was legitimate, it could offer itself as a resource to parishes in the diocese who were looking for new ideas. Priests and staffs from interested parishes visited the Sunday liturgies of the community just to see how it was done. In this way, the decision to stay within the limits of the Roman Rite opened up new opportunities for the community to be of service to other parishes in the diocese. It was not an easy decision to follow because many of the members wanted to try out new liturgical forms and new ways of structuring the Mass.

As the year of "legitimacy" drew to a close, the community evaluated what had taken place over the year. Three questions surfaced. The first was the education of children associated with the community. Should the community be responsible for their religious formation? It had always been understood that the group would consider itself an *adult* community. Up to this time the members had taken care of the religious development of their children by themselves or through their home parishes. One group of six families had formed its own family catechesis program, while most of the others had chosen to send their children either to parochial schools or to established parish religious education programs. This approach gave the Jesus Is Lord Community greater freedom to focus on the twice-monthly worship service without having to worry about an elaborate program for youth. Now that decision was being challenged by some of the members who felt that the community should begin the process of becoming a parish all its own, with a staff and parish council and education programs similar to those offered in a typical parish.

After much prayerful discernment and discussion (some of it quite heated) the community decided to continue with its present adult emphasis but to think about the possibility of having a paid part-time community coordinator or administrator who could handle the week-to-week organizational needs of the community.

A second question was whether the community should be reaching out to the wider community. So far it had existed of and for itself, providing an outlet for those who found it difficult to relate to their own parish situations. Some of the members proposed that the community take on an apostolate, perhaps an outreach program to alienated Catholics, perhaps sponsoring a refugee family, or perhaps addressing itself to an area of injustice. This suggestion was opposed by those who were already overcommitted in other projects and concerns. "The advantage of this community," one person said, "has been that it leaves people free to find their own apostolate and area of ministry. The community exists as a support and encouragement to those of us involved in these apostolates." After lengthy discussion the matter was dropped.

The third issue was the problem of limiting membership in the community. No one wanted to deal with this because it hinted at elitism and closed in-groups, but no one could deny that the group was getting very large, sometimes as many as 350 adults. The intimacy and informality of the group were dwindling. Some of the people were forming small groups on their own and holding prayer services in homes in order to preserve a feeling of community. The whole purpose of creating a close sharing community was being lost. Could that original spirit be recaptured?

Someone scrawled across the top of her evaluation sheet, "Has success spoiled Euphoria?" and it became the rallying cry of those who were losing faith in the Jesus Is Lord Community. Something had to be done. The group finally decided to try to get a statement of commitment from each member of the community for at least the coming year. It would mean that every person who wanted to belong to the Jesus Is Lord Community would make a commitment to participate in the planning and execution of bimonthly liturgies. It appeared to some to be too formal, but it did serve to make concrete an individual's desire to belong to the group.

The results of the year-end evaluation were sent to the bishop, along with a list of achievements, as a way of asking for permission to continue in existence for the next year. The community was not sure what to expect in return. They were suprised to find that they had been much harder on themselves than the bishop had been. He sent Chuck a flattering letter praising their work but cautioning them in a few areas, such as granting general absolution, encouraging non-Catholics to receive Communion, and not emphasizing enough the obligation of weekly Mass attendance. The community was guaranteed at least another year of existence.

Whether they would continue was in much more jeopardy than they had realized, however. Success might, indeed, spoil Blessed Euphoria. The problem had to do with Chuck, who was concluding his graduate studies and was being called back to his home diocese. The bishop wanted him to teach in the seminary and to be in charge of a new counseling and spiritual direction center in the diocese. Chuck was happy to be returning to his home territory, especially since he would be able to bring back with him such a wealth of practical as well as theoretical knowledge and experience. But he also knew he would miss the Jesus Is Lord Community after all the years of struggle and growth it had gone through. What would happen to the community? Who would be their priest? Everyone knew that Chuck would be leaving at the end of the school year, but no one wanted to talk about it. By this time the community did have a lay coordinator, who handled organizational details, but without a priest it was unlikely the group could stay in operation. Not just any priest would do. However, because the community needed a priest to stay in existence, it was hard to be choosey about who the priest would be.

The spirit of the liturgies toward the end of the school year was like that of a graduating class that knows that it may never be able to recapture the joy and companionship of its school days. The requirement that everyone commit himself or herself to the planning and execution of the liturgies went better than expected. It demanded new depths and commitment from all the members. People came more regularly to the Masses, so name tags were no longer needed. As the school year drew to an end the people entered into the themes of the Masses with great awareness and with a sense of urgency. Chuck tried to play down his role as presider, but that made his imminent departure all the more evident. Finally the day arrived—his graduation and the final Mass—and still no replacement had been found. The leave-taking was joyous and sad, celebrative and heavy—all the divergent emotions associated with departures.

However, on the day of his departure a solution was found. A retired priest—seventy years old—indicated that he might like to give the Jesus Is Lord Community a try. His letter to the community explained that he felt he still had a few good years left in him and he wanted to spend them, as he had most of his years, celebrating Mass with a worshiping community. People did not know how to respond to this offer. No one would be able to take Chuck's place; he had often reminded everyone that each person—priest included—was unique and that each person had a unique contribution to make to the life of the community. But the thought of having a priest who was twice the average age of the community was difficult to accept. Nevertheless, they sent an acknowledgment and accepted this new priest sight unseen.

The planning group met during the summer as they always had done, but very little could be accomplished since they did not know how the priest would react to their ideas and themes. There was much buzzing on the phones as people tried to learn about their new priest. What they learned was that he had been a pastor and a teacher. He was hard of hearing, was still energetic, and was well-liked in his former parish. Not too much was known about him in recent years, though, because he had been helping out at various parishes outside the diocese.

On September fifteenth the first Mass of the school year was held and *everyone* came, even old members who had moved out of the area, to see what it would be like. To their delight and surprise the new priest was a perfect choice— gentle, open to change, prayerful, outgoing, and very wise—

or so it seemed at first glance. He thanked everyone for making him feel so welcomed, explained that people would have to speak up a little for him to hear but that there was no need to shout. He talked about his past experiences, especially his recent years helping out with mostly rural and poor parishes, and said that he had been to see the bishop. The bishop, he explained, had been very kind and had given him free rein. Some people thought that they detected a hint of a wink at that last remark.

It is amazing how far the community has progressed in the few months that he has been part of it. He has celebrated the liturgies with informality and warmth. Although he does not depart from liturgical norms, he still has provided new modes of prayer and worship for the community to try in a style that is not self-conscious or artificial. The community members find themselves concentrating more on personal prayer, on striving for greater simplicity in their life-style, and on increasing their awareness of people in need. They find these new emphases strange since their priest—he said it was all right to call him "Pat" although he was not used to that— had not stressed these in his liturgies. People seemed to have experienced these emphases more through his presence than through anything he did or said. He never dominated the worship service and was content to let others plan the liturgies and give him cues when it was his turn.

Soon the Jesus Is Lord Community will be celebrating its seventh anniversary, which is a surprise to those who gathered for a liturgy in that small apartment a number of years ago. The community has survived many crises, even a change of priests. Eight of the original thirteen are still active, although they have given over their leadership roles to others. The founders are content to come and enjoy the community and the Mass every other Sunday. The school's gym is still being used for liturgies, but there is now a community office staffed by the administrator, himself a former priest. He and his wife share the job of keeping the organization running. No one is sure what the future will bring, but it does not matter. Enough has happened already to justify the community's existence. Maybe next year Father Pat will not be up to leading the group in liturgy, or perhaps the group will decide to disband and re-create the Jesus Is Lord Community in many different forms in their own parishes. Their only worry now is becoming too self-satisfied so that they stop struggling and growing in the Lord. The motto of the group has become "Don't let success spoil Blessed Euphoria!"

Part 2: Alternative Directions

It is obvious from the seven stories about parishes that there is no one ideal model. It all depends upon the background, expectations, and experience of the people who make up the whole parish community. The same is true for the Jesus Is Lord Community. Some would question whether it should even be considered a parish along with the others. Its origins lie outside the diocesan structure, and it had not been given the status of a parish. That may come in the future. It will depend upon the bishop and the desires of the people who belong to the Jesus Is Lord Community. They may decide to remain a loose collection of worshipers who relate to the larger Church through the parish that sponsors them, or they may decide to ask for permission to be a parish on their own.

I have included this community as one of the seven types of parishes, despite its uncertain future, because I feel it has a role to play in the life and growth of the Church. It is communities such as this that have tried new ministries, new approaches to worship, and new structures that eventually become part of the established parishes.

One characteristic of the Catholic Church is that it has allowed groups to experiment with new models and ways of acting. Throughout its history it has allowed people to challenge the accepted mode of religious behavior, at least to some degree. Religious orders and congregations were formed by people dissatisfied with the ordinary mode of behavior, people who tried out new approaches and apostolates. Eventually these groups traveled from the margin to the center of church life and practice.

In the growth of the American Catholic Church, for example, many ethnic groups who immigrated to the United States established worshiping communites that reflected their own culture and heritage. The local bishop was not always aware of these groups until they were well established, nor did he always understand or agree with their mode of religious behavior.

The pattern that was often followed then is still being followed today: new modes of worship, new approaches to ministry, new methods of leadership are tried out by individuals and groups not closely affiliated with the institutional Church or at least not with all of its official structures. These "marginal" members of the Church feel freer than do the majority to experiment with modes of religious behavior that fit their needs and their approach to God.

They are on the margin because they do not relate to the present accepted practice. It is too structured for them, or too formal, too theoretical, or superficial. Whatever the reason, these believers, while still wanting to be considered part of the Church, feel compelled to try other ways of being members of the Church.

Some of the groups that spring up soon dissolve; others split off from the Church entirely and start up a new religious group. But still others stay members of the Church and work for its growth and reform. They are willing to struggle through the painful crises, the doubts about their own motives, the inevitable difficulties with Church authorities, the feelings of being misunderstood and rejected by the regular membership.

Eventually the Church may begin to realize that some of its own modes of worship, teaching, and religious practice are no longer adequate. It may recognize that some of the mainstream parishes are incorporating the models and practices of the experimental groups into their own worship and religious behavior. As a result, the new models become accepted and incorporated into the main body of Church life and operation. Many of the recent liturgical changes, such as the Mass in the vernacular, Communion in the hand, Communion under both species, and women ministering in the sanctuary, were common practice in experimental groups before they were accepted as legitimate forms of liturgical ritual.

Once the cycle is complete, however, the experimenting does not come to an end. There will always be people in the Church who find it difficult to fit into established modes of behavior. They are the searchers, the innovators, the prophets who keep struggling to find a place for themselves in the Church, a place that feels comfortable and speaks to their needs and aspirations. They keep creating new models of worship, new expressions and understandings of belief, new areas of service.

The question is, How open can the Church remain to these new models and to the persons who propose them? Can it trust that the Spirit is operating through these experimental groups, as well as through the main body of the Church? Can the Church—both leaders and people—make room for the dissident, the prophet, the agent of change? These are not easy questions to answer. Change often causes disruption and confusion. Living in a state of flux requires strong faith and a confidence that this is the Lord's work and that he will guide his people to the realization of the Kingdom. These questions are also difficult to answer because it is the task of the leadership to make sure the Church remains true to its religious heritage and preserves for future generations the basic tenets of faith.

Nevertheless, if the Church is to remain alive, dynamic, and responsive to the needs of the people—needs that keep changing as the culture changes around them—then it must make room for the Jesus Is Lord Communities—the "Blessed Euphorias" of the Church. Experimental groups can make important contributions to the development of religious beliefs and behavior by exemplifying new and challenging ideas to the Church. The Jesus Is Lord Community demonstrated two such models by using the facilitating style of leadership and by increasing the role of women in its life and operations.

I have already described and discussed the facilitating style of leadership in Chapter Two; so I will not repeat that except to observe that the type of leadership used in a given situation is not always determined by those leading the group. The leaders do make a difference because of personality traits, training, and previous experience. But two other ingredients also help determine the style of leadership. One is the demands made by the group on the leader, and the other is the environment in which the leadership takes place.

Consider Father Pat, the retired priest who took Chuck's place as the priest of the Jesus Is Lord Community. This same person was at one time pastor of a typical parish and at another time the priest-presider of the community. The style of leadership he exercised in each situation, however, was different. He was not the one who inaugurated the change. The group changed and drew out different talents and capabilities from him. The parish and the Mass group had different needs and expectations, and these influenced the style of leadership he exercised. As pastor of the typical parish he was expected to make the final decisions, manage the parish plant, keep in touch with the diocese and take responsibility for the running and operation of the parish. But as priest-presider at the liturgies he became legitimator of the group and tone-setter for the Masses. It was a less conspicuous role but important nonetheless. His style changed because the group had changed.

Even if the leader and the group remain the same, a different location or environment can change the type of leadership. Move the community into a Gothic church building and the leadership changes. The community resisted the use of a church or even of the Newman Center because they felt it would not be conducive to the spirit of the group.

Hence all three aspects of leadership—leader, group, and environment—make a difference and have to be considered in any discussion of leadership.

A second changing model implicit in the Jesus Is Lord Community is the role women assumed as co-ministers of the community. It was never emphasized but was accepted as one of the unique characteristics of the group. The place of women in society and in the Church was often the topic of discussion during the liturgies and in the get-togethers that followed, and many divergent views were expressed. But no one in the community questioned the right of the women to share in the planning of the liturgies, to take an active role in the liturgical celebrations, or even to lead some of the parts of the Mass, such as the Liturgy of the Word or the Thanksgiving Rite. The fact that the women's roles were accepted as an integral part of the Masses served to heighten the feeling of frustration among the people that women were not allowed to be ordained and to take a position equal to men in the leadership of the Church.

There are signs in the Church that this may soon change, perhaps fifteen to twenty years from now. It is no longer unusual to see a woman reader or minister of Communion at parish Masses or to have women participating in the leadership of the parish as members of the council or staff, such as the women on the pastoral team at St. Joseph's, the parish described in Chapter Two. Judging from the rapidity of change in awareness and acceptance of women in positions of parish leadership and ministry in recent years, there may be women priests in the not-too-distant future.

The question at this time is what groups in the Church will keep these issues alive and give support and encouragement to the women. I see local groups as those who are willing to experiment with the changing roles of women in church leadership. These groups may not be like the Jesus Is Lord Community, but clusters of men and women will continue to come together to celebrate the Lord's presence in their midst and to speak out against injustices within and outside the Church. Women will be co-leaders of these groups, and much of the groups' struggles will be centered on the place of women in the Church and in the culture. These groups have the advantage of greater freedom than do typical parishes to try out changing models of leadership, ritual, and ministry. They can make mistakes and grow through them with fewer risks than can a typical parish. The people who belong to these groups do so of their own free choice and are more accepting of diversity and change. Eventually, either the group will dissolve because its experimental model has served its purpose or was not adequate to deal with the situation and needs of the people, or the group will endure and provide a resource and possible alternative to the Church as a whole. If and when the Church does allow women to be ordained priests, there will be women well prepared for the call to ordination through their lived experience of ministry and pastoral leadership. There will also be communities that have accepted women as their spiritual leaders and have grown accustomed to seeing them in positions of leadership.

This completes our parish storytelling. One characteristic common to all seven types of parishes is flux. They are in a continual process of ups and downs, growing and diminishing, living and dying. If a parish can look ahead far enough to see both the valleys and the hills, it will be better able to cope with the changes that are likely to occur. It is to that effort of prediction and visioning that we now turn.

CHAPTER NINE

Part 1: The Future—Cultural Movements

It is time to take a look at the future. What will our seven
parish types look like in ten or twenty years? Much depends
on what happens in the areas in which the parishes are located
and on changes in the country as a whole. Since the parish
is a social organization as well as a faith community, it is
influenced by the culture as is any other American organization and institution. The first part of this chapter, then, will
consider some of the cultural changes that are likely to occur
in the years ahead. The second part will consider the faith
dimension of the parish and the changes I would like to see
happening.

In this section we will consider four influences that come
from outside the parish but will influence the future direction
of the parish.

The first influence is a *shift in the age distribution* of our
population. Our country has been undergoing profound changes
in the last fifty years. First the depression, then World War
II, followed by the security of the fifties, the turbulence of the
sixties, and the uncertainty of the seventies. These changes
have influenced the number of children born into American
families. During the depression and World War II years the
birthrate was down. After the war and during the fifties and
early sixties the birthrate went up. Ever since the mid-sixties
the birthrate has been falling off. How does this affect American Catholic parishes?

Although this will vary by locality, a typical parish now has
fewer children than twenty years ago, a large group of people
between the ages of twenty and thirty-five because of the baby
boom of the sixties and seventies, and a smaller percentage of
people between thirty-five and fifty because of the depression

and the Second World War. This trend will change as the parish enters the latter half of the 1980s and the 1990s. It is likely that people will continue to have fewer children. The percentage of young adults will begin to decrease, and a larger percentage of the people will be in their forties and fifties. As advances in medicine continue to increase the adult life-expectancy, the high end of the age spectrum will maintain a steady but gradual growth. This distribution may be altered in locales experiencing high immigration from Hispanic cultures: in these regions the percentage of children will remain high.

What effect will this changing age distribution have on parish life? American Catholics feel freer today than in the past to select the parish they will belong to and to what extent they will participate in that parish. This level of participation is related to the age of the individual. Persons in certain age categories are more likely to become involved in parish functions than those in other age groups.

Parishioners between the ages of seven and eighteen, for instance, tend to have a high level of group participation whether in school, parish, or clubs. They receive encouragement, even pressure, from many sources to become part of group activities. Parents encourage their children to get to know others of their age through sports, parties, school- and church-related youth activities. Teachers and religious education coordinators create opportunities for youth involvement in the school and in the parish. Fellow students and friends make involvement the criterion for group acceptance and friendship. They themselves are looking for ways of "belonging" to the club, gang, inner circle, or sports group. If the parish does not provide opportunities for involvement, young people will look for other outlets since the drive "to belong" is strong in this age group. At present this is a struggle for parishes because there are so many young people to accommodate. It is likely, however, that parishes will have more success in the next few decades because the numbers of teenagers will be down and programs can be specialized to meet particular needs. The only danger might be that this group will be neglected as other age groups take over the attention of parish leadership.

Catholics between the ages of eighteen and thirty are in a low group-participation category. It is difficult for them to become involved in any group or organization, whether religious or secular. People in their twenties experience many demands on their time and psychic energy. They are busy acquiring an education, some attending school up to the age of thirty and beyond. They are trying to settle on a career, find a spouse, land a permanent job, and eventually start a family. All this takes a great deal of time and concentration. As a result, they are not able to commit themselves to any more than sporadic involvement in parish groups or activities. For some, even regular Mass attendance is difficult. This is one reason why campus ministry is a challenging, though at times frustrating, apostolate. Just when people have been trained to lead discussions, help at liturgies, run organizations, they are gone, sometimes with little or no explanation or warning. The same is true for parishes.

This problem of involving young adults is a worry for many staffs and parish leaders. "What can we do for our young adults? How can we invite them in and make them feel welcome? What are we doing wrong that they don't come?" Perhaps nothing. It is a difficult period for these people, and parish involvement is not high on their list of priorities. The problem was more obvious in recent years because there were so many people in this age group, but that will be changing in the next few decades. Because of the drop in the birthrate during the mid-1960s and 1970s, the percentage of young adults in the typical parish is falling off. The problem of finding ways of involving young adults remains, however, although not with the same urgency felt in recent years. Because of the many demands made on their time, the type of parish involvement that will prove most successful is the one that asks only limited and temporary commitment. Such a commitment, limited as it is, can be truly worthwhile. One good experience of liturgy each month, for instance, might prove more beneficial than four mediocre Masses on the Sundays of the month. One volleyball game, one dance, one ski trip, one day of canoeing, one visit to a nursing home every six months might have more impact than asking these people to commit themselves to biweekly or monthly involvement.

The next age group, those between the ages of thirty and fifty, will be growing in numbers over the next few decades. In recent years this group has been under-represented in the typical parish. This created problems since this is the age group that is most likely to volunteer for parish organizations and assume leadership positions. They are the ones who respond to appeals for parish ministers, who come to activities and help out at parish socials. This is because, other things being equal, they have greater motivation than other age groups to volunteer and become part of groups and organizations. If they have children, they become involved in the education and development of those children through education-related groups, such as teacher aids, parent-teacher organizations, school boards, sports, crafts, and socials. If they do not have children, they still are likely to become joiners, since they are more settled than when they were in their twenties and are looking for opportunities to grow and interact with others. The parish can provide an outlet for this group's desire for greater involvement and interchange.

In the next twenty years more people will be in this thirty-to-fifty age bracket than ever before. This will influence parish life. If a parish has nothing to offer these people, they will go elsewhere. Once they get involved in other organizations, perhaps elected to office in these groups, it will be difficult to entice them back to parish functions. Since many will be searching for group involvement, the parish ought to provide a variety of opportunities. It might appear as if there is a resurgence in parish life as more persons become interested in joining groups and coming to activities. This may be due, however, to the presence of more people who are looking for ways of becoming involved and not necessarily due to the parish itself.

Finally, there are the older parishioners, those over fifty years old. This group, too, will be growing in numbers in the years to come, but gradually. What is unique about this age group is that they usually join only those groups they belonged to in their earlier years. They are still willing to belong to groups but not become leaders or join new groups. If the older person moves or changes parishes, he or she is not likely to join groups there but is content to attend Mass and participate in parish life only to a limited degree. This trend may be changing as more people reach retirement age and look for ways of using their leisure time. The growing emphasis on senior citizens' groups is an example of the increasing level of group activity among older people.

As the percentage of older people continues to grow, the parish leader will have to figure out ways of utilizing their rich resources and experiences. The parish as a whole will benefit so long as not too much is demanded of the older parishioner, especially in new and, to them, strange activities and programs.

This, then, will probably be the complexion of the typical parish in the years ahead—fewer young and more middle-aged and older people. This change in age distribution will influence parish life, and leaders must become aware of some of the implications so they can plan for them well in advance.

One implication of this shift in age distribution is that competition may arise among parishes or parish groups. As people feel freer to make choices about what type of groups they will join, groups within the parish will try to attract prospective members. Competition can also arise among parishes as they attempt to attract new members. This tendency will have two phases. First, leaders may try to attract the most "desirable" individuals to join their group. Secondly, once the group approaches a desired size the leaders may then attempt to close membership. This is a natural human inclination in any volunteer organization. It takes a strong theology of openness to overcome this. Our religion teaches that the Lord extends the same call of love, salvation, and community to whoever responds to the invitation. Ours is a faith that allows people the freedom to pick the level and kind of religious involvement that best suits their needs and desires. This is the aspect of our faith that will have to come into play to overcome the natural tendency toward competition and the closing off of membership to "undesirables."

A second implication of the shift toward an older parish membership is the tendency toward conservatism. Many other factors can counteract this influence of age, but generally speaking, an older group will be less willing to change and more willing to endorse the accepted way of doing things. A younger group, on the other hand, will be more prone to take risks and to experiment. Because of an older membership, parishes in the future may tend to stress traditions more than changes. But the future always has a way of surprising us; maybe the elderly will get up in arms and lead a revolt from the left to counteract this swing toward conservatism!

Finally, the changes in age distibution will bring about an educational shift in parishes. It is happening already. With fewer children and young people, the educational emphasis has shifted toward the adults; notice how much attention is being paid to adult spiritual development and stages of adult growth. This will become even more prevalent in the years ahead. Furthermore, because parents will continue to have fewer children and are likely to bear them later in life, they will be able to devote more attention to their children and offer them special educational opportunities. The parents will be better educated themselves and will have more financial resources available. This means fewer, more specialized schools and smaller, more specialized parish religious education programs. Consolidation of educational programs among many parishes will be the trend, while more attention will be given to the adults and their continued growth and religious awareness.

The second cultural influence affecting the future direction of parishes, along with the shift in age distribution, is the *crisis of limits* that the world is undergoing and will continue to undergo for a number of years. More and more, we are realizing that our resources are limited and that we must act accordingly. The reduction of the speed limit to fifty-five is a good example of this. This apparently small adaptation brought with it a change of perspective: the realization that Americans no longer are able to go as fast or as far as they wish. Looking at the larger scene, we realize that the energy shortage, rising costs, unemployment, limited production and mobility are directly affecting every individual and institution in our country, including the Catholic parish. It has become clear that the American Catholic parish is no longer able to expand as fast or as far as it would like. What are some of the effects the parish will be experiencing in the late 1980s and 1990s?

For the parishioners, as for the American public generally, there will be less moving and less travel. Corporations are thinking twice about moving their operations because of the high cost of relocation. If they do decide to move, usually to the South because of lower labor and fuel costs, many employees are inclined to settle for a lower-paying job and stay put. They still come out ahead because of high relocation costs. Vacation travel will become more costly and therefore less frequent: People will not be as likely to pile everything into the station wagon and head for the hills or the ocean. The station wagon itself has changed; it no longer can hold all the gear it once did because it has shrunk to save on gas.

This shift in mobility patterns will influence parish life. People will be settling in more and will be thinking in more permanent terms about their own future in the neighborhood and parish. Parishes can count on greater continuity of membership. Involvement in the parish and neighborhood is likely to be year-round rather than just during the school year. Parish staffs may be surprised to have people asking for programs and activities during the summer, a time when the parish tempo usually slows down. Parishes in the southern states can look for an influx of Catholics from northern cities as people migrate to climates where fuel costs are not as high.

The rising costs of heating fuel and building materials will mean that parishes will not be able to expand facilities to meet increasing demands for meeting areas. Instead, old buildings will have to be maintained and some sections closed off to cope with rising costs. This will lead to smaller group liturgies and programs, many held in people's homes because of limited parish facilities.

Another cultural influence affecting American Catholic parishes is a *change in human interaction*. People are choosing to marry later in life, if at all. Once married, they are likely to have one or two children at most. Because of the high cost of care for the elderly, families are likely to have grandparents, aunts and uncles, parents and children all living under one roof. Because of the high cost of living on one's own, more of the children who have moved out of the home in their late teens or early twenties will return to live with their family as young adults.

I see several consequences of these changes. For example, the parish community will be composed of more single adults, more older parents with small children, and more extended families with a wide range of ages under one roof. Ministry to these people will need special attention. For instance, little attention is devoted at the present time to single adults, whether young or old. This will change as more and more single parishioners demand greater attention and a greater share of the parish budget. Many single persons may have children of their own, and this will have to be taken into account in planning ways in which single parents can enter into the full life of the parish and find answers to their specialized needs.

As for families, many couples will have children later in life, after both mother and father have completed their schooling and have become established in their careers. This means that these couples will be better equipped not only to participate in parish groups but to lead them. Since they will have fewer children, these parents will be able to devote more time, talent, and financial resources to the parish. But that will happen only if the parish speaks to their needs and expectations. Since both parents are likely to be working full-time, the little time left over from job and family will be more jealously apportioned.

The older family members—grandparents, aunts, and uncles—will probably remain closer to family and parish life than in the past. The trend toward home care for the dying that has given rise to the hospice movement, coupled with the emphasis on affirming the gifts and resources of older people, will be the occasion for new vitality in the parish, if parish leaders are able to tap these resources. This is especially true for programs that appeal to people of widely varying ages. The parish can help families who differ in age to grow closer together. These families can in turn become an example of community to the parish as a whole.

These changes in human interaction will become noticeable in institutions and organizations as well as in families. Within our society's larger institutions are many smaller communities or groups in which people feel comfortable and at home. Many ethnic parishes of the past were examples of these small, comfortable communities. But then as parishes grew in membership they became more structured and less personal. They became, in other words, institutions rather than communities. Parish leaders now realize that people need small, intimate experiences of community if they are to feel themselves a part of the parish. As a result, pastors and staffs are trying to encourage the formation of small groups such as neighborhood Christian communities, encounter groups, and Covenant households. This trend will increase because people will keep looking for an experience of belonging and companionship. If they don't find it in their parish they will find it someplace else. When parish groups do form, however, the tendency will be (as we have mentioned) to limit access to the group once the participants feel at home. The challenge for parish leadership in the next few decades will be to provide the opportunity for parish subgroups to form without at the same time fostering cliques, in-groups, and elitism.

Finally, changes in human interaction will influence the way men and women relate to one another. This change will influence parish life even more than it already has. More women will be assuming positions of authority and responsibility outside the home. It will no longer be unusual to see women as police officers, fire chiefs, corporation executives, or elected officials. More women will be assuming positions of authority and responsibility in parishes as well. Women are already heads of parish boards, council presidents, and in some places associate pastors. This trend will continue and will call less attention to itself. Pressure will continue to mount for the ordination of women to the diaconate and priesthood.

At the same time, parish leaders will be confronted with the problem of finding more men to become involved in parish life. Some of the men will feel that the women have taken over the parish, and this may cause them to pull away from parish involvement. This is likely to happen in other institutions of our culture and could lead to tensions between men and women as they strive to clarify their roles and identities with respect to each other. The parish community, rather than contributing to this tension, will have to seek ways to overcome the competition and hostility between men and women, especially those in leadership positions. The parish could be an example of community in which both men and women feel welcomed and encouraged to share their own unique gifts and contributions.

Another cultural influence that will shape parish life in the years ahead is the *shift toward democratic leadership*. In American society it is difficult for a group of people to accept a leader imposed from the outside. When a leader is needed to get a job done, the people in the group typically look around to see which person among them could best do the job, and that person becomes the leader. The group becomes critical if the leader does not include the group members in the decision-making process, at least on important matters, does not exercise leadership according to the wishes of the group, or does not remain open to evaluation and replacement at predetermined intervals. This criticism by one's peers can put pressure on the leaders. As a result it is sometimes difficult to find people to fill leadership positions. It does help, however, to have limited terms of office so that people know they will not have to be the group leader for a long period.

That form of leveling, democratic leadership, obviously, is not the type the Catholic Church is used to. Its form of leadership is hierarchical. Authority flows in an orderly fashion from superiors to subjects. The leader is appointed from outside and introduced into the group and usually is not subject to evaluation by the group. The appointment to a leadership position is often permanent, if not within the group or parish, then as leader of another.

This contrast between the two forms of leadership points to a vast difference between the American tradition of leadership and that of the Catholic Church. Compromises have been worked out during the history of the Church in America, but greater compromises will be necessary if it wishes to stay in touch with its people. Church leaders will have to accept a democratic approach to leadership, especially on the parish level. Parishioners have had a taste of what it is like to share in the decision-making, planning, and ministry of the parish. The present trend, far from slowing down, will continue in the direction of greater ownership of the parish by *all* active parishioners and not by just the pastor and parish staff.

These, then, are the four cultural influences that will shape the Catholic parish in the decades that lie ahead: uneven age distribution, the limited resources and rising costs of goods and services, the changes in human interaction, and the tendency toward participative, democratic-style leadership. The parish, because it is itself a social organization, is shaped and influenced by the culture within which it functions. It is influenced, but hopefully not swallowed up, by the surrounding culture. If the parish is to remain faithful to its transcendent purpose and origins, though, it must maintain an autonomy. In this way it can become a challenge to and critic of the culture. It is to this transcendent heritage that the second part of this chapter is devoted.

Part 2: The Ideal—Gospel Imperatives

I base my ideal for the parish on the ministry of Jesus Christ. This seems inescapable since the parish is the embodiment of Christ's Church on the local level. I consider the ministry of Christ to have been a sign/servant ministry. It had a sign quality in that, rather than drawing attention to itself, it emphasized a reality beyond itself. Christ's "sign" ministry pointed to two realities: the involvement of God in our world and the possibility of the Kingdom. Jesus, by his very being as well as by what he said and did, revealed that there is a God, that this God is a loving and caring God, and that this God is therefore concerned about the world and the people who dwell in it. Jesus often referred to God's will. He proclaimed that he himself came to do the Father's will and that he would obey his Father even to the point of death. These examples of the "sign" ministry of Christ reveal the love God has for us all.

Another aspect of Christ's "sign" ministry that frequently appears in Scripture is that of pointing to (becoming a sign of) the impending Kingdom. Jesus' presence on earth gave people hope. It told them that, yes, it was possible that good would overcome evil, that oppression would someday cease, that people would be free once again to love one another and live in peace. The possibility of this Kingdom was actually growing in people's hearts as they listened to Jesus' words and observed his actions. He pointed to that Kingdom; he convinced people it was possible; he encouraged them to drop all other concerns and devote their time and energy to making sure the Kingdom did occur. That is the power that Christ's "sign" ministry had.

But if the ministry of Christ had stopped there and had been only a "sign" ministry, then he would have founded a closed, sectarian church, one that did not become involved in the sweat and toil of everyday living. To give an adequate understanding of Christ's ministry there needs to be added to the "sign" ministry the notion of "servant." Jesus could not help but respond to people's needs, physically and spiritually. It angered the apostles to have to keep stopping along the road to wait for Jesus to heal someone or offer a word of support and forgiveness, especially when there were so many supposedly more important tasks to be done. Through this activity, though, Jesus was acting out the ministry of "service" to others. This reaching out to the needs of others through the simple gestures of healing wounded people and setting them free was the way in which Jesus broke through the boundaries of sectarian religion and founded a socially involved religion. He did this ministry on a personal, one-to-one level.

But the servant ministry of Christ goes beyond the personal response to people's needs and problems. Jesus also became a servant *for* the people as well as *to* the people. He took upon himself the responsibilities and commitments of his people. He *became* a symbol of the new Israel in order to lead the people to salvation. He *became* the faithful and obedient follower of Yahweh in order to fill up what was lacking in the commitment of the chosen people themselves. This is a notion of servant that is found in the Servant Songs of Isaiah. Jesus carried out this servant ministry, even to the point of dying for us, so that we might have new life in him. That was a servant ministry in which he took the place of his people and filled up what was lacking in their faith, in their praise of Yahweh, in their dedication to ministry, in their care for one another.

This, then, is how I picture Christ's ministry: as a sign ministry, pointing beyond itself to God's presence and to the promise of the Kingdom, and as a servant ministry that concentrated on being servant *to* people through healing and setting them free, and on being servant *for* others by taking upon himself their responsibilities and commitments. If this was the ministry of Christ, then it seems that the local parish must also aspire to the ideal of being a sign/servant community of believers. In fact, this is the mission of the universal Church, its way of carrying Christ to the whole world. Any other function it performs is secondary to this mission.

Some aspects of the sign/servant ideal are common to all types of parishes. All types, for instance, are called to become signs of a reality beyond themselves. The group reveals to others what kind of God we have: a God of love, concern, and involvement in the world. By coming together and sharing a common faith, they proclaim to themselves and to others that God lives in the world, that there is something or Someone beyond just ourselves. Our American culture needs people in its midst to keep alive this mystery of God's presence. The parish faith community is one place this can happen.

Americans seem particularly hungry for this sign. Too much of their lives is filled with impersonal, functional activity. They are beginning to realize that not all problems can be solved with a computer or with more advanced technology. The parish community can suggest other answers to our problems. Its people point beyond themselves to Another. When other people come in contact with such a community, this association leads them beyond the group in search of what gives that community of believers vitality and a sense of purpose. They discover a mystery, and in the midst of that mystery a loving, caring God.

But the parish is a sign of something else, too. Its very existence and way of acting becomes a sign of hope, a sign that a meaningful future is possible. Persons who are discouraged and in despair come in contact with a parish community, and through this contact they gain new hope and vitality. The parish holds out a hope that does not depend on human resources and power. It gains strength and support from another source, from the promise of the Kingdom.

Such a hope takes the pressure off people to make it on their own. They begin to realize that a life of love, happiness, and companionship is possible and exists in the Kingdom of God. They experience some of this love and happiness in their present situation. The realization of this new life in the Kingdom does not depend on their own achievements or prestige or possessions; it is a gift from a loving God.

The parish community becomes a sign to others that Christian hope is built on the paradox that to be weak, in need, and vulnerable is to be strong in the knowledge that someone else has overcome the frustrations, despair, and narrowness of a self-seeking world. We no longer have to do it ourselves.

Christ has done it and asks only that we trust in his support and strength.

Catholics have as much difficulty as do other Americans in letting go of the controls and allowing God to work in their midst for the growth of his Kingdom. They share in the country's competitive drive to be the best, the strongest, the most powerful, the one in control. But some individuals have had the courage to be witnesses and signs of hope to others by their life-styles. These people try not to be dependent on material goods. They share their time, talent, and resources with others. The parish faith community is called to provide this same hope of a meaningful future to others. Otherwise, people who are searching for a hope-filled community will find nothing new in the parish, only a reflection of the American culture as a whole. The parish does not become a sign of hope, and people do not feel any closer to a Kingdom of loving peace by belonging to such a parish.

But my ideal of a parish community is a limited dream if we stop here. A parish community could be an effective sign to others and yet never get outside itself; it could be a self-contained community of the "saved" with little outreach to those who are not in the group. This has always been a danger in forming faith communities. To avoid this the parish must see itself as a servant as well as a sign community.

A parish must be a group of people dedicated to serving others if it wants to share in the ministry of Christ. Many Catholic parishioners, however, find it difficult to see the connection between the "spiritual" side and the "social" side of their religion. They mention the American tradition of separation of Church and state as the basis for their views and the reason why the parish should not become involved in public or social issues. At the same time, many of these persons are caring for others in need through small and unnoticed apostolates: babysitting for a friend, driving an elderly person to the doctor, lending money to someone out of work, repairing a house or caring for the yard of a sick person, comforting someone who is grieving. It is these small gestures of care and concern that help to establish an environment of service in a parish community. These spontaneous acts of kindness need to be recognized, encouraged, supported, and celebrated by parish leaders as examples of how parishioners are carrying out their vocation as Christians and exercising a ministry of service.

Once these acts are recognized and encouraged, then people begin to realize that it is all right to connect the spiritual and social sides of their religion. The next step is to discover new areas of social service that parishioners can participate in without feeling threatened or coerced. These might include helping unemployed parishioners, contributing to poorer parishes, volunteering to help the sick and shut-ins, or sponsoring a refugee family.

These actions raise the awareness of the parish community to another level of commitment to service, where people begin to work together on service projects. (This, incidentally, is the level of service on which a new catechesis can begin.) People learn to listen and respond to larger issues of social concern and justice. They begin to feel the need, through their own service experience, to call to task the local community, or the nation as a whole, for the unjust and inhuman treatment of their brothers and sisters.

Through a gradual development of response to human needs, the parish establishes an emphasis on a service ministry. The parishioners begin to understand why it is important that the parish and Church as a whole speak out in defense of basic human rights and values, especially when these are endangered by public sentiment or behavior. Abortion, the death penalty, and reduction of nuclear arms are issues that come to mind. The parish faith community cannot stand aloof when human life is in danger. This imperative comes from the gospel message and from the example of Christ reaching out to those in need of healing and freedom from bondage. The parish community must carry on this servant ministry of Christ, both in the larger issues of peace and justice and in the smaller, less obvious acts of kindness to one another and to others in the larger community.

There is another way to continue it. Being a servant means "standing in the place of others." The parish community is called to take upon itself the responsibility of offering worship and praise to God on behalf of other people. People have a longing to pray and worship and relate to the Lord. But they do not always know how to do this or do not feel able to do it. There must be a group that speaks in the name of and stands in the place of others, a group that acknowledges God as their Lord and acts as a representative or "servant" for those who are unable to do so.

In this way shared ministry takes on a new meaning. All the believing community, and not just the priests and religious, shares the task of standing in the place of others before God. We need one another to fill up what is lacking in our own faith, because no one person can believe it all. Our faith is too rich a mystery to be grasped by any one person, or even by any one group of believers. A parish community needs to be an open community filled with people from different backgrounds and experiences and with different definitions of Church. Individuals in the community become servant *for* others, filling in the gaps and holes in other people's understanding of God, Church, parish ministry, and faith experience. Neither the parish community nor even the institutional Church as a whole can hope to contain within itself the whole mystery of the Christian faith. The Church needs other faith communities to fill in the gaps and holes in its own corporate belief and religious practices. An ecumenical dimension, therefore, is needed to fill up what is lacking in our own Catholic tradition.

Along with this mystery of "standing in the place of others" is the realization that an individual may not be able to be a believer all the time. There are moments of crisis and doubt in everyone's life when it becomes difficult to be a believer. During such times, others in the faith community take over the responsibility of filling up what is lacking, temporarily, in a person's faith. I remember being told by a friend, who at that time was a religious sister, that for about a year she did not believe in the real presence of Christ in the Eucharist. She didn't mention this to anyone while she was in the midst of her "unbelief," but she did say afterward that the only thing that pulled her through this difficult period was the belief of others around her. They went up to Communion, and it appeared to her that they believed they were receiving Jesus. Because of this she went to Communion also. They did not know at that time they were being servants *for* this sister. But she knew they were, and that made all the difference.

The sign/servant parish can experience many variations and modes of operation. Whatever its structure, however, it must seek to bring to life this ideal of a community of people gathered together to worship their God and care for their friends and neighbors.

No word was mentioned about the role of authority and leadership in this ideal parish. I believe the purpose of authority is to foster this sign/servant ideal in the parish. Authority will fulfill its duty if it itself becomes a sign/servant authority in the parish community. If the parishioners can look to their leaders, whether bishops, priests, or laity, and realize that the leaders themselves reveal God's presence in the world and lead people to a realization of the Kingdom, and if church leaders have the reputation of being servant to and for others, then the Church and parish will be well governed.

This is my ideal for the parish, then—that it become a sign/servant community. There remains the task of translating this ideal into concrete reality. The next chapter will spell out indicators I look for in seeking to determine how close a particular parish community comes to achieving this sign/servant ideal.

CHAPTER TEN

Indicators of a Successful Parish

A question I am often asked is: "How can we tell that the parish is doing well, or at least that we are headed in the right direction?" This is a difficult question to answer, for a number of reasons. For one thing, each parish is unique. Its people, leadership, location, crises, and triumphs are all unique. A judgment of success or failure is based on a combination of all of these. For another thing, a parish community never stands still. It goes through many ups and downs in leadership, priorities, membership, and involvement. Each change brings with it the necessity of changing expectations and criteria for success. Just when the leaders feel that they know where the parish is heading, all the parameters change, and they have to start over again. It's also hard to hold the Holy Spirit in check, much as people try. Our criteria for success may not be the ones that the Holy Spirit feels are important. Our view of the parish may be too narrow, too limited. We may have left out one or more important emphases. The Spirit has ways of pointing this out to us, ways that are not always gentle. The foundations shake, plans go up in smoke, and the pieces fall at our feet. If we can swallow our pride and think about the growth in holiness and the future of the parish as a whole, then there is hope we will be able to respond to the shakeup with openness and creativity. Our task is to put the pieces back together in a way that will come closer to what the parish is called to become by the gospels, by church traditions and the Spirit in our midst.

Having said all this, I still feel it is possible to identify a few indicators or signposts that point the way to a faith-filled, open, caring parish community. I have identified eleven such indicators. As I elaborate on each one it might be helpful to give your parish a score in each area from one to nine. One means the parish is doing poorly and needs much improvement. Three means the parish is only fair, five indicates the parish is average, seven means the parish is above average and into the good range. A score of nine means the parish is excellent in this area. Ten is an unrealistic score since this would mean that the parish is perfect in this regard and no further growth is possible. Once the list is completed and the scores are added up, if your parish comes out with a score in the nineties (99 is the highest score), throw a party for the parish. It deserves praise.

Adult Development

The questions to ask about the parish in this area are: Are the people growing in their faith? Are there opportunities for different age groups and interest groups to talk over common problems, to learn about new developments in the Church, to learn about stages in adult spiritual development? Do groups of people come together to pray or read and study the Scriptures? Are these opportunities offered in a way that will attract others besides the same faithful few who always show up? What formats are used? Who comes and why? What changes have occurred? Is the parish, in other words, composed of parishioners who realize that to be a Catholic means to be on a journey of faith, with new roads to follow, new terrain to be explored? What a person learned in school or religious education programs as a youth, while appropriate for that time in life, is not adequate for adult living. The experiences of later years change the questions being asked. New answers and solutions must be found. Is that mentality of ongoing growth and development prevalent among the people? Does the parish leadership foster this understanding of adult spiritual development? Are parish Masses directed to the spiritual growth and updating of the adults? For most of the parishioners, the Mass will be their only contact with the parish or the Church. How would you describe the efforts toward adult growth in spirituality in your parish: poor, fair, good, or excellent? Put down your score, from one to nine.

Bridging Gaps

Because it is a gathering of human individuals, every parish is a collection of small groups. These clusters of people form because of a common interest or activity. Through their common experiences people form bonds with one another. They create a structure for keeping their small group alive and functioning. The structure may consist of regular meetings, set agenda, and elected leaders, or the group may have an informal structure with loosely organized meeting times, shifting leadership, and undeclared membership. The parish is filled with such groups. The informal ones include weekday Mass-goers, neighborhood coffee groups, sports followers, carpools, parents of Scouts. The more structured ones might include Marriage Encounter, Charismatic Renewal, religious education teachers, and the choir. Strong friendships are built up among members of these groups, friendships which last a lifetime. These groups are the lifeblood of the parish.

However, it can happen that these subgroups become so strong that they attain a life of their own. They either control the operation of the parish or retreat from involvement in the larger parish and keep to themselves. Neither benefits the parish as a whole. The parish dissolves into a collection of in-groups and cliques, coexisting in a sort of frozen violence. "If you don't get in our way, we won't get in your way."

One thing I look for when I visit a parish is whether the subgroups in the parish are in opposition to one another or whether they work together toward the good of the whole parish. The question to ask, then, is, Does your parish provide a means in which the individual groups and organizations can interact and learn from one another? Are there, in other words, a means for *bridging the gaps* between parish groups? Are there opportunities for different age groups to interact, such as teenagers with senior citizens? Are there joint projects and celebrations for different ethnic groups or for those from different social backgrounds and occupations? Do those who always go to the same Mass ever come in contact with those who go to other Masses? Do the choir and the folk group ever sing together? Do the school and religious education teachers ever have joint meetings? How long has it been since the entire staff was at the altar together as a sign of unity in the parish? Do the men's and women's groups occasionally meet in common? Parish subgroups must spend time creating their own identity and purpose, but it is important that they also establish links with the larger parish community and with other parish organizations. Some parish groups appear to have nothing in common. After contact is made, however, members from these groups often discover that they have been talking about similar issues and problems, each from their own perspective. Seeing the problem from another's perspective gives new insights into a solution. Locate the bridges and links that exist between different groups in your parish, and give the parish a poor, fair, good, or excellent score, from one to nine points.

Celebrative Rituals

Does the parish know how to celebrate in ritual and festival the high and low moments of its existence? Of course, the regular weekly Masses are important. They provide the continuity in the parish. People come to these Masses knowing what to expect. These Masses will vary, depending on the time they are offered and on what type of people attend. These weekend Masses reveal a great deal about the tone and climate of the parish. But other special Masses and celebrations, ones held at unique moments in the history of the parish, are also important. These are essential to the life of the parish because people use them as gauges of how healthy and alive it is. They look back on these unique moments and, depending on whether their impressions are negative or positive, judge the parish accordingly. It is a way of taking the parish's temperature.

Parishioners will recall that Easter Vigil Mass when all those adults were baptized and the music was so lovely and everything went so well. They will remember that festival when each parish organization put on a skit and how much fun it was, or that play put on by the combined school-religious education classes and how cute the children were. They will recall the crises and how well the parish responded to these.

They will remember when their beloved pastor died and what a moving experience that wake service and funeral was. They will recall when the roof caught fire and everyone pitched in to clean up the smoke damage. They will remember the severe summer storm when the parish organized a relief shelter for the homeless and collected so much food and clothing that the surplus was sent overseas.

These moments are the memorable threads out of which the fabric of the parish myth is woven. If the leaders know how to use these moments well, parish spirit is enhanced and people take pride in belonging to the parish. Think back on the last year and see how well key moments were recognized and celebrated. Did many of these moments pass by unnoticed? If they were noticed, were they used to best advantage for the growth of community spirit? Are any special moments coming up in the next year that may be used to best advantage—anniversaries, feast days, patron saint's day, change of pastor or associate? Judge how well your parish has celebrated its extraordinary moments, both high and low, and give it a score on a scale of one to nine, from poor to excellent.

Facilitating Leadership

I consider leadership, especially that exercised by the pastor, as the most critical determinant of whether a parish comes close to, or retreats from, being the ideal parish. When I work in a parish, I look to see how decisions are made, who makes them, and how well they are carried out. For example, if at a meeting of parish leaders a person in a position of authority has to leave temporarily, I watch to see what happens. Suppose the staff is discussing the Holy Week liturgies and the pastor must respond to an urgent call. If the group stops all deliberating and takes a break until he returns, then I would consider that the pastor is in charge of the parish and nothing can be decided unless he is present. This is not a facilitating style of leadership.

Suppose the staff continues its discussion but reaches no decisions until he returns. The group can function, but only tentatively. This style comes closer to facilitating leadership, but the pastor is still at the top of the decision-making pyramid. He has to be consulted and approve all decisions before action is taken.

Suppose, though, that the group continues with its task as if the pastor had never been there. This is an indication that individuals are working independently and come together only when group decisions are necessary so as not to get in each other's way. The pastor has an area of responsibility, as do other members on the staff, but the staff members do not share with one another their own ministry or the decisions of the parish as a whole. This is a laissez-faire approach to leadership, everyone doing her or his own thing. It is not a facilitating or supportive style.

If, however, the group continues to deliberate when the pastor leaves, and comes to a conclusion but acknowledges that the absent person may influence the result, this is closer to what I consider a facilitating style of leadership. The role of the leader (pastor) is not to make the decision but to create the environment in which each person has the freedom to speak up, to give ideas, and to offer suggestions and criticize solutions. Then the group reaches a decision based on the input from all members. It is a decision that is accepted and "owned" by each person in the group. Those who are absent trust that the decisions arrived at will respect their own feelings and ideas.

The question to ask, while reflecting on recent decisions in the parish, is: Who were included in the deliberations, and who made the final decision? If the pastor or the staff as a whole made the final decision, they are the ones who "own" the parish. If the council shared the decision-making process with the pastor and staff, then the authority is shared by a few more persons. If the parishioners felt they were being consulted, at least for important decisions, and that their ideas and suggestions were taken seriously, then the leaders are coming closer to establishing the atmosphere of facilitating leadership. A warning about scoring this area. Do not be too hard on the parish leaders. It is a heavy weight to bear; even the most facilitating style falls short of the ideal. The parishioners have been taught for a long time to be passive recipients of, rather than active contributors to, parish decisions. Add a few points to the score to give people credit for trying.

Fostering Community

The question to ask in this area is, How well do the parishioners understand the parish as a community, rather than as a collection of buildings, a place to attend Mass, or a spiritual service station? Do the weekend liturgies show signs of people getting to know one another, spending time talking afterward, going out to one another during the greeting of peace, being aware of persons missing because of sickness or vacations? It is difficult to foster community if the Masses are attended by hundreds of people. But it can be done if planned for and worked at. Having people act as greeters and hosts helps. Spreading singers throughout the congregation to encourage singing also adds to the community spirit, as we mentioned earlier. These are some of the things I look for in a parish as indications of a community spirit at the Masses: how well people sing, how interested they are in the Mass, how they respond to humor in the sermons, whether they spend time greeting the celebrant and one another after Mass, and whether there is a place to gather for coffee and conversation.

Building community works best if groups are not large. A gathering of thirty or fewer is a good size for people to get to know one another's names, backgrounds, and concerns. Do many such gatherings take place in the parish, whether related to the liturgies, educational programs, recreation or social service? If the parish can count on more than fifteen percent of the membership becoming involved in activities and gatherings, other than coming to the weekend Masses, it is above average in its attempts to draw people together as community. Rate the parish from poor to excellent on community spirit, taking into account both the Masses and other parish gatherings.

Ownership

Who owns the parish? This is a question not easily answered. Even the parish with the most progressive style of ministry, the most active programs, and the most vibrant liturgies may not belong to the people. I have worked in one parish that possessed a beautiful new church building that was artistic, meditative, multi-purpose, and yet foreign to the people. It was the product of the pastor's creative imagination, but it was too advanced for the people. It took many years before the people felt comfortable coming to pray in the new church and before they considered it their own. Ownership by the people is an obvious but not always evident indicator of a successful parish. But it requires taking people as they are and not as the staff or leadership would like them to be.

Results of a survey I have taken over the last ten years have revealed large gaps between parishioners' and staffs' attitudes on liturgy, activities, education, and social service. It is one function of good leadership to challenge people and to introduce new understandings of Church and Christian commitment. The parish, however, does not belong just to the pastor or staff; it belongs to all the parishioners. Over half the parish staff members in a typical parish come or go every four years, compared with only seventeen percent of the parishioners. By rights, then, the parish should belong to the people. When I visit a parish, I ask, Do the parishioners feel it belongs to them to the extent that their attitudes and opinions are listened to, their needs and expectations acted upon, their criticisms and objections valued? I was working in one parish when a new pastor was appointed. People were surprised that he was interested in how they felt. It was as if the lid had come off the parish. "The parish actually belongs to us! If we don't take responsibility, no one will. If we don't contribute, parish projects will be cut. If we don't help run it, the event will fold. If we don't take initiative, it won't even get started." It was a shock to the parishioners, but eventually they caught on.

The pastor and staff should be servants to the people. They should provide professional resources. The misfortune occurs when a parish community does come to realize that the members share the ownership of the parish, and then a new pastor with an authoritarian, hierarchical approach to leadership is appointed. The lid is clamped back on the parish once again. When this happens, what gives me hope is that people are beginning to realize that the authoritarian approach is not the only way to run a parish. If they have had an experience of what it is like to "own" the parish, they will not be discouraged by an authoritarian pastor. How does your parish rate on ownership by the people? Give it a score from one to nine.

Planning

A parish without a sense of where it is going is in trouble. A parish must be prepared to deal with the many changes that take place in the Church, the country, and the local area. The crises that faced parish schools in the 1970s could have been dealt with better if leaders had spent more time investigating birthrates, assessing parishioners' opinions on school support, and anticipating changes in parish membership. Crises will always occur, but a parish that devotes time to long-range planning is not as easily thrown by these crises as one that is unprepared to meet them.

A successful parish, especially if its resources are limited, must devote a great deal of its time and energy to figuring out what changes are likely to occur in the neighborhood and in the parish, what can be done to prepare for these changes, and what alternatives are open to the parish over the next five to ten years. This effort at long-range planning is necessary in order to focus the limited resources of the parish and to make sure that at least some part of the leaders' vision or dream comes true.

Does your parish have a vision or ideal? Does each area of the parish—liturgy, organizations, education, leadership, social service, outreach—fit into the dream and contribute to its realization? Are liturgies and programs evaluated periodically to see if they are carrying the parish toward fulfilling it? Are changes in the neighborhood and country noticed and included in the plans for the future of the parish? Are the staff and lay leaders committed to planning so that the parish becomes a loving and sharing community? Answers to these questions reveal to what extent a parish is committed to long-range planning and what type of planning it does. Give your parish a score from one to nine.

Room for Marginals

Are there ways in which those who choose not to belong to the parish can still feel welcomed? Does the parish have a welcoming image so that people can belong without feeling pressured or coerced? Sometimes a parish can stress involvement and personal commitment to such an extent that people who are not able or willing to take an active part, even temporarily, are made to feel unwelcomed and are forced out. Do leaders tell people that if they want to be members of the parish they have to come to certain meetings, or donate so much to the parish, or be associated with certain services or programs?

Some small or more voluntary parish communities, such as the Jesus Is Lord group, might be able to get away with such heavy emphasis on participation, but even there it is risky. It is difficult to determine what level of parish involvement makes a good parishioner. Some people need room to maneuver; they need to be able to move in and out of the parish community. They may not be able for a time to commit themselves to regular attendance at Masses or parish functions. Perhaps some day they will be able to make a commitment, but this will happen only if they experience the parish as understanding and welcoming, and not as pressuring or judgmental. In your parish, what impressions are given at the parish Masses? Are some people made to feel like second-class parishioners? Are requirements for attendance at sacramental preparation programs or other educational programs absolute? Can people have a loose association with the parish and still feel they belong there? Have some people felt pressured and given up all association with the parish? Or, on the other hand, do people feel that they are welcome to come to parish liturgies and activities if and when it is possible for them to do so? The obligation of weekly Mass attendance is an ideal to be encouraged, but it does no good to force people into a practice that produces only negative feelings. Wooing people back to church and giving them a positive experience of belonging and of companionship will produce more lasting results. Give your parish a score, from one to nine, on how well it makes room for the marginal, less active Catholics.

Servant Image

A parish community does not exist for itself. If it does, it is a sect and not a Catholic parish. A sect is self-contained. It provides within itself all that it needs for existence. No effort is made to relate to those outside the circle. If others want to join the sect, they must conform to the group's standards and modes of behavior. This cannot be an ideal for a parish. Rather, a parish must struggle to break down the barriers that separate it from its surrounding area and cultures. It must respond to people in need, share with other churches, be committed to overcoming injustices in its midst. One thing I look for in a parish is its relationship with other groups in the area. It may not be possible to isolate specific examples of service, but the parish should be known as one that is not concerned just for its own advantage. It should be known as responsive to needs and crises. It should, in other words, have an image of being a servant parish. Whether it is located in a wealthy neighborhood or a poor one, it establishes this image or reputation because it is known as the servant of the needy, the forgotten, and the powerless. Even if its own resources are limited and it has barely enough money to keep operating, it still is able to look beyond its own needs and help the unemployed, the homeless, the elderly, and those on government aid or fixed resources. It is the responsibility of the wealthier parishes to share their riches and resources with others in need. It is difficult for these parishes to look beyond their own needs since they experience many internal demands on the budget, such as running a school, paying salaries, and maintenance and renovation. But the parish must be willing to share its limited finances and people-resources with those in need: poor parishes, refugee families, disaster victims. Does the parish have this image or reputation of generosity in the local neighborhood and in the diocese as a whole? Are the consciences of parishioners being challenged to simplify their life-styles, curtail material possessions, and redistribute their wealth? How many parish programs or liturgies have been held jointly with other churches and groups? What community actions and movements have been sponsored by the parish, what families cared for, which public policies challenged within the last year? This is a complicated area, one filled with counter-arguments and qualitative statements. But it is possible to determine whether a parish is committed to social service and whether it has created an image for service and outreach. Does your parish have this image, or does it have an image of being self-serving and narrow in its relationship with those in need? Give it a score on its servant image: poor, fair, good, or excellent.

Shared Ministry

To what extent are your parishioners involved in ministry? Does the pastor or the staff or do a few of the faithful leaders do all the work? Do the leaders keep inviting people to minister to one another and to others in the parish and in the larger community? Are there training sessions for these ministers? Are there opportunities for them to come together and reflect on their experience? Is there frequent freshening of the ranks so the burden does not fall on the shoulders of a few? Are the ministers given frequent support, acknowledgment, and thanks by the pastor, staff, and parish leaders? Are there periodic evaluations of the ministers' work? Does the shared ministry reach all aspects and levels of parish life: old and young, single and married and separated, liturgy, health care, maintenance, education, outreach, organizations, leadership? How long are people asked to minister? Are they given frequent breaks and vacations, and are their other commitments to family and occupation respected? Are parishioners challenged to realize that all Christians are called to be ministers of the gospel in their individual and family lives? Do parish leaders help people hear and respond to this call to ministry? Are there support groups for people to learn about this wider notion of ministry, to talk over personal experiences, and to discover what aspects of their lives could be considered ministry? Give your parish a score, from one to nine, on how well it shares ministry.

Transmitting Traditions

Unless the local Church has provided for ways to pass on its ideals, traditions, and tenets of faith to the next generation, it will lose its identity and purpose. The parochial schools, the common rituals, the calendar of feasts that were part of American Catholic parishes in recent decades provided this continuity and transmission of traditions. Everyone knew not only what days were feasts of important saints but also the dates of the parish bazaars and picnics, the pastor's birthday, the fast days and the schedule for novenas and Benediction. Parishes have changed, and many traditions have been left behind. As these traditions were dropped, the question arose about the essentials of the Catholic faith. What beliefs and traditions are important to keep and pass on to the next generation? What new rituals and traditions need to be established? Traditions are necessary ingredients of the Catholic religion. They take the pressure off parents, educators, and parish leaders to start over with each group of neophytes. Year-to-year traditions and rituals carry the weight of passing on to new groups the essentials of the religion and the spirit of the parish. How do the children learn to pray? How do they experience Eucharist? How are they prepared to receive the sacraments? What means exists to keep the youth interested in learning more about their faith? How do newcomers to the parish learn about the faith? Are they invited and encouraged to be part of parish gatherings? Are there regular events in the life of the parish that carry it through the year and give people something to look forward to and to reflect back on with fond memories? These traditions, even though they may have been introduced into the parish only recently, are important for providing the people with a sense of continuity, identity, and permanence. They are vehicles through which new members, young and old, learn about the essentials of the faith and incorporate these into their lives. How well does the parish treasure traditions and pass on the essentials of the faith to the younger generation? Give your parish a score for how well it transmits tradition: poor, fair, good, or excellent.

This list of eleven indicators is not complete or definitive. Others can be added, and the ones mentioned can be redefined and expanded. What I have attempted to do is provide a means for judging the effectiveness of a parish as measured by general criteria that should be present in a well-functioning, authentic Catholic parish. These criteria will have different nuances depending on the locale and makeup of the parish, but to some degree they are applicable to all parish situations. The scale given below is meant as a help in evaluating your parish. Members of the staff or a group of leaders could give the parish a score individually and then compare the results to see which areas the group agrees are going well and which are weak and need more attention.

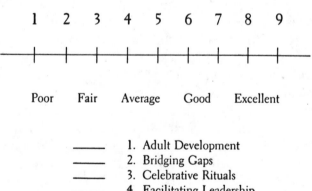

1   2   3   4   5   6   7   8   9

Poor   Fair   Average   Good   Excellent

_____	1. Adult Development
_____	2. Bridging Gaps
_____	3. Celebrative Rituals
_____	4. Facilitating Leadership
_____	5. Fostering Community
_____	6. Ownership
_____	7. Planning
_____	8. Room for Marginals
_____	9. Servant Image

_____ 10. Shared Ministry
_____ 11. Transmitting Tradition

_____ Total (99 = highest score)

CHAPTER ELEVEN

Helps for Parish Leaders

This chapter contains eight short subjects. Most of these issues were lightly touched upon in the parish stories of the previous chapters. They are expanded here and are arranged in alphabetical order for easy reference.
1. Case Studies
2. Census-taking
3. Communiques
4. Deciding Big Issues
5. Forming Dreams
6. Instant Agenda
7. Roots and Histories
8. Surveying

Case Studies

Case studies are an effective tool for helping parish staffs and lay leaders deal with decision-making. The seven stories contained in this book are case studies. Even though they are fictitious accounts of different kinds of parishes, each one is true to life and provides ideas for dealing with actual situations. The seven stories do come to optimistic conclusions. A case study, on the other hand, does not have a conclusion. It leaves the situation up in the air and asks the participants to come up with a solution. The following account is one way a case study can be used in a parish.

The staff and council have come together for a full day of decision-making and planning; they will have to make many decisions for the coming year. Rather than beginning with parish business, though, the group decides to spend half an hour in prayer and reflection. After the prayer, people split into small groups of three or four, making sure that these small groups have a mixture of both staff and council members. Each group is given the same case study, along with some newsprint, magic markers, and masking tape for taping the newsprint on the wall. The groups have forty-five minutes to come up with a solution to the problem posed by the case study. The people will then reassemble in one large group to report on their activity.

The case study can of course be made up to fit each parish situation, but the following is one example:

St. Jerome's Parish

The Steeple Case

St. Jerome's is a parish dating back to the turn of the century. It has a membership of 1200 families, 400 of them active in the parish. The people are diverse in age and interests. The parish has a council that has been in operation for the last five years. The Administration Committee of the council is responsible for matters involving money and physical assets. The Christian Service Committee directs social action programs that sometimes involve modest expenditures of funds. The council has four other committees, but our case study involves these two committees in particular.

On a Friday night in September, lightning struck the steeple and ignited a fire that caused severe structural damage to it. The Administration Committee, after consulting contractors, decided that the steeple should be rebuilt at a cost of $60,000 and that a special "steeple" campaign should be organized to raise the money. The Administration Committee presented its recommendation to the parish council. The response was immediate.

"In a time like this, with all the poverty and problems in the city, and world refugees and hunger and all, how can we justify this much money on a steeple that has no function?" asked Dan Fitzpatrick, chairman of the Christian Service Committee.

Fred Thornton replied, "Because if we don't fix it, it will fall down, and if we take it down, who will know this is a Catholic Church?"

Charlotte Raynor, a member of the Religious Education Committee, who said she had joined the parish because she thought it could work to bring changes in society, was aghast at this, and literally shouted to the meeting, "The world is going to pot, and we sit here discussing spending money on a steeple! It seems to me we have our priorities turned upside down. Jesus sent the church out to minister to human beings, not to make monuments out of our buildings."

An elderly gentleman, Richard Casey, a loyal parishioner and substantial giver, who had come to observe the council meeting, then offered to contribute a set of bells to go in the repaired steeple so that the whole neighborhood would hear them and know where the Catholic Church was. Although there were some negative reactions to this, Harriet Gibson, a council member, came to his support, saying, "This church is the church of my childhood, and I want the steeple to stay on. I know there are many others who feel the same way about it. The Administration Committee voted unanimously to fix the steeple, and if Mr. Casey wants to put bells up there, we ought to go along."

During the ensuing month, Father Anderson, who had kept his opinions on the matter to himself, preached on the virtues of compassion, forgiveness, and acceptance and reconciliation.

Wallace Berry noted that although his liturgy committee, in a private poll after the last meeting, had voted three to two in favor of retaining the steeple and the bells, he personally opposed it and was uncertain how to vote when the motion would be brought before the next council meeting. The permanent deacon of the parish responded, "I think this whole thing is getting out of hand. Let's let those who want to have the steeple replaced raise the money among themselves and leave the rest of us out of it."

Another member of the liturgy committee answered, "But that is no way for a Christian community to behave—we must learn to work and worship together!"

Eventually the motion was brought to a parish council vote. It lost eleven to nine, with Father Anderson abstaining. A resolution was then passed that respectfully declined Mr. Casey's gift but thanked him for his generosity and thoughtfulness. Through Christmas the atmosphere was tense. The Administration Committee refused to do anything at all about arranging for the removal of the steeple. Father Anderson, bearing the brunt of well-intentioned but often harsh criticism from some parishioners, began to feel isolated and alone.

Finally, in mid-January Mr. Berger, the parish council president, was informed that a meeting of the congregation was being called by a group of parishioners, including several on the Administration Committee, to consider a motion that would reverse the council vote and approve rebuilding the church steeple. Should this motion carry, a second one would request that the council president appoint a committee on governance to consider changing the bylaws so as to involve the congregation more directly in decision-making in the parish.

It was in this situation that Mr. Berger pondered the nature of the parish's purpose and what, if anything, he could do to help resolve St. Jerome's current dilemma.

What suggestions do you have for Mr. Berger?

When the small groups reassemble, each reports on how the crisis was dealt with, how the group members interacted, and whether they reached a consensus. This process can take two or three hours, but it is time well spent since it prepares the staff and council to deal with real parish problems. It gives them a chance to be creative and resourceful in solving problems, without getting bogged down in vested interests or hidden agenda. Dealing with such a case study can help create an atmosphere that makes the decision-making process more enjoyable and beneficial for the whole parish.

Census-taking

On the average, about twenty percent of the members of a typical Catholic parish moves in or out of the parish every three to four years. In some suburban areas over half the parish membership can change in that same length of time. It is important to keep in touch with the new membership of the parish. This can be done in a number of ways.

First, parish leaders must make a continual effort to get the names and addresses of new members. Frequent bulletin and pulpit anouncements about where new parishioners can sign up is a beginning. A welcome wagon or hospitality committee can then follow up with a visit to the homes of new parishioners. Periodic parties or get-togethers for new members will give them a chance to meet the staff and lay leaders and to learn how the parish works and where newcomers can fit into its tempo and activities.

Every three to four years it helps to update the census. The best place to begin is at the weekend Masses, preferably during October or March, because these are the months when the highest percentage of Catholics attend Mass. Census update cards are put into the pew, and one member of each family is asked to fill out a census card and give it to the usher. These update cards are matched with the parish files. This Mass census will provide an update for about eighty percent of the parish membership.

But what about the remaining Catholics, those who are not regular Mass-goers? What about the baptized Catholics living within parish boundaries who are not registered in any parish? According to statistics, these account for about twenty-eight percent of the Catholics living within the boundaries of a typical parish. How can the parish get in touch with these marginal Catholics? The only way is through door-to-door personal contact. At Immaculate Conception Parish described in Chapter Four, the call for volunteers to do a census became a turning point for the whole parish. It is a way in which parishioners can volunteer for a project without signing their lives away. It is a one-shot commitment with a simple, realizable objective: to contact every home in a given area and get the names of those who wish to become members of the parish.

Using volunteers for a census takes organization. The temptation is to call in outside help or hire additional staff. That is a mistake; it is a job for the whole parish. Two options are possible for door-to-door canvass: Either cover the whole parish at once, or spread the job out over a number of months. In either case, the parish is divided into sections, and each section is under the leadership of two persons. Packets prepared for the subregions within a section include flyers about the parish and its operation. These flyers are given to every household visited, regardless of religion. The packet also includes census cards with instructions about how to ask the census information. The volunteers have a list of parishioners in their subregion whose names are already on the parish lists. There is no need to visit these people, except as a friendly gesture.

The best time to do the census is in the fall or spring, say October or Lent. Whether it is done all at once or over a number of weeks, the same procedure is followed. It starts with a call for volunteers. The call includes a clear description of the job and how much time it will take. The volunteers are asked to come to a Saturday morning meeting, which will last no more than one and a half hours. This Saturday meeting is run by the area team leaders. They explain the reason for the census: to locate and welcome the people who might like to join the parish, to inform the others about the parish and its activities, and to learn what concerns people have about the church and neighborhood.

The leaders describe how the census is done. They explain that they are sending out the volunteers in pairs, just as Jesus sent out his disciples in pairs to announce the coming of the Kingdom. The volunteers are encouraged to pair up with those they would not ordinarily choose so those of different ages and backgrounds work together. Each pair chooses an area to cover, usually including no more than thirty homes, and is given the packets for that area. Several possible situations are brought up, and ideas are given as to how to deal with them.

"What if there's no one at home?"

"Go back at another time of day."

"What if the people won't open the door?"

"Show your parish identification card through the window and shout louder."

"What if there's a big dog?"

"Be quick about getting in or out, depending on where the dog is."

"What if the people are hostile?"

"Smile a lot!"

The Saturday meeting and the following week of canvassing are done in the spirit of prayer and ministry. It is a way of sharing in the Lord's work; each person has a part to play. The workers are encouraged to knock on every door over the weekend and to return to the "no-answers" sometime during the week. They are told to come to the Mass and celebration on Sunday afternoon at the end of the week with census cards in hand.

As a way of giving support to the efforts of the volunteers, the Masses over the two weekends talk up the census. All the parishioners are asked to pray for God's blessings on the census-taking.

The Sunday afternoon get-together is a time for celebrating and sharing experiences. The volunteers come closer together and feel themselves part of the parish community through their generous commitment. The results of their canvassing are collected, along with personal impressions that add feeling-tones to the census information.

The area leaders collate the information and put it into the parish files. They also take note of the people who showed interest in becoming active members of the parish or who expressed a desire to be visited again, perhaps by a member of the Social Service committee or one of the parish staff. In this way the new members do not become merely cases in the parish file but persons who are integrated into the life of the parish community.

Communiques

A parish communicates its life and operation in many subtle and unspoken ways. The tone of the liturgies, the types of organizations and programs, the interaction among staff, council, and people—all these reveal what kind of parish it is. But there are also vehicles of communication that the leaders use as explicit ways of keeping in touch with the parishioners. These include pulpit announcements, bulletins, newsletters, letters from the pastor and staff, financial reports, parish handbooks, and directories. We will focus on the parish bulletin and the newsletter.

I rarely find parish bulletins interesting. Most are too cluttered and monotonous. They contain everything happening in the parish, along with Mass intentions, last week's collection totals, and advertisements. The purpose of the bulletin becomes clouded because everything appears to have equal weight. As a result, not much is communicated.

A few bulletins have caught my attention, no doubt because their purpose was clear and the layout uncluttered. They contained all the necessary information for newcomers and visitors: the time for Masses, names of parish leaders, and the focus or purpose of the parish. They also discussed the weekend Scripture readings and reflected briefly on the significance of the readings for everyday life. They contained one or two (no more!) features about an important event or issue in the parish or in the neighborhood, or about a group that deserved attention. The pastor or staff might have a word of thanks to an individual or group. The bulletin also had plenty of open space, perhaps a drawing or picture or two, and usually no advertisements.

This type of bulletin not only communicated the essentials for the week but provided a tone or feeling about the parish as a whole. The parish leaders were saying that the purpose of the parish is to worship the Lord together, to reflect on God's Word, to focus on key issues, to become aware of important problems, and to thank and support those who have done a good job. In short, the *bulletin* is a *vehicle* used by the pastor and staff *to educate, stimulate reflection, raise parishioners' consciousness, and create a community spirit.*

But what about all those other parish events and happenings that didn't get into the bulletin? These can be communicated through a monthly newsletter. The purpose of the *newsletter is to publicize parish events and get feedback from the parishioners.* This newsletter is more difficult to establish and maintain in operation than the bulletin is, but it is an important vehicle of communication. The bulletin comes from the staff and pastor. The newsletter is supported by the staff but comes from and is owned by the people. For that reason it may not be as organized, neat, or regular as the bulletin, but it will probably be read by more people. Each month a group of parishioners puts together a calendar of events and a description of parish programs and activities, and mails it out to all parishioners. This means that it gets into all the homes and is seen even by those who are not regular Mass-goers, the young people especially.

Since the newsletter belongs to the people, it will include room for their opinions. It can include letters to the editor, reactions to activities, congratulations for last month's projects, pitches for getting people interested in the coming month's activities, and many pictures. It can include regular columns by the staff and perhaps some thoughts from the pastor, but the newsletter is the creation of the parish community. The more people who own it and contribute to it, the more successful it will be.

If you have tried a newsletter and find it didn't work, then I suggest you try it again . . . and again . . . and again. It's that important. A few practical hints might help bring it to life and assure its continuance. First, give it staff support and back it up with money. The benefits will be far beyond the amount of money spent. Find a pair of good editors to spell each other, and pay them for their efforts; it is too great a burden for one person. Before all else the newsletter must be interesting, even catchy—neither too long nor too crowded. The editors should be able to present the news in a clear and appealing format. Add humor along with the news, and include the names of as many parishioners as possible. Be sure all the names are spelled correctly. Have a newsletter staff out in the field gathering information in person about parish organizations, events, and programs, as well as about individual parishioners who deserve a writeup. Keep deadlines! In this way the newsletter becomes the primary vehicle in which the parishioners learn about what is going on in the parish.

Deciding Big Issues

Decision-making is part of the everyday life of the parish. The decisions range from routine matters to critical decisions that influence the direction of the parish for years to come. Between these two extremes is a wide range of decisions that affect parish life to varying degrees, depending on the importance of the issues and the number of people affected by the outcome. Some decisions are handled with comparative ease; others take more time and deliberation.

Occasionally a major issue affects the entire parish. The school enrollment is dropping and expenses are climbing. Some decision will have to be made about the future of our school. The weekend Masses are overcrowded. Should we construct a new building? The sanctuary needs remodeling. What is the best plan to follow?

These are questions that affect a large proportion of the parish community. How can a decision be made that will be accepted by the people, especially when these issues touch their vested interests? The answer lies in a process of discernment, a process that includes prayer and sincere group effort. The discernment process follows these steps.

The Process of Discernment

Suppose a decision must be made about the future of the parish school. The first step for parish leaders is to *define the issue for the parishioners*—to gather all the information related to the school stuation, including cost patterns in recent years and projected costs, the present state of the buildings and expected repairs, enrollment figures from previous years and expected enrollment for the years ahead.

But the leaders must do more. They also must *provide a possible solution* as a means of focusing the attention of the parishioners. For example, the staff and council and/or school board might appoint a fact-finding committee to gather all necessary information related to the school. The commitee might also submit a recommended solution. As a result of the information, closing the school might seem to be the best solution.

The committee, however, does not make the decision. Nor does the staff, council, or school board. This is far too large an issue to be settled by parish leaders without consulting the parish as a whole. Instead, the leaders *take the issue to the parishioners,* in this fashion.

First, the leaders compile all the information about the school in a clear manner so that the parishioners can understand all sides of the issue. Next, the pastor, perhaps in conjunction with representatives of the council or school board, presents the information to the parish. He can do this at the parish weekend Masses since most of the parishioners can be reached then. He invites the parishioners to participate in a period of discernment. He describes the history of the issue, the process that will be used for making the decision, and why it is critical to arrive at a decision at this time. He invites everyone to help discern in what direction the Lord is calling the parish.

The people are asked to spend the next two weeks in prayer and discernment. (The time intervals will vary according to the rhythm of the parish.) Parishioners are to think of all the reasons *against* choosing the solution offered—in this case, closing the school. They are to find reasons even if they feel the school should be closed. The pastor invites people to talk the matter over in their families, in their neighborhoods, and in parish gatherings. A worksheet is provided along with the information materials so that people can write down on it all the reasons against closing the school.

At the end of the two weeks, the pastor asks the parishioners to take the opposite position and think of all the reasons *for* choosing the proposed solution, even if they do not agree with that course of action. They write these reasons on the worksheet opposite the reasons against. At the end of the month the people are asked to look over their worksheet carefully and then come to a conclusion.

At the weekend Masses a card is given to each adult with the single question and direction: "Do we close the school? Yes or no, and give one reason for your response." The pastor makes clear that this is not a parish vote but a way of learning how the Spirit is working in the parishioners during the time of discernment.

The *result of the people's discernment is given to the decision-making group*. This might be the staff, the council, or the school board, or some combination of these. The *parishioners are asked to pray for this decision-making group* for the next two weeks, asking that the discerning group remain open to the urgings of the Spirit about what course would be the best.

Often the result of the parishioners' discernment will be split, perhaps forty percent for closing the school, forty-five percent for keeping it open, and the rest having no opinion. But along with the responses come many reasons why people made a particular choice. The *decision-making group takes all this information, adds it to the results of its own discernment, and comes to a tentative decision*. The decision may be neither to close the school nor keep it open but some other option that lies on the continuum between these two poles.

The *tentative decision is made public* so that all the parishioners are aware of the result of the discernment and the reasons for that choice. The decision is tentative in order to give the parishioners time to react. The parishioners are given the opportunity to air their opinions and to ask questions about what is implied in the decision. This gives people time to learn what the decision will mean for the future of the parish. The discerning group pays attention to the parishioners' reactions to see if the people can accept the result. If a significant group of people is not willing to support the decision, it may be an indication that the process of discernment must continue until a more acceptable alternative can be found.

If after a suitable period of reflection, prayer, and reaction it appears that the parish as a whole is willing to accept and support the proposal, the *decision-making group makes a final decision. Steps are then taken to implement the decision.*

This process of discernment will serve to draw the parish together rather than create conflict and division. If enough time and effort is spent on helping the people see what the Lord is urging in this matter, then it is more likely that they will accept and even rejoice in the decision. They know that the parish community has been heard and respected in trying to decide the Lord's wishes.*

Two notes of caution are necessary. First, the staff and parish leaders must be honest about their intentions. Perhaps they have already decided what course of action will be followed and want parishioners to accept their own solution, so they go through the motions of a discernment process. It will probably not succeed, however, because the people will see through the charade and reject the process. When a solution has already been chosen, a better process is to sell the people on the reasons why. Good communication and public relations are necessary in this case. But don't call it discernment, since a final decision has already been made.

A second caution is that this process should not be used very often. Save it for only the critical issues that require consultation with large groups of parishioners or for those areas where vested interests are likely to impede the decision-making process. An adaptation of this process can be used for decision-making within staffs and councils and other parish groups, especially when difficult decisions must be made that affect the members of those groups. But the process does take time and effort and may not be necessary for most kinds of group decision-making.

To sum up, the discernment process follows these steps:

1. Define the issue or critical situation and provide a possible solution.
2. Give everyone all the information necessary for arriving at a solution.
3. Invite parishioners to spend time in prayer and discussion as a means of getting in touch with the Spirit.
4. Ask parishioners to list all their reasons against the suggested solution.
5. After a suitable time interval, ask them to list all their reasons for the suggested solution.

*The subject of decision-making is treated in William Rademacher's *The Practical Guide for Parish Councils* (West Mystic, Conn.: Twenty-Third Publications, 1979), pp. 143-52.

6. At the end of the discernment period, ask each person to choose for or against the solution and to give one reason for his or her choice.
7. Give the results to a discerning group for deliberation.
8. Ask the parish to pray that the discerning group be attentive to the movements of the Spirit.
9. Have the discerning group arrive at a tentative solution and present this to the parish as a whole.
10. Invite parishioners to give reactions about the tentative solution.
11. Have the discerning group make a final decision.
12. Invite parishioners to ratify the result of the discernment process, perhaps through a special Mass or parish celebration.

Forming Dreams

A successful parish knows how to dream dreams. With no vision or sense of direction a parish community flounders. But not everyone finds dreaming easy; some have to be given direction and support. Here is one way to give it.

A day has been set aside for the parish staff and council to establish a dream for the parish community. The day begins at two o'clock on a Sunday afternoon. The twenty participants spend thirty minutes in prayer and group reflection, focusing on the parish and on their own role as its leaders. While still in the spirit of prayer and reflection, each person is given a worksheet and is told to spend forty-five minutes filling it out. The worksheet contains six sections and begins with the statement: "As I reflect on what I would like to see the parish look like five years from now, this is what I come up with."

The six sections of the worksheet are:
1. *This is the way the parish worships and prays* . . . (Describe your dream for the parish Masses, prayer experiences, individual and family spirituality, etc.)
2. *This is the way the parish is given direction* . . . (Describe your dream for the parish leadership, whether staff and/or council, and how decisions are made, etc.)

3. *This is the way the parishioners relate to one another . . .* (Describe your dream for parish groupings and activities and how community spirit happens, etc.)
4. *This is the way the people—old and young—learn about their faith and traditions . . .* (Describe education in your dream parish and what is included, etc.)
5. *This is the way the parish relates to the larger community . . .* (Describe your dream for outreach, social service and awareness, ecumenical and civic involvement, etc.)
6. *This is the size, age distribution, types of persons involved in the parish . . .* (Describe what changes are likely, and what changes should be encouraged, etc.)

At the end of the personal reflection time, the participants reassemble in one group, and their dreams are listed on large sheets of newsprint taped to the wall. This takes at least an hour. If some of the dreams conflict, note the diverse views. By then it is time for dinner.

After dinner, the participants break into five groups, one to deal with liturgy and worship, one with leadership, one with community building, one with education, and one with service and outreach. Each group takes the newsprint list of dreams for its own area and identifies both the common elements and the points of disagreement. Each group then tries to formulate a common vision or dream for the parish in its own area that will give the parish direction over the next five years.

Each of the five small groups is given a worksheet that asks three questions. The first question is: What do we want to have accomplished five years from now in the area of _____ (specify worship, leadership, community building, education, outreach)? When the group members settle on the common dream or vision, they all write it on the worksheet.

They go on to the second question: What are we already doing that is helping us come closer to our dream? The group then lists all the activities, groups, programs, and individuals that are contributing to the parish vision in that area. These are the persons and programs that should be given support, since they are helping the parish reach its ideal.

Once this list is complete, they address the last question: In light of what we consider our dream and what is already happening, where do we want to spend our energies over the next year? The group then tries to plan for the coming year to cover the aspects of the dream that have not been dealt with. The result will be one, or at most two, plans of action.

The final task of the small group is to determine what groups or individuals are responsible for these actions and how to get the actions into operation.

Not all of the five groups will be able to complete this task in the few hours given them, but the task does provide a focus for subsequent meetings. At the end of the day the five groups reassemble and present to the whole group the common vision for the parish in each area and indicate what actions need to be taken over the coming year to help the parish come closer to this dream.

Instant Agenda

Good meetings have an agenda. But a meeting can become a disaster if a pressing problem comes up after the agenda has been set and there is no time to deal with it. Another difficulty is that people are so busy that they fail to get their item to the person preparing the agenda and therefore get frustrated because their business will not be dealt with at the meeting. A solution to this difficulty is to create the agenda just prior to the meeting. It works this way:

A parish staff comes together for its weekly meeting. Each person brings along the items he or she wants addressed. The person chairing that meeting (it need not be the pastor) passes around the "instant agenda" sheet. It looks like this:

Agenda Item	Staff Member	Information	Decision	Feedback	Planning	New Business
1.						
2.						
3.						

As the sheet is passed around, each member may enter an agenda item, his or her name, and a check in the appropriate column. These columns will differ according to the parish, but usually they are as follows:

A. Informational items: These include various announcements, names of persons who are sick, information on meetings, dates. They can be handled quickly and with little discussion.

B. Decision items: These have been talked about in prior meetings, but some decision must be reached. They take more time but can be handled relatively quickly if people have been thinking about them.

C. Feedback items: These have to do with existing programs and/or the way someone is doing his or her job. They presume a high level of trust in the group and are put in the middle column so that eveyone knows there will be room to air feelings and raise questions about the subject.

D. Planning items: These require some thinking by the staff, both during the meeting and afterward. They may involve immediate planning for an upcoming event or longer-range issues. If the planning item needs a great deal of discussion, then time is set aside at a future meeting, or a special meeting is called to deal with the issue. But the issue is at least raised at this meeting.

E. New business items: These are new issues that members want to bring up, usually to be dealt with later, but mentioned now to get others thinking about them. They come at the end of the meeting as time permits.

After each staff member has put down his or her agenda items, the person chairing the meeting calls on the persons who have checked informational items, in the order the names appear on the sheet.

Once all the informational items have been completed, then the second-column items are dealt with, and so on, until the agenda sheet is covered or time has expired. Those items not covered are put at the top of the column for the next meeting. *

*I am grateful to the pastoral team of St. James Parish in Chicago for sharing this process of setting an instant agenda.

Roots and Histories

The American culture is only beginning to reflect upon its past and look for links that will provide present generations with a sense of continuity. The immigrant experience of Catholic parishes is a field ripe for the harvesting of our past. A parish contains many traditions, customs, and rituals that are part of its history and contribute to its present image and operation. A group experience of reflecting on these past events can add interest and vitality to the parish. What follows is one of many ways of recapturing the past.

Suppose a parish anniversary is approaching. It need not be a momentous one, such as a fiftieth anniversary or centennial. Any one will do. During the week before the event everyone is invited to an evening of "remembering." The participants are divided into small groups, with twenty or thirty in each group. The groups are distributed far enough apart so as not to disturb one another (the experience usually generates laughter and loud talking). It may help to have them meet in different rooms.

Each small group gathers at a wall of the room on which are posted several pieces of blank newsprint. The writing surface should be at least five feet wide and two feet high. A line is drawn across the paper, with the present date to the right side of the line and the founding date of the parish to the left.

The session begins with some quiet reflection. The group leaders encourage people to think about key moments or events in the history of the parish, whether they happened yesterday or a number of years ago. They may be either positive or negative experiences that have helped or hindered the growth of the parish. Whatever the case, the people consider them important enough to have influenced the direction and life of the parish.

After a few minutes of individual reflection, the leader asks the participants to share with the group the events that came to mind. The leader writes these events on the newsprint with a magic marker, trying to locate them on the history line at about the time they occurred. Some of the events will be serious, some humorous, some painful; all are listed.

When the task is completed, the history line will probably include key people such as pastors, associates, staff members, teachers, or noteworthy parishioners. It will show when buildings went up, when changes in school enrollment occurred, when parish crises happened, when shifts in parish membership occurred, when parish organizations and groups were formed and disbanded, and how the parishioners reacted to changes and innovations.

Once the people have exhausted their memories of the parish (or more likely, when the time has run out), all are given an index card and are asked to reflect prayerfully on what is before them on the history line. Then they write on the card a word or two (no more than five) that describes the parish at the present moment, given the past out of which it has come. After five minutes of personal reflection, the people are invited to read their cards, and these results are listed on a blank piece of newsprint posted to the right of the parish history line. This last part of the exercise helps link the past to the present.

The entire task usually takes from an hour to an hour and a half. At the conclusion of the evening all the small groups reunite to talk about the experience and to compare each group's history line and description of the present parish situation.

The history lines from all the groups are taped to a wall, one above the other, to see which events were remembered by all groups and which appeared in only one or two. The meeting concludes with refreshments, perhaps including snacks that remind people of the parish in days gone by.

A few persons are given the responsibility of combining the history lines into one line and typing up the results. These summaries are given out to all parishioners at the anniversary celebrations. The history lines are displayed in the church hall (provided the people who made them give their consent) so that others can share these remembrances of the parish.

Surveying

A parish that consists of five hundred families or more should think about conducting a survey of attitudes among the parishioners to discover their needs, opinions, and expectations. The attitudes of the more active and vocal members can be known without surveying, but those who do not come to parish functions or who hesitate to express their opinions should also be encouraged to share their ideas and feelings.

One way to get at the feelings of all the parishioners is through surveying. This is not an easy task, and care must be taken to do it well and within a reasonable time. Otherwise the information will be inaccurate or out of date before it is put to use.

A parish-wide survey should be made with outside help, using either diocesan resources or other experienced professional groups. Even surveying subgroups within the parish takes time and skill. As a guide to those who are thinking of conducting parish surveys, I have a list of questions that should be asked during the surveying process.

The first question to ask is: *Why are we taking this survey?* Is it to seek information, or is it meant as an educational tool? Do we want to tell people something about the whole parish, or about a particular program? Is a survey the best way to do this? Those conducting a survey must be candid about why they want to do it. If education is the intention, then there are easier and more beneficial ways of doing this: through letters, communiques, or other publicity efforts. If, on the other hand, the reason for doing the survey is to get in touch with the ideas and the feelings of the people, then surveying is a good way to do this. The intention of those doing the survey should be to listen to the parishioners, not to tell them something.

The next question is: *What are we looking for?* Those who are conducting a survey must limit its range. Are we interested in the people's reaction to all the parish liturgies, or just to the weekend Masses? Are we interested in how they participate in the Masses, or in what they think about the music used at Mass? Are we interested in all the music used at Mass, or only in those songs used for congregational singing? Are we interested in all the congregational singing, or in the singing at just a few Masses? This series of specific questions can help narrow the scope of the survey to something like this: What do the people at the 9, 10:30, and 12 o'clock Masses think about the songs used for congregational singing, and how can we get them more interested in joining in with the singing? The sharper the focus at the beginning of the survey, the easier the task throughout.

How will we do the surveying? A number of options are available. The first is to choose between personal interviews and written surveys. Each approach has advantages and disadvantages. Interviewing allows the people to express their feelings and explain their responses more fully. This approach also has a high response rate. Interviews, however, are more difficult to tabulate and analyze than written responses. Also, a smaller group of people is usually surveyed through interviewing than through written surveys because it takes longer to complete each interview. One way of interviewing a larger group is by telephone, although this approach reduces the number of questions that can be asked.

I have found the best method to be a combination of these approaches. I encourage parishes to send out a written survey asking two types of questions—those that have clear-cut alternatives that respondents must choose from, since these can be easily tabulated, and those that do not specify answers, or open-ended questions. Open-ended questions allow people the freedom to make up their own answers and to give their impressions. This combination of different types of questions allows people to express their feelings but also makes it easier to compile the results of the survey. A follow-up telephone call is made to encourage those who have not returned the written survey to do so. Those who do not want to respond to the written survey are asked interview questions over the phone. In this way at least some information is obtained from nearly all the people who were sent surveys.

Where will we do the surveying? If interviews are going to be conducted, then a choice will have to be made among calling door-to-door, contacting persons as they come to Masses or activities, or calling them by phone. If written surveys are going to be used, then a choice has to be made about mailing them or giving them out at the Masses. I have discovered that people tend to be more positive toward the Church and parish when they fill out surveys during or just after Mass, but that they give a more candid response if they take the survey home and fill it out there. Also, if a survey is given out at Mass, then only those who attend Mass can respond, but if we want the opinions of less active members, then mailing is better.

Who will be surveyed? If the topics on the survey relate to only one group in the parish, such as the parents of children in the religious education program, then these are the only ones who should be surveyed. Nor is it necessary to survey every parent who has children in the religious education program. If gathering information is the reason for the survey, then this can be done by selecting a smaller sample of parents. This saves a great deal of time in the tabulation of the responses.

In choosing the size of a sample, the first consideration is to estimate how many surveys are likely to be returned to work with, especially if the responses are going to be divided up into age, sex, or education subgroups. If, for instance, there are 500 families associated with the religious education program, then surveying 100 parents, either father or mother, would be a large enough sample. About 70 surveys are likely to be returned, and this will be enough to uncover the attitudes and feelings of the parents toward the program. Suppose a survey is to be given to the people who attend the Sunday Masses in order to find out what they think about the congregational singing, and that the total number of adults attending the Masses is about 1500. In this case 300 surveys would be plenty to hand out at random as people leave church. This way about 200 surveys will be returned, and this is enough to find out what the entire congregation thinks about congregational singing.

In my own surveying of parishes, I usually give out 300 surveys to individual adults, eighteen years and over, who are registered members of the parish. If the adult population of the parish is over 5000, then I give out as many as 450, but no more. The people who are to receive surveys are picked at random from the parish files, using a set of random numbers. Because the persons who are picked to receive a survey know that they belong to a special group, they tend to return the survey in greater numbers than if the whole parish received it. The same is true for subgroups in the parish. If the 100 religious education program parents realize that they have been selected (at random) to represent the attitudes of the whole group, they are more likely to take the survey seriously and send back the completed questionnaire.

What questions will we ask? Whether the surveyers plan to conduct interviews or to send out a written survey, great care must be taken to make the questions clear, simple, and unbiased. Narrowing the topics to include only those that will be used is the first step. The next step is to divide the topics into specific, uncomplicated questions. Then a rough draft of the survey or interview questions is distributed to a number of people for their advice and corrections. Once the survey is in its final form it should be given to about ten or fifteen people as a pretest to see if they can understand and respond to the questions. These few sample surveys are tabulated as if they were part of the regular group of respondents. Final corrections and changes are made, and the final version is then prepared for distribution. The rule of thumb is: Every hour spent in preparing a survey before it is sent out will save ten hours in tabulation and analysis afterward. In other words, the more work that goes into narrowing down the topics, refining and culling the questions, rearranging and ordering questions, the less work will be necessary when the surveys are returned. Once the survey is sent out, no more changes can be made, and its designers are stuck with any mistakes or errors that were made in preparing it.

How will we tabulate the results? This question must be asked *before* the survey is sent out. There are ways of constructing a survey or conducting an interview that make tabulation much simpler. Think about using a computer to summarize the results. Even if a computer is not used, try to get the results into numerical categories so that summations and comparisons can be made. Figure out in advance how to deal with written comments: how they will be categorized and how the divisions of age, sex, and education are going to be used in subdividing the answers.

How will we write the report? Again, it is best to answer this question before doing the surveying. Otherwise it will take too long to put the information into usable form. A good technique for writing the results is comparison. Try to uncover differences and similarities between different groups and in that way learn the significance of each group's response. Are there differences between the way teachers and the parents feel toward the religious education program? Do the parents of different-aged children feel differently? Do the parents' attitudes change if they have more than one child in the program?

Surveying is a helpful tool for assessing the attitudes and feelings of a large congregation. But it cannot be done overnight. It demands a good deal of thought and perspective.

APPENDIX

What Parishioners Are Saying

The first step in parish renewal and planning is to discover the attitudes and expectations of parishioners. During the past ten years I have asked people their opinions about the parish and the Church. I have surveyed over twelve thousand Catholic parishioners living in seventy parishes across the country. I did not select these parishes; they requested my help in my capacity as director of the Parish Evaluation Project.

As a result, the information contained in this appendix does not represent a scientifically constructed sample of Catholic attitudes in the United States. But because of the wide variety of parishes I have worked with, I am confident that it does represent the feelings and attitudes of Catholic parishioners from all parts of the country and all walks of life. The sixty parishes that are the basis of my information cover a wide geographical area. Twenty states are represented, from Arizona to Massachusetts, and from Florida to the state of Washington, as well as the District of Columbia. Many different types of parishes are included, moreover, such as those serving predominantly Black, Hispanic, or Eastern European congregations. Represented are older parishes located in large and medium-sized cities, parishes from both well-established and developing suburban communities, and those situated in small towns and rural settings. Because of the variety of locations and types of congregations, I think I am in touch with the opinions and desires of a representative group of American Catholic parishioners. The end of this appendix details the sample size and distribution of the parish surveys.

I will be reporting information gathered from parishes I surveyed between the years 1978 and 1982. This is the most up-to-date information available on what Catholic parishioners are saying about the parish and the Church during the last few years. Because I have been collecting surveys of Catholic opinion since the early 1970s, I have been able to observe shifts in attitudes during the decade and to put the present data into a larger perspective.

A general survey instrument was sent to a sample of about three hundred individual adults in a parish, not to family units. The sample was selected by using a set of random numbers that was matched with the membership file in each parish. Because the selection of parishioners was random, it was possible for both a husband and wife to receive a survey. The description of Catholic parishioners' attitudes contained in this appendix is taken from the responses to the general survey instrument. Also sent along with the general survey was a set of questions unique to each parish's situation. The average response from the parishes I surveyed has been high, usually sixty-five to seventy-five percent and sometimes more than eighty percent.

Some of the people's attitudes have changed over the last ten years; some have remained the same. One example of a change in attitude is the reaction of people toward the institutional Catholic Church.

In the early and mid-1970s, fewer than half of the parishioners polled (47%) said they were favorable or very favorable toward the Catholic Church as a whole. This attitude was in contrast to the reaction toward the local parish, where 63% said they were favorable or very favorable toward their own parish. In the last few years, however, reactions toward the institutional Church have become more favorable. At the present time, 57% say they are favorable toward the Catholic Church, an increase of 10%. During the same time span, positive reactions to the parish have remained unchanged.

The more favorable reaction to the Church can be related to a number of causes, such as the election of Pope John Paul II and his visit to the United States, fewer changes in the liturgy, and more opportunities for people to learn about new emphases in the Church since the Second Vatican Council.

An attitude that has not changed over the last 10 years is the reaction toward Benediction of the Blessed Sacrament.

About 3 out of 4 people surveyed say they are favorable or very favorable toward Benediction. Parish staffs and lay leaders are as surprised today as in the early 1970s that so many of the parishioners like Benediction. One pastor exclaimed when he learned that over three-fourths of the people—young and old—favored Benediction, "How can this be? We've not had Benediction in this parish for the last three years!"

A favorable response from the people does not mean, of course, that they will come to Benediction if and when it is offered. But they associate an aura of mystery and reverence with Benediction, and a feeling of being in direct contact with the Holy. This appeals to people, and they feel that it might be good if the parish provided opportunities for Benediction to those who might like to attend.

In reporting the attitudes of Catholic parishioners, I will concentrate on seven areas: liturgical preferences, reactions to parish activities and programs, areas of concern and worry to parishioners, personal moral attitudes, social awareness, opinions about parish decision-making and Church authority, and finally, personal and family religious experience and practice.

Liturgical Preferences

The Mass has undergone many changes in the last two decades. Some of the changes have been welcomed by the majority of the people; others have been resisted. Reactions to liturgical changes vary with the age and background of the individual, as well as with the way the changes were prepared for and introduced.

In recent years a greater percentage of the parishioners have reacted more positively than negatively toward changes in the Mass. People appear to be growing accustomed to the new rhythm and emphases of the post-Vatican II liturgies. Proof of that is found in response to a question on the survey that asked, "What is your present attitude toward changes in the liturgy?" My results show that there has been a gradual increase during the last ten years in the percentage of parishioners who are satisfied with the present rate of change in the liturgy. In the mid-1970s just over half of the people (54%) said they were satisfied with the present rate of change or would like even more changes taking place. By the beginning of the 1980s, the percentage of people open to change had increased to almost two-thirds (64%).

Despite this openness to change by the majority of parishioners, many people still respond favorably to traditional forms of prayer and worship. About 3 people out of 5 favor parish novenas and rosary devotions. As I have already mentioned, 3 out of 4 parishioners favor Benediction of the Blessed Sacrament, and 1 in 3 favors a Latin Mass, at least as an occasional experience.

Much of the favorable reaction toward traditional forms of worship is based on memory. People look back to their younger days and recall many positive experiences associated with the Latin Mass, Gregorian chant, familiar hymns, incense, novena prayers, the nine first Fridays. They wish others could have the same experiences they had. For that reason, they feel the parish should make these traditional forms of worship available for those who would like to attend. At the same time, many people who said they favor the traditional forms would not attend these services themselves because they do not feel the need or cannot find the time because of other interests and commitments.

On the other end of the spectrum, the post-Vatican II emphasis on people's participation in the Mass has taken hold. Only 25% favor a quiet Mass with no singing, and 20% favor a quiet Mass with no responses by the congregation. Over three-fourths of the parishioners (76%) said they favored participation at Mass in which the people take part in the singing and the responses. A majority of the people say they favor a guitar or folk Mass in which contemporary songs are used. Parishioners are growing accustomed to seeing lay persons reading at Mass, making petitions during the Prayer of the Faithful, and giving the greeting of peace to one another. This last practice has undergone a significant increase in acceptance over the last few years. In 1975 results showed that only about a third of the people (37%) were in favor of the greeting of peace. At present, twice as many people (67%) favor the practice. That represents a 30% change in five years.

Another liturgical practice that has only recently been introduced was favored by a majority well before it became accepted practice: Communion under both species for the congregation. The favorable reaction is the same today as it was in the early 1970s. Three out of five parishioners over the age of eighteen favor providing the cup as well as the altar bread for Holy Communion.

Communion in the hand does not seem to be favored by more young people than old, nor by those with college background more than by those with less formal education. It is accepted by a majority of all groups. Because it is a matter of personal choice, and people do not feel pressured to receive Communion one way or the other, the favorable attitude among the parishioners has been high ever since the American bishops gave permission and it was introduced into parish liturgies.

This is not true of the reaction toward lay ministers of Communion. Although this practice has been part of most parish Masses since the mid-1970s, less than a majority favor the laity distributing Communion. People are more accepting of deacons and religious sisters or brothers distributing Communion, but many feel it is not fitting for lay persons to be extraordinary ministers of Communion. They find it difficult receiving Communion from their neighbors and friends, people they are well enough acquainted with to know their limitations and faults. This task, they feel, is a sacred duty reserved for priests, deacons, or religious. This is one reason that priests are ordained and have their hands blessed, they say: so as to be able to touch the Sacred Species. If "ordinary people" can give out Communion, then what about other areas of priestly work, such as offering Mass, hearing confessions, blessing weddings? One person who filled out a survey added this comment when responding to the question of lay ministers of Communion: "I think it is disgusting. I would rather not receive. Pretty soon they will start mailing it home. I think it was more special when just the priest was allowed to handle it."

Despite the opposition many people feel toward lay ministers of Communion, people are receiving Communion in growing numbers. In the mid-1970s about 60% of the parishioners in the parishes I surveyed said they received Communion at least twice a month. At the present time, 70% of the registered parishioners eighteen years of age and over say they receive Communion twice a month or oftener. There is no single reason for this increase. In their emphasis on greater participation in the Mass, parish priests and staff members have encouraged all who attend Mass to receive Communion in order to enhance the sense of celebration and feeling of community. The custom of going to confession before each reception of the Eucharist, which was prevalent before the Second Vatican Council, is not as much so today. Many people feel freer now than in the recent past to receive Communion even though they may be at odds with the official Church's stand on such issues as the use of artificial means of birth control or divorce and remarriage.

This raises the issue of confession, or as it is now called, the Rite of Reconciliation. Twenty years ago all "good" Catholics were encouraged to go to confession every other week, or at the very least, once a month. Many Catholics followed this advice. At present only a few parishioners go to individual confession once a month or more. This is also true of the staffs and lay leaders of the parish. Three out of five parishioners I surveyed go to confession once a year or less often.

This shift in the practice of frequent confession was most evident in the late 1960s and early 1970s. In the last six or seven years I have not noticed a significant change in the infrequent use of private confession by Catholic parishioners despite recent emphasis on the New Rite of Reconciliation and efforts by parish priests and staffs to explain and put into use the reconciliation room and the option of face-to-face conversation.

Although the practice of private confession has gone through a profound downward shift in the last few years, the use of Communal Penance has become more popular. Many priests and staffs are surprised at the numbers that attend Communal Penance services held during Advent and Lent. Because of the large number of people who came to these services, one parish I worked with now has a regular monthly Communal Penance service following the last Mass on Sunday. In the mid-1970s just under half of the parishioners I surveyed said they felt favorably or very favorably toward Communal Penance services. Many did not have an opinion because they had never attended one. At present, 55% of those asked favor this form of reconciliation, and the positive response is growing as more people experience Communal Penance services.

The general survey instrument contained thirteen questions related to liturgical and devotional practices. The people were asked to give their reaction to these practices whether or not these were used in their own parish. I have rearranged the questions, listing first those that received the highest percentage of favorable reactions. Here is the list, along with the percentage of people who favored each practice: Benediction of the Blessed Sacrament (76%), participation in Mass with hymns and singing (75%), the greeting of peace during Mass (67%), novenas and rosary devotions (61%), receiving Communion under both species (60%), lay persons receiving Communion in the hand (57%), guitar Masses with contemporary songs (57%), Communal Penance Services (55%), informal Masses in homes (47%), lay persons distributing Communion (45%), the Mass in Latin (32%), Mass with responses but no singing (25%), quiet Mass with no responses by the people (20%).

Reactions to Activities and Programs

The parishioners were asked in the survey to give their reactions to a number of different kinds of parish activities and programs, even if these did not exist in their local parish. The list included fund-raisers, adult religious education, women's and men's clubs, school-related groups, and social action, to name just a few. All but three of the twelve types of activities and programs listed received a high favorable response from the parishioners, over 70%. The three types of activities that received a low positive response were: parish social action groups that deal with race relations and peace-and-justice issues, personal-growth groups such as sensitivity and encounter groups, and pentecostal or charismatic renewal groups.

The favorable response toward parish social action groups is low because many parishioners are reluctant to have the parish or Church become involved in social or public policy issues. Only a minority of the people feel that religion has a role to play in the public sphere. Most feel there should be a clear dichotomy between the activities of religion and the activities of the state. Attitudes toward parish social involvement have not changed over the last ten years. Many of the fears associated with the social action movement of the 1960s still remain in the people's consciousness. The majority of the parish staffs and lay leaders, on the other hand, do favor parish involvement in social and public policy issues. Since this is an important area of parish life, a section of this appendix will be devoted to attitudes on social awareness.

The parishioners I have surveyed in recent years have grown more positive toward sensitivity groups and encounter groups than were the parishioners in the mid-1970s. At that time only two out of five people favored these types of activities in the parish. Now, almost half of the parishioners (48%) are favorable toward personal-growth groups. Marriage Encounter, parish-support groups, and the Cursillo Movement have become more common and have helped overcome people's fears about these types of activities. Some of the written comments made in reaction to these activities mentioned apprehension and suspicion that these groups were too emotional and self-revelatory. Many other people mentioned having no knowledge of these activities. But most of those who had participated in these personal-growth groups had had a positive experience that helped lessen the fears of others in the parish.

Some of the suspicion and apprehension toward personal-growth groups is also associated with the Charismatic Renewal Movement. Those committed to the movement are enthusiastic, and their written comments showed how much they had gained from the experience. But the majority of parishioners view pentecostal groups and the Charismatic Movement with mixed or negative feelings. Only about a third of the people surveyed (36%) said they were favorable or very favorable toward charismatic groups in the parish. A quarter of the respondents were not aware of these groups and had no opinion. The rest, about 40%, had mixed or negative reactions.

These three types of activities received a positive response from less than the majority of the parishioners; all other types of activities and programs are favored by most of the people. Only one kind of activity received a favorable response from less than 80% of the parishioners: devotional activities such as fostered by the rosary or novena societies. But even in this area, 72% of the people said they were favorable or very favorable toward such activities.

It usually comes as a surprise to parish staffs and leaders that as many as 82% of the parishioners said they favor adult religious education programs, that 85% favor parish administrative groups such as the parish council and school board, and that 86% favor liturgical groups such as the choir, lectors, and commentators. What surprises the leadership is that so many people said they favor these types of activities and yet so few people show up for the adult education programs, or volunteer for the choir or act as lectors at Mass, or that so few are willing to run for the parish council. This is the same phenomenon that was apparent in people's liturgical preference. The fact that a person says he or she is favorable toward a type of parish activity is no guarantee that the person will choose to become involved. Attitudes and behavior do not always coincide.

Fewer than half of the parishioners (45%) said they were members of any parish groups or participated in any parish activities other than the weekend Masses. Only 20% of the people came to parish activities and programs once a month or more. This percentage of participation dropped significantly if the types of activities were narrowed to include only adult education programs or parish service projects. People were even less likely to belong to religious or Church-affiliated groups outside the parish. Only 23% said they were members of such groups, and it was usually the same people who were already involved in parish activities who joined religious and Church-related groups not associated with the parish.

· When the parishioners were asked why they were not active in parish activities and programs, most of them said they were too busy with other groups or did not have any time after taking care of commitments to their family and occupation. Many,

-234-

especially older people, indicated they did not feel qualified to participate in parish programs. Others, especially younger adults, said they did not know how to gain admittance into existing groups. This indicates that walls are often built up around parish organizations without members becoming aware of it. The members wonder why more people don't join, especially the young people. They do not realize that an image of a clique or in-group may have been attached to their group or program and that "outsiders" do not feel welcome or encouraged to attend.

Not only did most of the parish activities and programs receive a largely favorable response from the parishioners; most of the parish staffs and lay leaders also favored these activities. There was one type of activity mentioned, however, to which the leaders' response was less positive than the people's: fund-raising activities, such as bazaars, bake sales, and bingo. Although 83% of the people favor such events, only 70% of the parish councils and 62% of the parish staffs do. Fund-raising events do not fit into the leaders' ideal for the parish. Some of the written comments from the staff and lay leaders revealed an ambiguous reaction toward bingo and fund-raising since these activities demand so much time from leaders in preparation and cleanup. But the parishioners love them and remember them for many years as high points in the life of the parish.

Although a high percentage favor parish activities and programs, only a minority participate in parish functions other than the weekend Masses. They like to belong to an active and dynamic parish, one that has an image of growth and vitality. But becoming personally involved is another matter. On the average, about 13% of the adult parishioners are "core" members of the parish: the people who belong to parish organizations, take part in parish programs, and volunteer for areas of ministry.

The most active age group in the parish is the 35 to 55 group. Those 55 and over have a more difficult time participating in parish functions, especially if they have joined the parish after reaching that age. The young adults constitute the lowest percentage of "core" parishioners. Most of their attention is devoted to attending college, learning a skill, seeking a mate, raising a family, or settling into an occupation. What participation is possible for those between 18 and 35 is sporadic and of short duration.

Three-fourths of the adult parishioners are regular Massgoers. These are the people who support the parish financially and occasionally participate in parish activities. They find it difficult to make an extended commitment to parish programs, however.

The remaining 12% to 15% of the registered adults are infrequent visitors. For various reasons, whether lack of initiative, reaction to a particular person or parish event, or because of a marital problem, they no longer attend Mass regularly. They continue as registered members of the parish either through default, the urging of a spouse, or a sense of loyalty to the Church.

Areas of Concern

People are burdened with many anxieties, and the parish should be a help to them in these cares and concerns. The most pressing concern on people's minds is the fate of the country. Seventy-eight percent of the parishioners, 77% of the parish council members and 72% of the parish staffs are worried, either a great deal or at least to some extent, about the future of the United States. This worry crosses age, educational, and parish involvement lines. The young and the old, those with college and those with only high school background, the core members of the parish as well as the marginal members are all worried about the country and its ability to cope with inflation, unemployment, limited goods, and inadequate services. This high percentage of people worried about the fate of the country has remained constant over the last six years.

Do parishes provide help to people who are worried and in need? I asked the parishioners whether they felt the parish had given them assistance and support in times of need. Almost half (48%) said they had found the parish helpful when they were in need. Twenty-nine percent thought the parish had been no help at all or had been of little help to them. The remaining 23% said they had never needed help from the parish.

The help requested by the people was in areas other than financial aid or moral support as they tried to cope with the pressures of the economy and the culture. But these are the issues of greatest concern to the parishioners, and they are issues that received little attention from parish leaders. The staffs and councils themselves are faced with the problems of rising costs and diminishing funds and resources as they struggle to keep the parish plant and programs in operation. This financial pressure makes it difficult to reach out and care for others who are experiencing the same worries and anxieties.

A second area of concern for many is personal salvation, including such issues as being in the state of grace, going to heaven, or whether to go to confession. Two out of five people I surveyed, and this includes both active as well as inactive parishioners, said they are concerned about these matters. If priests and parish leaders wish to speak to the cares of the people, these are the questions on many people's minds: Will I go to heaven? Will I be forgiven? Can God still love me? What is this life all about? What is being asked for is a ministry of comfort, support, hope, and assurance of God's lasting love and mercy.

My results showed that the leadership is providing help to people, especially in the areas of learning about the faith and knowing how to pray. Sixty-three percent of the parishioners said they have been helped by their parishes through sermons, study groups, counseling, and programs for forming their faith and beliefs. Fifty-two percent said they have been given guidance by the parish in learning how to pray. At the same time, only 38% said they have been helped in family and marital matters. Many do not look to the parish for assistance in such matters, but this still leaves many who are suffering through doubts and worries who do not feel they have been assisted in personal and family problems.

Recent attempts by parish staffs to deal with these areas of concern are encouraging. The growth of support groups for divorced, separated, and widowed Catholics is one example.

So is the increasing number of singles groups. We must conclude that parish leaders are trying to touch the everyday experience of people and are seeking ways to help people cope with their problems.

Personal Moral Issues

The Church's position on personal moral issues such as birth control, divorce-remarriage, and abortion has been much discussed in recent years, especially since the publication of Pope Paul VI's *Humanae Vitae*. This encyclical, published in the late 1960s, upheld the Catholic Church's ban on artificial means of birth control. Since that time attitudes among American Catholic parishioners toward personal moral issues have become more liberal. At present only about 15% of the people consider artificial means of birth control to be always wrong. Another 30% said it depends on the circumstances of each situation. But the majority of the Catholic parishioners that I have surveyed in recent years said they do not feel it is wrong for married couples to use these means of birth control. Fifty-two percent disagree with the statement "It is wrong for married people to use artificial means of birth control."

Age does make a difference in the way people react to personal moral issues. Those parishioners under 35 are less likely to consider the use of artificial birth control to be wrong than are older people. But only 29% of those parishioners who are 55 or older said they consider these actions always wrong. The majority of the people, young and old, appear to have settled the issue for themselves: that artificial birth control is not wrong, despite the Church's official stand to the contrary.

The response toward the morality of divorce and remarriage shows a different trend. Most people do not consider divorce-remarriage as always wrong, but neither do they consider it as always permitted. Twenty percent of the parishioners said divorce-remarriage is always wrong, and 35% say that it is not wrong. The highest percentage response (43%) is in the middle range of "mixed feelings" and "it depends on the circumstances." The age of the respondent does make a difference.

Almost half (48%) of the younger adults, those under 35, do not feel it is wrong for Catholics to divorce and remarry, no matter the circumstances.

Just over half the parishioners of all ages agreed with the statement "It is wrong for people who are not married to have sexual relations." Twenty-four percent have mixed feelings, and 17% disagree with the statement. The parish staffs and councils showed about the same response as the parishioners. Fifty-nine percent of the councils and 57% of the parish staffs agreed with the statement that premarital sex is always wrong, no matter what the circumstances.

The reactions from different age categories in the parish was significant. Only one in three parishioners between the ages of 18 and 34 agreed that premarital sexual relations are always wrong, compared with 3 out of 5 between 35 and 54, and 4 out of 5 of the persons 55 and over. More women than men consider premarital sexual relations always wrong.

On the abortion issue, the parishioners were asked to react to the statement "It is wrong for a woman who wants an abortion in the first three months of pregnancy to have one." About 3 out of 5 respondents (61%) agreed with the statement. One out of 4 said it depends on the circumstances or has mixed feelings about abortion. Only 10% of the parishioners I have surveyed in the last few years disagreed with the statement. Three percent had no opinion. The parishioners under 35 showed a higher percentage of "mixed feelings" or "it depends on circumstances" (32%), but all ages had about the same percentage (10% to 12%) of those who do not feel abortion is wrong.

Reactions toward the morality of abortion have changed in the last 5 to 7 years. In the mid-1970s, only 54% of the parishioners I surveyed considered abortion to be always wrong. Now the percentage who feel this way has increased to 61%. I am not able to isolate the reasons for this change in attitude. Parish leaders would like to believe it is because of their own efforts to point out to the parishioners the immorality of abortion. Some of the change may have come as a result of the moral guidance provided by the Church and parish leaders, but it is also possible that cultural attitudes toward abortion are changing, and Catholics are following the same pattern as the general public.

I asked parishioners whether the parish has given them help or guidance in personal moral issues. The percentage who said they had been helped by their parish through such activities as study groups, counseling, or homilies has not changed significantly over the past ten years. It is stll the minority (45%) who say they have been helped in personal moral areas. About a third of the respondents said they feel the parish has given them no help or has been of little help. The rest said they do not need the help or guidance of the parish in these matters. In other words, although the amount of help people said they had received has remained the same, attitudes among parishioners toward the morality of abortion have grown closer to the Church's stand in recent years.

Social Awareness

Seeing the connection between social issues and religious belief is a difficult area for Catholic parishioners. They are apprehensive about the Church and parish becoming involved in the secular world. The parish staffs, on the other hand, see a close connection between the Church and world, and consider it the role of the parish to call into question any social and political judgments that threaten the rights of the poor, the helpless, and the oppressed.

To sample the difference in opinion between the parish staffs and the majority of the parishioners, I asked both staffs and people to react to the statement, "The institutional Catholic Church should take public stands on social issues." Seventy-three percent of the staff members agreed with the statement, but only 35% of the parishioners agreed. The rest of the people had either "mixed feelings" (36%), disagreed with the statement (21%), or had no opinion (8%). The parish council members had about the same reaction toward Church social involvement as did the parishioners. Forty-one percent of the council members agreed with the statement. There does not appear to be much difference between the attitudes of the young and older adults on the question of social involvement.

Another example of the differences between the staffs and the people in attitudes toward this question is their reaction to the formation of parish social-action groups that would deal with race relations and peace-and-justice issues. Eighty-four percent of the staffs favored such groups, compared with just half of the council members and 46% of the parishioners. Only one parishioner in four feels the parish should take an official stand on public-policy issues. One person included this comment: "Parish involvement in political affairs irritates me. I particularly dislike the Church condemning our involvement in Vietnam and Israel. My feeling is, if the Church can publicly interfere in government policy, what is there to prevent the government from interfering in Church and religious freedoms?" In most of the parishes I surveyed the people were split on whether weekend homilies should deal with social issues. The people were asked to react to the statement "Sermons should stick to spiritual matters and not deal with current social issues." On the average, a third of the parishioners agreed with the statement, 25% had mixed feelings, and 38% disagreed. The remaining 4% had no opinion.

Only two out of the ten questions on the survey that dealt with Church and parish social awareness received a positive response from a majority of the parishioners. One of the two questions was whether the parish should make an effort to welcome all races and classes into the parish. The response varied with the location of the parish. The predominantly Black and Hispanic parishes showed a high favorable reaction to accepting all races and classes. So did suburban parishes that are not experiencing an immediate threat of an ethnic or racial turnover. The parishes that showed a low positive response to welcoming all races and classes are the ones who are experiencing an ethnic or racial change in membership. Even in parishes where people are willing to open the doors to different ethnic and social groups, many parishioners are reluctant to welcome these groups into the neighborhood or into the local school. In response to the statement "Provided the education is good, I prefer sending my children to a racially integrated school," 41% of the parishioners surveyed agreed, and an equal amount had mixed or negative reactions. That response is in contrast to the 87% of the parishioners who agreed to the welcoming of all races and classes into the parish.

Since the mid-1970s, however, parishioners' attitudes toward the racial integration of schools and neighborhoods have become more open and accepting. Five years ago only 25% of the people agreed they would send their children to a racially integrated school. Now the percentage of agreement is 41%, an increase of 16% in half a decade.

The second question that received a positive response from the majority of the parishioners was whether the parish should encourage parishioners to participate in community-wide social-action groups. Fifty-four percent of the people agreed that the parish should do this, compared with 73% of the parish council members and 85% of the parish staff. The parishioners said they are willing to have the parish give encouragement and support to people who wish to become active in social issues but that the parish itself should not become directly involved in this area.

The level of support by the people for parish social involvement is also related to how much would be asked of the individuals themselves. More persons, for instance, are willing to allow social-action groups to use parish buildings (45%) than are willing to have the parish form social-action groups or set up discussion groups on public-policy issues (35%). There is no significant difference in the way the older or younger parishioners respond to these questions on parish social involvement. A majority of all age groups is apprehensive about the parish getting involved with public-policy issues.

Most of the parishioners said they had not been given help or guidance by the parish on social moral issues. Twenty-seven percent said they had been given help through the homilies, parish programs, and counseling, as compared with 45% who said they had not received any help or that the parish had been of little help to them in giving guidance on social issues. The remaining 28% said they did not need the help of the parish in these matters. It seems, then, that the parish has not neglected to give guidance but rather that many parishioners do not want the help of the parish in social moral issues.

The majority of the parishioners, however, is not willing to go so far as to say that the parish should not become involved in *any* way with social issues and public policy. Only 22% of the people said the parish should play no part. Most of the parishioners were undecided. They realize that religion and the Church do have a part to play in public and social issues. They also realize how ambiguous and complicated many of these issues can be. As a result, they are reluctant to give unqualified support to the parish becoming involved in the public sphere.

A number of questions on the parish survey asked opinions about specific social issues such as capital punishment, welfare benefits, and the American system of government. The staff responses were different from the people's. For instance, 42% of the parishioners agreed that capital punishment is a just sentence for a selected set of crimes, such as killing a police-man, 32% expressed mixed feelings, and 21% disagreed. The parish council's response was almost identical to the people's. A comment often received in connection with this question was that it is a just sentence for *any* murder and not just for a selected group. Only 19% of the parish staffs, on the other hand, agreed that the death penalty is a just sentence.

Thirty-nine percent of the parishioners agreed with the state-ment "Most people on welfare could support themselves," and 18% disagreed. In contrast, only 19% of the staff members agreed with the statement, and 41% disagreed. The parish staffs, councils, and parishioners were also asked to agree or disagree with the statement "The American system of govern-ment is the best there is in the world today." Three out of four members of the parish council and two out of three pa-rishioners agreed, compared with only 37% of the parish staff members.

The parish priests and professional staffs hold significantly different opinions from the majority of people on capital pun-ishment, welfare, and the American system of government. While unlike in their reactions to personal moral and sexual issues, young and old parishioners do not differ significantly on social moral issues. The income level of the parishioners does make a difference. Those in the upper income brackets have a higher percentage who agreed that the American system of government is the best in the world than do those with lower incomes.

Decision-making and Church Authority

It often comes as a surprise to parish leaders that only a third of the people I surveyed agreed with the statement "Catholics should follow the teachings of the pope and not take it upon themselves to decide differently." When I begin working with a parish I ask the parish staff members to predict how they feel the majority of the people would respond to this statement. Most staff members think that the majority of the parishioners would agree with it and accept the teaching authority of the pope. But at no time in the ten years of my survey experience has a majority of the parishioners agreed with the statement. When Pope John Paul II visited the United States, more people were willing to agree that the authority of the pope should come before individual decision-making, but positive response to the above question peaked at 41% and then returned to the same level as in the mid-1970s. At present, about a third of the people (34%) agree that Catholics should follow the teachings of the pope and not take it upon themselves to decide differently. Thirty-seven percent expressed mixed feelings, and 25% disagreed. It is difficult to find a more divided response to a question than in this one.

The difference in people's responses to this question depends upon what issue they had in mind. For some people the Church's ban on artificial birth control is uppermost in their minds. They find it difficult to follow the pope's teaching on this issue and respond accordingly. Others feel that the Church's teachings have become too lax; they want Church law and discipline reemphasized. These Catholics tend to agree that Catholics should follow the teachings of the pope and not decide for themselves. Still others respond to the question with mixed feelings because they feel it is the Church's duty to give direction and guidance. But they also feel that in the past the authority of the Church has been too strict and overbearing.

These people are looking for a blend of Church law and individual decision-making.

Whatever the reason behind a person's response to this question of the pope's authority, the majority of the parishioners are not willing to give precedence to the pope's teachings over their own assessment of what is right and wrong. Members of parish councils reacted to the question of the teaching authority of the pope in the same way as did the parish staffs. A minority of the staff members were willing to agree that Catholics should follow the teachings of the pope and not take it upon themselves to decide differently. Seventeen percent of the parish staff members agreed with the statement, 38% had mixed feelings, and 44% disagreed.

One area of Church authority that most parishioners are willing to accept is the obligation to attend Mass on the weekend. Sixty-four percent of those questioned agreed that "It is a sin to miss Mass on Sunday (or Saturday evening) when I could easily attend." The obligation of weekly Mass attendance is still strong, especially among older parishioners. Four out of 5 persons 55 and older agree with the statement, compared with 2 out of 3 of the people between the ages of 35 and 54, and only half of the younger adults between the ages of 18 and 35.

Age makes a difference in questions related to Church law and authority. The young adults have a much more difficult time accepting the teaching authority of the Church than do older parishioners. One exception is the reaction to the question of married priests. This issue is associated with Church law since there does not appear to be a theological or scriptural argument prohibiting a married clergy. The parishioners were asked to react to the statement "Catholic priests should be allowed to marry and still function as priests." The overall response was 39% agreeing, 25% with mixed feelings, and 32% disagreeing. Five percent had no opinion. Dividing this response into age categories revealed that there is no significant variation in the response between older and younger people. Forty-six percent of people under 35 said they would agree to a married clergy, compared with 43% of the middle-aged group, and 32% of the people 55 or older. No age group had a majority willing to accept a married priesthood. Almost 60% of the staffs accept it.

One area of Church law that has been challenged in recent years is the exclusion of women from Holy Orders. The issue began to be raised in the early 1970s, and in 1978 I included it in the general survey instrument. Since that time there has been little change in attitudes among the parishioners toward women's ordination. One out of five parishioners agreed with the statement "Women should be allowed to be ordained to the priesthood." Another 19% had mixed feelings. Most of the people (55%) disagreed, indicating their unwillingness to accept a priesthood that would include both men and women. Even of those between 18 and 35, only 30% said they would favor the ordination of women to the priesthood. Half the parish staff members, including priests, religious, and laity agreed that women should be ordained to the priesthood.

The people were asked to give their opinions about the way in which decisions are made in the parish. They were asked to react to the statement "I feel the parishioners should have a greater share in the decision-making of the parish." Two out of five parishioners agreed with the statement, a response that has remained unchanged during the last eight years. In some parishes I have worked with there is a tradition of lay involvement in the planning and running of the parish. In these parishes the parishioners feel that there is already enough lay involvement in decision-making. It is curious, however, that in these same parishes the parish staffs and council members react differently. They would like the parishioners to be even more involved in running the parish, and as a result most of the leadership agrees with the statement.

I have received a number of comments from parishioners in reaction to the question of lay persons taking a greater part in parish decision-making. Many of the comments indicated that parishioners do not trust their neighbors and friends to assume a greater share in that task. As one person wrote, "Better let the priests do it. That is what they are trained for."

Parishioners are beginning to realize that if they do agree to greater lay involvement in the parish, they themselves might be asked to take a more active part in parish life. It is easier and less demanding to have the professional staff members make the decisions. Another reason for the reluctance to agree to greater lay leadership is that parishioners have been trained for many years *not* to share in the decision-making and running of the parish. To ask them to change and agree to greater lay involvement demands personal contact and gentle persuasion.

Another question asked the people whether they should be consulted about which priests are to serve in the parish. They were asked to react to the statement "I feel the parishioners should have a say in the choice of priests to serve in the parish." On the average, only 27% of the parishioners agreed, compared with 35% of the parish council members and 47% of the parish staffs themselves. The written comments made in connection with this question frequently mentioned the politics that could enter into choosing an associate or pastor, the divisions that this could cause in the parish, and the difficulties that some Protestant churches experience when the congregation is involved in the selection of the minister.

Efforts are being made by diocesan personnel boards to consult the parishioners before assigning priests to a parish and in this way to match the priests with the needs and expectations of the people.

Religious Experience and Practice

The parishioners were asked whether, as adults, they had ever had the feeling of being in close contact with something holy or sacred, whether they have had an experience of the presence of God, or whether they were aware of God directing them to some goal in life.

More of the parishioners said they were aware of God leading or directing them to some goal than had experienced the presence of God or being in close contact with something holy or sacred. Seventy percent said they were sure or at least *thought* they had had the experience of God leading them. Two-thirds said they were aware of being in close contact with something holy, but only 60% were willing to admit they had had a personal experience of God in their adult lives.

There is a relationship between persons' involvement in the parish and an awareness of religious experience in their lives. For example, 72% of the active members of a parish—those who not only come to Mass regularly but also participate in parish activities and programs—said they had had an experience of God's presence. Only 62% of the Mass-goers and fewer than half (47%) of the inactive members of the parish admitted to having had this experience. (The inactive members are those who attend Mass once a month or less.) Where there is a greater level of parish involvement, there is greater awareness of God's presence.

This same connection between parish involvement and religious experience is evident in the degree of individual and family religious activity. Sixty-five percent of the active parishioners indicated a high level of family religious activity, such as saying Grace at meals, discussing religious activities in the family, and establishing religious traditions in the home. Only a third of the Mass-goers—those who attend Mass regularly but do not take part in other parish functions—said they have religious practices with their families. The level of family religious practice falls off to almost nothing for the inactive members of the parish. Only 13% of the people who attend church once a month or less perform religious activities with their families. This indicates that personal and family religious practice is connected with one's level of involvement in parish life. The two reinforce each other.

If we group together the responses from questions associated with individual and family religious practice, the level of "at home" religious practice is not great. Only 30% of the people said they read from the Bible oftener than on rare occasions. This percentage has gradually increased in recent years, however, as more of the parishioners participate in Bible study or prayer groups in the parish. In the mid-1970s only 22% of the people I surveyed said they read the Bible oftener than on rare occasions. At the same time, however, when I ask council members and lay leaders to select a Bible passage for group prayer, I still hear "I've never used a Bible before. Where do I begin? I have no idea where to look for a passage."

About half of the parishioners said they read religious books or periodicals at least once a month. Fifty-seven percent said they discuss religious issues with others that often. The women are more likely to engage in religious reading and discussion than are the men, but the age of a person does not make a difference. The younger adults showed about the same level of personal religious activity as did the older people. Only a small percent have ever had a Mass or religious service held in their homes, so this is still a rare occurrence for most parishioners. Only a tenth of the parishioners said they read the Bible together in their homes. Eighteen percent said they have prayers together with their families once a month or more often. A third said they discuss the meaning of their faith with one another at least once a month, and about three in five say Grace at meals on a regular basis.

This information on religious, social, and moral attitudes drawn from a number of Catholic parishes from across the country provides some idea about what Catholic parishioners as a whole are saying. However, each parish is unique, with its own set of issues, crises, and responses. The tone and style of the community is shaped by the quality of the leadership, the history and background of the people, and the locale of the parish.

TABLE ONE

Size, Type and Location of the Parishes Surveyed

Size:	Under 500 Families	23%
	From 500 to 1200 Families	47%
	Over 1200 Families	30%
Type:	Central or Inner City .... (Predominantly Black or Hispanic)	17%
	Outer City .... (Established neighborhood, formerly ethnic)	20%
	Young Suburb .... (Developing area with young families)	12%
	Established Suburb .... (Middle- and upper-middle-class families)	32%
	Rural and Small Town .... (Agriculture and small businesses)	17%
Location:	Northeast (Mass., N.Y., D.C.)	15%
	South (Fla., Ga., La.)	8%
	Central (Ohio, Mich., Ill.)	53%
	Northwest (Minn., N. Dak., Mont., Wash.) ...	12%
	West (Mo., Colo., Okla., Tex., Ariz.)	12%

Bibliography

Adams, Arthur Merrihew. *Effective Leadership for Today's Church.* Philadelphia: Westminster Press, 1978.

Bauman, William A. *The Ministry of Music: A Guide for the Practicing Musician.* Washington, D.C.: The Liturgical Conference, 1977.

Bausch, William J. *The Christian Parish.* Notre Dame, Ind.: Fides/ Claretian, 1980.

——————————. *Traditions, Tensions, Transitions in Ministry.* West Mystic, Conn.: Twenty-Third Publications, 1982.

Biersdorf, John E., ed. *Creating an Intentional Ministry.* Nashville, Tenn.: 1976.

Bishops' Committee on the Parish. *The Parish.* Washington, D.C.: National Conference of Catholic Bishops, 1980.

Bradford, Leland P. *Making Meetings Work.* La Jolla, Calif.: University Associates, 1976.

Broholm, Dick, and John Hoffman. *Empowering Laity for Their Full Ministry: Nine Blocking/Enabling Forces.* Newton Centre, Mass.: Andover Newton Laity Project, 1981.

Bruck, Maria, ed. *Parish Ministry Resources.* New York: Paulist Press, 1979.

Champlin, Joseph M. *The Living Parish.* Notre Dame, Ind.: Ave Maria Press, 1977.

Coleman, William V., et al. *Parish Leadership Today.* West Mystic, Conn.: Twenty-Third Publications, 1979.

——————————. *Planning Tomorrow's Parish.* West Mystic, Conn.: Twenty-Third Publications, 1976.

Cooke, Bernard. *Ministry to Word and Sacraments.* Philadelphia: Fortress Press, 1976.

Donnelly, Dody. *Theory and Practice of Team Ministry.* New York: Paulist Press, 1977.

Downs, Thomas. *The Parish As Learning Community.* New York: Paulist Press, 1979.

Dulles, Avery. *Models of the Church.* New York: Doubleday and Company, 1974.

Dunning, James B. *Ministries: Sharing God's Gifts.* Winona, Minn.: Saint Mary's Press, 1980.

Fagan, Harry. *Empowerment: Skills for Parish Social Action.* New York: Paulist Press, 1979.

Fenhagen, James C. *Mutual Ministry: New Vitality for the Local Church.* New York: Seabury Press, 1977.

Fuller, Robert D. *Adventures of a Collegial Parish.* West Mystic, Conn.: Twenty-Third Publications, 1981.

Geaney, Dennis. *Emerging Lay Ministry.* Kansas City, Mo.: Andrews and McNeil Publishers, 1979.

_____. *Full Church, Empty Rectory: Training Lay Ministers for Parishes Without Priests.* Notre Dame, Ind.: Fides/Claretian, 1980.

Gerzaitis, Loretta. *The Church As Reflecting Community.* West Mystic, Conn.: Twenty-Third Publications, 1977.

Greeley, Andrew, Mary Durkin, David Tracy, John Shea, William McCready. *Parish, Priest, and People.* Chicago: Thomas More Press, 1981.

Harms, William C. *Who Are We and Where Are We Going?.* New York: Sadlier, 1981.

Harris, Maria. *Portrait of Youth Ministry.* New York: Paulist Press, 1981.

Hoge, Dean R. *Converts, Dropouts, Returnees.* New York: The Pilgrim Press, 1981.

Hughes, Alfred C. *Preparing for Church Ministry.* Denville, N.J.: Dimension Books, 1979.

Jacoby, John O., and Robert P. Edwards. *Christ Renews His Parish.* 3rd ed. Cleveland: Christian Life Services, 1979.

Johnson, Douglas W. *The Care and Feeding of Volunteers.* Nashville: Abingdon Press, 1978.

Kay, Melissa, ed. *It Is Your Own Mystery: A Guide to the Communion Rite.* Washington, D.C.: The Liturgical Conference, 1977.

Keating, Charles J. *The Leadership Book.* New York: Paulist Press, 1978.

Killian, Davis. "Basic Christian Communities in Boston" in *Developing Basic Christian Communities, A Handbook.* Chicago: National Federation of Priests' Councils, 1979.

Kleissler, Thomas A. *RENEW: A Program for Parishes.* New York: Paulist Press, 1980.

Krause, Fred, OFM Cap. *Liturgy in Parish Life.* New York: Alba House, 1979.

Lange, Joseph. *Renewing the Catholic Parish.* Notre Dame, Ind.: Fides/Claretian, 1980.

Larsen, Earnest. *The Renewed Parish.* Liguori, Mo.: Liguorian Books, 1977.

Lassey, William R., and Richard R. Fernandez, eds. *Leadership and Social Change.* 2nd ed. La Jolla, Calif.: University Associates, 1976.

Lewis, G. Douglas. *Resolving Church Conflicts.* San Francisco: Harper and Row, 1981.

Lindgren, Alvin, and Norman Shawchuck. *Let My People Go: Empowering the Laity for Ministry.* Nashville: Abingdon Press, 1980.

——————————. *Management for Your Church.* Nashville: Abingdon Press, 1977.

Maxwell, John. *Worship in Action: A Parish Model of Creative Liturgy and Social Concern.* West Mystic, Conn.: Twenty-Third Publications, 1981.

McBrien, Richard. *Catholicism.* Minneapolis: Winston Press, 1980.

McKenzie, Leon. *Creative Learning for Adults: The Why/How/Now of Games and Exercises.* West Mystic, Conn.: Twenty-Third Publications, 1977.

——————————. *Decision Making in Your Parish.* West Mystic, Conn.: Twenty-Third Publications, 1980.

Murnion, Philip. *Forming the Parish Community.* Washington, D.C.: United States Catholic Conference, 1977.

Nouwen, Henri. *Creative Ministry.* New York: Doubleday and Company, 1971.

O'Brien, J. Stephen, ed. *Gathering God's People: Signs of a Successful Parish.* Huntington, Ind.: National Catholic Education Association with Our Sunday Visitor, Inc., 1982.

Quinn, Bernard. *The Small Rural Parish.* Washington, D.C.: Glenmary Research Center, 1980.

Rademacher, William J. *The Practical Guide for Parish Councils.* West Mystic, Conn.: Twenty-Third Publications, 1979.

Schaller, Lyle E. *Effective Church Planning.* Nashville: Abingdon Press, 1979.

Sloyan, Virginia, ed. *Touchstones for Liturgical Ministers.* Washington, D.C.: The Liturgical Conference, 1979.

Sweetser, Thomas P. *The Catholic Parish: Shifting Membership in a Changing Church.* Chicago: Center for the Scientific Study of Religion, Chicago Theological Seminary, 1974.

Whitehead, Evelyn Eaton, ed. *The Parish in Community and Ministry.* New York: Paulist Press, 1978.

Whitehead, James D., and Evelyn Eaton Whitehead. *Community of Faith.* New York: Seabury Press, 1982.

——————————. *Method in Ministry*. New York: Seabury Press, 1980.

Worley, Robert C. *Dry Bones, Breathe!*. Chicago: Center for the Study of Church Organizational Behavior, McCormick Theological Seminary, 1978.

DATE DUE

AUG 24 '88			
APR 19 '89			

DEMCO 38-297